Maine Horse Doctor
On the Road with Dr J

David A. Jefferson, DVM

PUBLISHED by PRGOTT BOOKS

PO Box 43, Norway, Maine 04268

www.prgottbooks.net

Maine Horse Doctor
On the Road with Dr J

David A. Jefferson, DVM

Front cover photo by:
Duncan Miller Photography
duncanmiller@duncanmillerphoto.com

ISBN: 978-1546764175

Published by PRGott Books

Printed in the United States of America

Dedication

To all our horses, so strong, so fragile,
and to all those who love and care for them.

Table of Contents

Table of Contents, cont.

Table of Contents, cont.

Table of Contents, cont.

Acknowledgments

To my wife, Bonnie, who has stuck with this equine vet for 52 years! She reviewed each essay of this book before it was published as a monthly article. There were always run on sentences and severe comma shortages. Just as importantly, she tried to understand each one at first reading. Bonnie has no equine background, so if she didn't get what I was trying to say, she asked for rewrites until she did. If you find them understandable, she is the reason.

Lynda McCann is the founder and editor of *The Horse's Maine & NH,* the monthly equine newspaper that northern New England has come to depend on. Lynda gets my thanks for her continued support and encouragement. She has graciously given full permission to have the 10+ years of articles appearing in her paper made into this book.

Huge thanks to the staff of Maine Equine Associates. Erin Austin is our manager and also serves as my driver, technician, and talented horse handler. Backing us at the office is Lizzy Soucie, MEA's Client Care Coordinator and the caring voice of MEA. Without these two I wouldn't have had time to even think of writing. They have been unswervingly loyal to me, my family, and Maine Equine Associates. Thanks, Ladies.

For their encouragement and wise council, thanks to Pat Gott and Laura Ashton of PR Gott Books, Norway, Maine, who took the idea of this book and made it happen.

Final thanks must go to our clients and their horses, who have provided all of the material for this book. It has been a joy working for and with you in our joint effort to keep your horses sound, healthy, and happy!

Dr J

Maine Horse Doctor
On the Road with Dr J

1

A Plea
(help your vet out)

U

A while back I had an appointment at a barn to take a Coggins test on a mare. Prior arrangements had been made with the owner for us to meet during the noon hour. It was a beautiful fall day, and I was enjoying Cumberland County as I drove toward the farm. I pulled into the driveway at 12:15, grabbed a needle and blood tube, and walked to the barn. There was no one there, four legged or two. I walked over to the house. A few knocks on the door and a hollered "hello" brought no response. I was just wondering if I had the wrong day when the door opened.

"Oh, it's you, Doc! Be just a minute." Eddie began lacing his L.L.Bean boots. "The mare is running out at pasture. Don't worry, she's easy to catch. She's probably standing right by the gate." In a few minutes the boots were laced up. Right to the top. He hadn't missed an eyelet.

We walked to the pasture gate. No mare. Five minutes later we found her at the far end of the pasture by the wood line. I hung back so that he could catch her without my spooking her. He almost did too, four or five times. We tried cornering her once or twice and almost got her, once or twice. After ten minutes of back and forth the mare's owner decided that she might respond to some grain. Back to the barn he went. I sat down on a rock and tried to recapture my earlier, happy mood. The mare got curious, came over and stuck out her nose toward me. I managed to snag her halter. I had the blood drawn by the time that my client returned.

"Had some trouble with the grain bag, Doc, but I see you caught her all right. It's like I said, she's never hard to catch if you can just get

13

close enough." Nearly an hour after my arrival I climbed back into my truck with my one blood sample. If I kept you waiting that day, I'm sorry. Now you know the reason.

It was about a month later that I made a visit to a large but rather unorganized barn. It was late afternoon and my last stop after a long day. The appointment was to vaccinate two horses. I noticed a bunch of kids standing around. Once I was in the barn, the stable owner, Ann, sprung her trap: "I just thought that while you were here you wouldn't mind floating two others and doing a lameness exam. I've invited my 4H group to watch you work, and I told them you probably wouldn't mind giving a little talk." This is the kind of news that drives vets from large animal practice. I like to leave a barn knowing I've addressed all the health problems, but it's a huge help knowing how much work is ahead of you before you arrive.

The reason behind this is not only your vet's sanity, but there is usually someone else down the road who is waiting. I'm sure there isn't a horse owner alive who hasn't been kept waiting for the vet to arrive. It seems like every day brings at least one emergency call, and these, of course must be taken care of while the scheduled work waits. Most people understand this and appreciate the fact that when they have an emergency, *they* will get help right away. The problem comes from those who are inconsiderate of everyone's time.

***

So, this article is a plea. I may not be your vet, but I'm sure that whoever is would second my request. When arranging a visit, give your vet a list of what needs to be done so he can budget that time. Have your animals in the barn, and be available yourself. This kind of respect for a veterinarian's time will repay itself in his respect for you.

2

ADR
(Ain't Doin' Right)

———————— ♆ ————————

ADR. It's a term used by veterinarians to describe a horse that isn't really sick, but isn't really well, either. The initials stand for "Ain't Doin' Right." We use ADR to describe the horse that might be off his feed a bit, or seems a little depressed. It's that horse that just isn't himself or herself. Your vet listens to your observations and starts checking all those things we are trained to do. The horse's temperature and pulse are taken. We listen to heart and lungs, look at oral membranes, listen for gut sounds and maybe do a rectal exam. There are times when we are as thorough as we can be, but still are mystified. Sometimes even ultrasounds and blood samples don't help to pinpoint the problem. During the exam the horse may seem BAR, another shorthand term which stands for bright, alert, and responsive.

When I was just out of school I would say, "There is nothing wrong with this animal." It didn't take me too many months to learn that just because I can't find it, doesn't mean that there isn't a problem. The fact is that no one knows that horse better than you, his owner or trainer, the person who is around that animal every day. You get your clues from the little ways that a horse just doesn't seem to be on his game. You might live with the situation for a day or two and finally call for professional help.

Stop and think about it. You and I have days when we are ADR You don't know exactly what's wrong, but you just aren't feeling right. Someone who just met you wouldn't pick up on it. However, a spouse, relative, or close friend might be aware of your state even before you are. If you go to the doctor he, like your vet with your horse, may not find a thing.

Lots of horses that are ADR will snap back in a day or two, just like you often do. Others don't. The ADR state may be a prelude to more serious problems. Two syndromes that come to mind that may start with a horse being ADR are Lymes and gastric ulcers.

So, what do you do when your horse is ADR? First, listen to, and trust that inner voice that is telling you that something isn't right. If you think your horse is off, he probably is. When behavior or attitude seems different, take note of it. Nothing makes a horse so much "not himself" as a fever. If you don't have a thermometer in your tack trunk or first aid kit, get one the next time you go by a drug store. The oral digital thermometers work great for taking rectal temperatures. Take it before he gets sick so you know what normal is. If you don't know how to get a pulse rate on your horse, ask someone who does, and get taught. Learn what a normal gut sounds like. Keep a separate loose leaf or spiral notebook for every horse and record your findings on a good day and then when your horse is in that ADR state.

Learn these skills, and then your vet will be more comfortable with saying, "Keep an eye on him and give me a call tomorrow." If you have taken the ADR condition seriously early on, and your vet knows that you can accurately assess your horse's condition, everyone benefits.

3

Before You Call

U

Something interesting happened a few weeks ago. It was early on a Saturday morning, and I was the emergency vet on duty. Within the space of 10 minutes I got pages from two horse owners with horses that "weren't right." Both farms are about an hour's drive from me, and wouldn't you know, one was directly north and the other straight south. Here's what they said when they called, and what happened that day as a result.

Caller #1 said, "Patches seemed OK last night but is off feed this morning. I don't know if he is sick enough to have you come out. What do you think?" Of course I didn't have enough information to know what to think, so I started asking questions. "Have you taken his temperature and heart rate? How is he acting? Does he have gut sounds? Is he making manure? What do his membranes look like?" The owner replied that she didn't have a thermometer, didn't know how to get his heart rate or listen for gut sounds, and didn't know what I meant by membranes.

Caller #2 also told me that her horse, a mare named Suzy, was off feed this morning. I asked the same questions, and this was her reply. "I knew you'd ask, so here is what I've found out. Her temperature is just 99.5, the heart rate is 42 and she is making manure. There aren't many gut sounds on the left, but on the right she sounds more active than normal. Her membranes are pink."

I told both callers that I would get back to them within 15 minutes and then sat down with a cup of coffee and thought about how I was going to handle the two calls. It would be tough to get to them both within a reasonable time because they were so far apart geographically. Did I need to see both, or neither?

I knew from experience that caller # 1, no matter how I might instruct her over the phone, would not/could not get me the information that I needed. The only way I would be able to tell if Patches had a serious problem would be to go and check him out. On the other hand, caller # 2 had given me enough to know that there was not an immediate crisis, and that I might not have to go to her place at all. I called her back, and thanked her for gathering the information on Suzy. I said that from what she had told me I thought we could wait a bit, but that she should stay in touch. I then called owner #1 and told *her* I would be right out.

By the time I saw Patches he actually was looking pretty good. His temperature was normal, and he was breathing easily and at a normal rate. His heart rate was normal, and gut sounds were good. When I offered him some hay he took it readily. Perhaps he had suffered a bout of gas colic that had since passed. His owner had spent a good deal of money getting me out on an emergency call and evaluating her gelding. Had I known what was going on before I left, I could have told her to hold off for awhile and maybe she wouldn't need to pay for that farm call. Before I left, I gave her a lesson on how to do the simple evaluations that tell so much about a horse's health status. I was on my way back and wondering how Suzy was doing when her owner called me on my cellphone. She reported that her mare had started eating, had made manure, and would probably be fine.

The point of this is that there are a few simple observations that you can do yourself with diagnostic equipment that will cost you less than $25. Be ready to report your findings when you call. The information you give over the phone will be a tremendous help to your veterinarian. The important questions will be asked. If you have the answers ready for your vet, you will have his respect.

It's better for your horse *and* your wallet to know how to take a temperature, check for heart rate, listen for gut sounds, and check for membrane color. If you aren't totally sure on how to make the observations or don't have the thermometer and stethoscope to do them with, my suggestion is to corner your vet next time he is on the farm. Tell him you would like to learn how to evaluate your horse. I can assure you that he will be happy to take the time. Down the road this might save *you* money and *him* a midnight trip.

4

Before You Leave

─────────── ♘ ───────────

A few weeks ago Janet called and left a very detailed message on our office answering machine. Although I have changed the names and details, it went something like this: "This is Janet Brown calling. Chet and I are going on vacation for a week. Our neighbor Amy will be watching over the barn. If Charlie gets colicky, please limit his treatment to medicine. We have decided that he is too old to go through colic surgery. If Blossom gets in trouble, don't forget that she is very sensitive to tranquilizer, and whatever you do, don't use Bute on her." The message went on for two more minutes, detailing all of the medical dos and don'ts for the other horses in the barn. She added that if the two boarders' horses got in trouble, we should call their owners directly to get their input on treatments. She reminded us that her credit card was on file with us should we have to see any of the horses. She ended the message by saying that her friend June (phone number given) should be called if a decision needed to be made about any treatments.

I appreciate two things. One is that Janet will be taking some time off. It's important for all of us to take time away for a bit, if only to appreciate what we have at home. Secondly, Janet cared enough about the horses in her barn to have made the call. However, as I listened to her message, I wondered just what I was supposed to do with it. It felt a little like, "tag, you're it."

Like most equine practices, we do our best to provide 24/7 emergency coverage. We share emergencies with four other practices, for a total of seven equine vets on a rotating schedule. So, here is my dilemma. Should I call the other 6 vets and give them all the many details set forth in Janet's message? Maybe spend ½ an hour writing her message down and then send an email to each vet detailing what to do and what not to do for every horse in case that an emergency call came from the farm? What about the other similar message I received the same week? Send that one as well? I also wondered whether the other two practices were getting the same kind of phone calls, and whether they would be calling our practice with all that information.

Here is my suggestion. Hopefully you already have a plastic protected information sheet on your horse's stall door with information about your animal and numbers to call in an emergency. When you are going away, take the time to write down all the current information that would be needed for your animal in case of any problem. Do this well in advance of your going. Don't wait until the night before when you are distracted by packing. Go beyond the basic information that is on your stall sheet. For example, is this horse a candidate for colic surgery if medical treatment would not be enough? Is there someone that you are designating to make such decisions? Are there any peculiarities about your horse that a veterinarian who has never seen him should be aware of? This is important, because although you probably prefer to have your own vet treat your animal, he or she may not be available when a problem arises. Once you have written out all your thoughts, please do not call your veterinarian's office with it. It will just cause frustration on their end.

Tack the sheet to your horse's stall door. If you are a boarder, make sure that the stable owner has read and understands your directions. The advantage of this written plan over a phone call to your vet is huge. If your own vet is away, then any vet that comes will have some guidance on any decision to be made, and you will have a more relaxed time away.

5

Bent Frames

(on buying horses)

⟨U⟩

We didn't have a car in my family until I was 12 years old. It was a big green Buick with plenty of miles on it. She was the first of several used cars. Every few years the current one would start to fail, and my father would go out and start kicking tires. I'd try to steer him toward the chromed models with the good looking paint jobs. He would say, "A good coat of paint can hide a multitude of sins." So he'd look a little deeper. The hood would get opened to see if the motor might be older than what the odometer showed. Down he'd go on his back to slide under the car and check out the vehicle's frame. Finally he'd settle on some not so fancy transportation that would usually prove to be pretty dependable. We all set out to buy cars with an idea of what we want. At the same time, there is wisdom in knowing what to *avoid*.

Buying horses is a good deal like buying used cars. You have to look beneath the shiny hair coat and long pedigree to make sure you aren't purchasing tomorrow's problem. I'm talking about looking specifically for some fundamental problems that will cause you nothing but heartache and money down the road. If you find a bent frame under a used car, you should pass. The car has been in an accident and probably won't hold the road correctly. At the very least, you'll go through more tires than you should.

You can consider some problems in horses as "bent frames." One of these problems is the respiratory condition called "heaves." The official name is chronic obstructive pulmonary disease (COPD). Whatever name you use, it's a heartbreaking situation that is similar to emphysema in people. My understanding is that at least 90% of COPD in people is caused by smoking. In horses in northern New England at least

21

90% is caused by moldy hay fed to horses in barns with poor ventilation. In COPD the lungs have lost a good deal of their capacity and most of their elasticity. Breathing becomes a real effort, and ultimately the horse becomes a respiratory cripple.

There is a way to spot this problem without a stethoscope. If you are like me, you like to size a horse up generally before getting down to details. Stand at least ten feet back to get a whole body appreciation. You don't need to be any closer to spot a horse with heaves. Normally, the act of breathing should be effortless, with a natural and easy rhythm. Heavey horses literally struggle to exhale. They get most of the air out, but have to give an extra push to get the rest out. This type of breathing is called a double lift. When the problem is well established, affected horses have little time to do anything but breathe.

Months of COPD breathing will cause an overdevelopment of the muscles along the rib cage. This inappropriate long muscle bulge is called a heave line. Heavy horses tire easily and often have coughing spells. They can't take a full breath, so they have to take many more breaths per minute to get enough oxygen. A normal horse will take 8-15 breaths per minute when at rest. The heavey horse will almost pant at 30-60 breaths per minute. Each breath is a struggle. When a horse has advanced heaves, you can hear a crackling noise coming from the lungs if you put your ear near the horse's nose or use a stethoscope over the lungs. There are some visuals of heavey horses on You Tube. To bring them up, Google "Heavey Horses aka COPD."

I recommend a veterinary check before you buy any horse. However, heaves is one of those "bent frames" situations that you can spot yourself. Even if you love everything else about this animal, my advice would be not to buy. The animal will eventually not be able to do anything beyond a walk without wheezing. He or she will have an increasingly hard time breathing as time goes on. Watching them suffer is no fun. There are medications that help, and environmental changes that can be made, but there is no cure for heaves.

I warned against buying a used car with a bent frame. A vehicle with a bent frame will never really be right on the road. I described one type of "bent frame" in a horse. That was the condition known as heaves. Another horse to avoid if you intend to ride or drive is one that has obvious signs of some specific foot problems.

Whenever you are evaluating conformation, always stand several feet back. Front and side views are best for foot evaluation. From the front, visually check to see if the front feet are the same size. At the ground level they should be the same circumference. You won't have to measure. This is a difference you can see at a glance. If one is markedly smaller, it is an indication that the horse has had a long standing lameness issue. If the horse has consistently been putting less weight on one leg, that foot becomes smaller. Within a few months of going sound, the feet will again be equal in size.

While in front, take a look at the circumference of the foot at ground level and compare it to the circumference at the coronary band. The ground level circumference should always, always, be greater. If it is not larger at the bottom than at the top, that horse, even under minimal work, will go lame. These narrow footed horses tend to be "mincy" gaited and reluctant to stride out.

The side view of the foot may reveal other problems. First, look at the foot angle. Draw an imaginary line through the middle of the pastern. That same angle should be carried in a smooth, unbroken line through the foot to the ground. If the angle of the foot is lower than the angle of the pastern, it can mean a couple of things. The horse simply might have extra-long toes and be way overdue for a trim. It can also mean that the horse does not grow a good heel. If the horse goes barefoot, it means constant shortening of the toe to try to maintain angles. If the horse is shod, you may have to use degree pads to get the angle corrected. Horses with chronically lower heels are hard to keep sound and are an expense to maintain.

If one of the feet looks more upright (higher in the heel) than the other, this could be another deal breaker. If the angle is so high that the coronary band is jutting forward, you are looking at a club foot. It's difficult to keep a club footed horse sound. Any experienced farrier will tell you what a headache they can be to trim or shoe. Only X-rays will reveal exactly how the bones of this foot are aligned. It's best to avoid a horse with a foot with an upright conformation.

The side view is also best for evaluating those ripples or rings on the surface of the hoof that run around the hoof wall. They are as normal as the annual rings seen on the stump of a cut tree. Just as a woodsman can interpret rings on wood, the rings on a hoof also tell a story. Major feeding changes or a period of an extended fever will change the ring thickness. An example would be the thicker ring that becomes evident a couple of months from when horses go out on spring grass. It takes almost a year for rings to move from the coronary band down to the ground surface, so there are literally months of history written in them. The important thing to remember is that the rings on a normal horse will be parallel to the coronary band from the front of the hoof all the way back to the heel. If the rings start off parallel and then slope acutely downwards toward the ground as they approach the heel, put your money back in your pocket. Rings like this are most often a sign that the horse has had at least one severe attack of laminitis (founder). This disease seems to weaken the feet so that further attacks are common. If you suspect this condition, don't purchase without a set of X-rays to evaluate the coffin bone. If this animal has a marked tendency to put his heels down first as he walks, it's time for you to walk.

By all means, have an examination performed by your veterinarian before buying a horse. However, if you spot one of these "bent frame" items yourself, my advice would be to eliminate that particular horse from your shopping list.

6

Big Fat Legs

"**D**oc, stick a needle in it and let some of that fluid out, would ya?"
I spent several years working on the race track. Every so often one of the horsemen would say these words as we were looking at a horse with a big fat leg. Swollen legs are always a concern, and sticking a needle in one to drain it is almost never the solution.

Below the knee and hock, a horse is pretty much trimmed down. The powerful leg muscles end at the knee or hock and have tapered into long, strong tendons. There is no fat to speak of, even in a roly-poly overweight horse.

You can usually grab a handful of skin in places on the upper body, but never in the lower legs. Beneath that tight skin the outlines of the tendons, bones, and joints are sharp and clear. For this reason, any swelling in the lower legs is immediately noticeable. This is true for 100-pound foals and one ton draft horses. Equines are apt to get all kinds of bumps and swellings on their legs. Splints, bowed tendons and swollen joints are easy to identify if you know your anatomy. In this article I am ignoring all of these localized bumps and will be talking about the leg that is "stocked up." A stocked up leg is one that is swollen from the knee or hock down and is big all around.

At its worst, the leg looks like a stove pipe. It is hard to tell where the ankle begins and ends. From the coronary band up, the leg circumference may be as much as 3 times bigger than normal. In other cases the swelling is mild and barely noticeable.

The swelling is edema, which is a collection of excess fluid. However, if you were to try to drain the fluid with a needle, it wouldn't work. You would never get more than a drop or two. The fluid is in the spaces between the cells, and not just under the skin in a big pool. If you push your finger into an edematous leg, it will leave a dent. Edema can occur anywhere in the body, but partly because of gravity, it tends to collect in low spots.

There are several causes of big legs, but the most common is a problem with the lymphatic system. You may be familiar with the fact that arteries carry blood from the heart and veins return it. Veins were not designed to handle all of the return. In the lower leg, the lymph vessels are almost as important as veins in getting fluids back up. Large protein particles, bacteria, and contaminants are picked up by the lymphatic system and are filtered out in the lymph nodes. The lymph vessels generally follow the course of the veins and have many one-way valves along their course which prevent the fluid from draining back down.

The lower leg has no extra room, and the fragile lymphatic vessels are right under the skin. Anything that interferes with the movement of the lymph up the leg will cause it to accumulate. When the lymph is not moving, the leg starts to fill. The most dramatic filling of a leg occurs when the lymphatic system becomes infected. This condition is called lymphangitis. It can start with any break in the skin, including a simple scrape or even scratches. If enough bacteria enter a wound, the lymph system, which is built to handle infection, may be overwhelmed. The vessels become swollen, choked off, and unable to carry the fluid. The lymph leaks out of the vessels and collects quickly, sometimes in just a few hours. The swelling that results can be alarming. The horse may run a fever and go off feed, and the leg is often extremely sensitive.

If lymphangitis is not treated, the edema may reach all the way up the leg to the body and sometimes spread down the other leg. In extreme cases, because of the pressure, the skin may break open and let the fluid seep out. If the horse is treated early and intensively, the response is usually good. An animal with lymphangitis should be seen by a veterinarian. Antibiotics alone are often not enough to correct the problem.

Mechanical blockage of the lymph vessels may also cause a backup of fluid, even if there is no infection. The most common example of this is a scar across the front of the hock joint. This is usually seen within a week after a wire cut. The scarring goes deep, and beneath the skin it acts like a dam across the lymph vessels. The barrier blocks the fluid from getting back up the leg. Other conditions such as an enlarged suspensory may push against the skin and also retard the upward flow.

I have known several brood mares with swollen hind legs. The swollen udder can cause a blockage of the lymph return up the leg. Whenever possible we try not to medicate pregnant brood mares. Often moderate exercise will take the swelling down considerably, and, of course, once the mares are nursed the problem is over.

Any horse that is stocking up should be examined by your veterinarian so that the source can be diagnosed and treated. Big legs are one of those situations where early treatment may make a big difference and prevent a temporary problem from becoming permanent.

7

Blocking Out
(nerve blocks)

———————— U ————————

Most lameness can be diagnosed by using our senses. If we are watching from the ground, our eyes tell us that the horse is not moving right. If we are riding, our seat bones tell us. Our ears can tell us which leg is hitting the ground the hardest. By using our hands we can make the horse flinch when we squeeze on a tender spot.

On a surprising number of horses, the exact area on the leg that hurts cannot be diagnosed this easily. We watch the horse go, identify the lame leg, and then run into a snag. No matter how much we bend, twist, push, or pull the limb, we can't get the horse to respond. This is always a little embarrassing. "My horse hurts so bad he can't put his heel on the ground, and my vet can't even tell where he is sore." It is probably no reflection on the examining veterinarian. There is an explanation.

As a horse's foot hits the ground, the impact is sent up the leg. It travels up the bony column, and when it reaches a sore spot, the horse reacts by favoring that leg. That's simple enough. But let's use the example of a damaged cartilage deep inside a stifle joint. As the weight of the leg passes over that spot, there is pain. We often can't duplicate this pain by manipulating this largest of all joints. We can flex, extend, twist, and stress test the joint as much as possible, and may still not be able to get a reaction from the horse. That deep problem is not being affected by our puny efforts. There might not be sufficient damage to cause heat or swelling. This is also the reason that hoof testers sometimes aren't any help even when we know there is a foot problem. So this leaves us with a lame horse and no idea of why.

It is vital to know exactly where the pain is coming from so that we can radiograph, ultrasound, or otherwise image to know what the source of the pain is. It is true that nuclear scans can find inflamed areas, but sometimes several areas "light up," and we are no further ahead. If our senses aren't giving us the clues, then "blocking out" is the next logical step in lameness location. Blocking is pretty unique to horse work. It isn't really indicated in human medicine where the patient can talk. "It hurts right here, No, a little to the left. Ouch! Yes, that's it, right there."

Let's assume that we have a horse lame in the right fore, but we are stumped as to where in the leg the pain is coming from. Through the process of nerve and joint blocks we can selectively numb different sections of the leg. After each injection or block, we wait several minutes and then move the horse. When the correct area has been numbed, the horse's gait will improve, and the sore area is identified. This is not just a good theory. Blocking out horses is done on a daily basis in equine practice. Vets dealing with sport horses use far more numbing agents than the busiest dental practice.

Done systematically the procedure is usually begun at the level of the foot. There is a pair of nerves that run down the back of the pastern that go to the back third of the foot. When a small amount of anesthetic is injected directly over these nerves, that portion of the foot loses sensation. If the horse is still lame after this block, the entire foot or the joints in that area will be next, and so on, up the leg. We start at the bottom and work up because if we started with the high (closest to the body) nerves, the whole leg would be anesthetized, and not much would have been gained. After a number of nerve blocks, it might turn out that the problem is high in the leg, and so a good deal of time will be invested before the lameness source is located. For this reason, the vet on your farm may only have time for a couple of blocks before recommending that you take the horse to a clinic where they can work on other horses during those waiting times for blocks to work. Ever notice how your dentist will leave for about 10 minutes after he numbs an area of your mouth? He's waiting for that block to work, and let's be truthful, you are in no hurry for him to get back as you want to be sure that that troublesome tooth is completely anesthetized. Your dentist does the blocks so that he can drill or extract your tooth. We do it for diagnostic purposes.

When blocks do locate the area, the difference it makes is amazing. Horses that were hopping lame become sound. Of course, the relief is temporary, and the painful condition returns after the anesthetic wears off. This might take an hour or two. Once the area is pinpointed through the nerve blocks, X-rays or ultrasounds can be used to see what the problem is.

An occasional horse remains lame even after blocking up to and including the highest joint. This is frustrating and can be due to different causes. One is that some problems are mechanical in nature and don't involve pain. An example of this is a case of navicular disease that has caused adhesions between the navicular bone of the foot and the tendon that rides over it. This causes a stumbly gait that cannot be effectively blocked out. Other cases may involve a very deep pulled muscle that may hurt but cannot be effectively located.

The process of nerve blocking requires a very precise knowledge of anatomy. Miss a nerve by a quarter of an inch, and there may be little or no effect. Nerve blocks are not indicated for every lameness, but in many cases they are a valuable tool in reaching a correct diagnosis.

8

Blood Loss In Horses

———————— ♘ ————————

Equine veterinarians are always getting calls about horses with cuts. Often the owner is very concerned over the amount of blood that may have been lost. It takes very little blood on the ground to look like a bucket's worth. Usually by the time I arrive, the horse that the owner thought was bleeding to death is quietly eating, and the bleeding has stopped on its own.

The word hemostasis means stopping blood flow. Horses have an unusually good hemostatic system, and even large diameter blood vessels that have been sliced will retract back into tissue and seal themselves off. Another hemostatic feature in horses is the huge reserve of red blood cells in the spleen. Within seconds of excitement from any source, adrenalin is released. The adrenalin causes the spleen to contract, sending out pints of red cell rich blood. Horses also form good blood clots which further slows the hemorrhage.

In a horse losing quantities of blood, other changes are occurring to maintain blood pressure. Fluid is pulled from the spaces between the cells of the body and is shifted into the blood vessels. Arteries supplying non-essential areas constrict. This keeps most of the blood going to vitally important structures like the brain and the heart. That shift results in a lower body temperature and cold skin. The heart rate increases to pump around the now decreased volume of blood. However, if enough blood has been lost, the emergency measures will start to fail, and the animal will go into shock.

There is a rough rule to determine how much blood a horse has. Depending on the breed you can estimate that 6-10% of the body weight is blood. Arabians and Thoroughbreds would be the highest, draft horses the lowest. A 1000 lb. Thoroughbred would have about 100 pounds or roughly 100 pints (50 quarts) of blood. In my research I found that a horse can lose up to 30% of its blood (in this case 15 quarts!) and still live. It would be very rare for a horse to bleed to death from a laceration.

If your horse has been cut and is bleeding profusely, don't move him. Check his temperature, pulse and respiration. Roll back his lip and check for extreme paleness. Call us. Be ready to describe exactly where the cut is and how deep. Estimate, unemotionally, how much blood is on the ground. Now with a clean piece of cloth apply firm steady pressure directly over the wound. Maintain that pressure for at least five minutes. Remove the pressure slowly. If the bleeding continues, reapply the pressure and double the time. Don't worry about scarring. Most sutured lacerations in horses do not leave a scar. Above all, don't panic. The blood system has plenty of built-in reserves, or as the old horsemen used to say, "It's a long way from his heart."

9

Bloody Noses

The call came in before 8 AM. "I think we have a problem. Our old mare Chiclet must have been bleeding from her nose all night. She's not bleeding now, but there are puddles of blood all around her paddock." Judy is an experienced horse owner and trainer who has been a client for years. She is not one to panic. I told her that we would rearrange our day and make her farm our first stop.

An hour later we were walking around Chiclet's paddock and saw that Judy had not been exaggerating. The "puddles" were actually foot wide clumps of clotted blood scattered across the paddock. The white board fencing looked like someone had taken a red paint brush and smeared it randomly on the boards and posts. Chiclet herself was standing quietly, head down, nose crusty with dried blood. Her pulse rate was a fairly rapid 70. Her temperature was 98 degrees, a bit below normal for a warm morning in July. Her gums were pale. Her lungs sounded normal.

There are a few reasons that horses can get bloody noses, but only two that are known to cause this amount of bleeding. The first is seen almost exclusively on the race track and is from blood coming up from the lungs. This is so common that it is known by its initials, EIPH, which stands for Exercised Induced Pulmonary Hemorrhage. Toward the end of a race, horses are in oxygen deficit, meaning that even with them gulping for air, they aren't getting enough oxygen to keep up with their body needs. The lungs are working hard, and the blood vessels are apt to rupture. The blood gets carried up the trachea and out the nose. While there can be a great deal of blood, in most cases it's just a trickle as most of it gets reabsorbed in the lungs. There is no way that any horse could run around a paddock the size of Chiclet's fast enough to rupture a lung blood vessel, nor was the ground torn up as it would be from a galloping horse. EIPH was not the cause of her bleeding.

The other thing that can cause *this* much bleeding is a leaking of one of the large carotid arteries. The carotids are paired blood vessels that run up the neck under the jugular veins to the brain. Every time the heart beats, about a quarter of its output goes through these two blood vessels. The carotid arteries have thick walls. How could they possibly start to bleed, and how does the blood get out the nose? To understand how it happens, we need to look at the anatomy of the horse's head.

Just like people, horses have Eustachian tubes. These are air passages that run from each ear to the back of the throat into an area called the pharynx. The Eustachian tubes act to equalize air pressure. When you are on an airplane, the tubes are what make your ears pop with altitude changes.

The guttural pouch is an air pocket which is located along the tract of the Eustachian tube, under the brain, just behind the back angle of the jaw. There is one on each side. Of all our domestic animals only the horse has guttural pouches. Each has the capacity of a coffee mug. If you were an inch high and stood on the floor of the pouch and looked up, you would see a big pipe suspended from the roof. That pipe, throbbing with every heart beat is the carotid artery which carries blood to the brain.

Because the pouch is warm and dark, it is an ideal place for a species of fungus to multiply. The condition is called "guttural pouch mycosis." The fungus grows on the walls of the pouch, or in Chiclet's case, right on the exposed carotid artery itself. If the fungus is aggressive, it will erode the arterial wall. Just as a puncture on a car tire leaks air, the artery starts to leak blood. The heart is pushing the blood through this artery on the way to the brain, and the pinhole leak can become a squirt and then a serious bleed. Anywhere else in the body, the blood would pool and clot. The surrounding tissue puts pressure on the blood vessel and slows the flow. But the pouch is an *air* space, and as the artery continues to bleed with no back pressure, the pouch fills with blood. From there it pours into the pharynx through a valve at the back of the throat. Then it's down the nose and out the nostrils. A horse with a good size hole in the artery can bleed out within hours.

In Chiclet's case the bleeding had stopped before we arrived, probably because of a decrease in blood pressure due to the blood she had lost. When I ran an endoscope up her nose, I could see that the guttural pouch was where the blood had been coming from. We talked about the situation. I told Judy that we could send the mare to a hospital for immediate surgery. Surgeons approach the pouch from behind the jaw and use either a balloon catheter or a metal clip to stop the blood flow from the artery. There also was the possibility the trailer ride could get the artery bleeding again and that she might not make the trip. Sometimes surgery is not an option, and such horses are kept quiet and treated with an antifungal medication. Some heal with no recurrence. Given that Chiclet was an older mare, it seemed that the sensible thing to do was wait at least until she was more stable. I left the farm and told Judy that she should call my cellphone if the bleeding started again. We had been gone less than an hour when Judy called. The blood had started coming out of her nose again. When I arrived back at the farm, the mare had a steady stream of blood from both nostrils. It was obvious that she wasn't going to make it and that she would not survive a trip to the hospital. Chiclet staggered as we walked her down to the edge of the pasture where we put her to sleep.

To review, both EIPH (lung bleeding after strenuous exercise) and guttural pouch mycosis (carotid artery bleeding) can cause massive bleeding. There are other causes of nose bleeds in horses which are usually less severe. One is bleeding from the ethmoids. The ethmoid area is a very vascular area in the back of the nasal cavity that has many folds. Its purpose seems to be to warm the incoming air. It is an area that is subject to hematomas (swellings filled with blood) which may rupture and start to leak. No one knows exactly what causes them, but pathologists say they are not cancerous. The blood coming out the nose is usually a trickle rather than a flow, and there is often a smelly green discharge along with it. The blood may continue to drip from the nose for days. Surgery is sometimes the cure.

Horses can also get nose bleeds from direct trauma to the head, usually from a kick by another horse. These are usually not massive bleeds and often just drip for a day or two. There is often an obvious painful swelling over the face when that is the cause. The origin of nose bleeds can often be diagnosed by your vet using a flexible endoscope run up one of the nostrils to the back of the throat. Sometimes X-rays are helpful. It is definitely wise to call your vet if you have a persistent nose bleed. Most prove not to be serious, but some, like Chiclet, don't end well.

10

Brakes
(beware these conditions)

---- ♘ ----

Erin is my practice manager and personal technician. She has a ½ hour commute to work. When she got tired of filling the tank on her big SUV, she bought a used VW Passat. For a few months she raved about the stick shift, the quick response, and the $20 she was saving every week. After a while I didn't hear as much and asked her how it was running. She said that it just didn't seem to have the same get up and go, and it was costing more to fill the tank. Erin assumed that it needed a tune up but had been putting that off. Finally she started to hear a noise from the wheels that she couldn't identify and got the brakes checked. It turns out that the calipers on the two front wheels had grabbed the brake drums and had not released. As soon as that was fixed, the car, which had literally been held back by its brakes, was back to its economical and zippy self.

There are times that our horses have their brakes on and as a result are giving suboptimal performances. Our tendency is to blame the weather, the feed, or maybe the fact that we haven't been riding as much lately. The fact is that there are many potential health brakes, and most are correctable.

In New England, a common brake is Lyme disease. In our practice, at any given time, we are always treating at least one horse for this tick-borne disease. A common symptom is increased skin sensitivity. Horses that normally like to be groomed or fussed over tend to back away. They are often grumpy. The Lyme literature talks about a lameness that is in this leg today and that leg tomorrow. We do see that, but early on it's that sensitivity to touch and the attitude change that is most telling. For sure, they won't be themselves under harness

37

or saddle. If you suspect Lyme, get your animal tested. The tests are accurate, and treatment is usually successful if started early.

There is an expression used by veterinarians to describe the horse that isn't obviously sick or lame, but is just "ADR" (see Chapter 2). The ADR horse has brakes partially applied, just like Erin's VW. When a physical exam doesn't give us the answer, we often turn to blood tests to try to help figure things out. I've already mentioned the Lyme's test. There are specific tests for many diseases, but the basic screening blood test that is used most is the CBC and blood chemistry. The CBC checks the number and type of white and red blood cells to see if the horse has anemia, an infection or an allergy. The chemistry part checks the enzymes of the muscles and liver. It also assesses kidney function and gives protein, electrolyte and glucose levels among other things. The screening blood test is never the wrong thing to do when you and your vet are scratching your heads.

Right now I am thinking of a horse that I'll call Sammy. Sammy is a 14-year-old "American Warmblood" gelding, a cross between a Percheron and a Thoroughbred, and one of the sweetest horses I have ever known. Sammy's brakes are his front feet, which have to be trimmed and shod so that the angles are exactly right. There are some underlying issues that can be seen on his X-rays, but no matter what they show, if everything from the pastern down isn't in perfect alignment, he will be lame. An extended trial period without shoes was a disaster. When his feet are right, Sammy is sound and stays sound for a few weeks. As his feet start to grow, and the angles change, he goes lame again. The current problem is that only one farrier has been able to "fix" Sammy, and he has recently left the profession. Sammy is an extreme example of how important foot care is in keeping horses sound. Good farriers have a great working knowledge of the anatomy and physiology of the foot. Great ones know when they should throw away the science and fall back on the art. The old saying, "no foot, no horse" is as true now as when it was first said in some other language hundreds or maybe even thousands of years ago. Poorly cared-for feet will eventually put on the brakes.

It's interesting how horse's mouths can so markedly affect their performance. A horse that has never had his wolf teeth extracted may put on the brakes by throwing his head when contact is made with the bit. The chewing molar teeth invariably develop sharp edges and can lacerate the inside of the cheeks and cause poor performance. As horses age, other dental problems may develop that can have a significant effect on attitude and work. A thorough exam of the mouth should be part of your horse's annual physical exam. Ask that it be done.

There are an infinite number of brakes that can drag your horse down. Things can potentially not work right from the tip of the nose right through the tail. No one really knows a horse as well as an attentive owner. If you suspect a slowdown, it's time to call in your veterinarian. All problems are easier to deal with in the early stages. In vehicles and in horses, don't wait until things start to get noisy.

11

Buttons
(suturing big wounds)

U

I'll never forget my first solo attempt at surgery on a horse. A workhorse in the next town was cut and needed suturing. I got directions to the place and was there shortly. No one was around when I drove in, but tied to a ring on the side of the barn was a big Belgian. He was facing me with his head down. I walked up to him and patted him on the left shoulder. This side seemed OK. I ducked under his neck and around to his right side, looking for a wound. Nothing there. I walked all around him, checking each leg, because that's where horses usually get cut. Nope. I guessed that I had the wrong horse.

I stood back a few feet, and then it caught my eye. You have to understand that this was close to a one-ton horse which means that there is a lot to take in at a glance. I just hadn't been looking high enough. There it was, right in front of my face, the most awful looking sight I had ever seen. I took a step back. No good. I still couldn't take it all in. I took two more steps back. Now I could see the whole ugly thing. He was cut from the top of his croup down across his hip and down behind the stifle. It was a huge gash. Without exaggeration, this laceration was over three feet long, and at one point was eight inches deep. The muscles near the wound edge had already started to pull back the skin, and at its widest point there was a foot of separation.

I had been out of vet school just a month, and all of my surgery to this point had been under very controlled situations with instructors looking on. I felt like I had been hit with a pail of ice cold water. As I was staring at the wound with my mouth open, Leonard came out of the barn. "Sorry, Doc, didn't hear you drive up. That's Bob, and he's a mess, ain't he? He come 'round the corner goin' full tilt and hooked hisself on a piece of steel roof that I ain't tacked down since that last storm ripped it. Do you think you can fix him, or should we just lay him away?"

All the possibilities and their implications flashed through my brain. Finally I spoke. It was just one word. "Buttons."

"Buttons?"

"Yes, buttons. I'll need lots of buttons. See if your wife can dig out a couple of handfuls from her sewing basket. The bigger the buttons the better." I needed both the buttons and the chance to be alone for a few minutes to fight the panic rising up from my gut. By the time Leonard had returned with the buttons, I had everything that I needed from my vehicle. I threw the two dozen buttons into a disinfecting solution. As I cleaned up the wound, I explained the purpose of the buttons.

In very large gaping wounds, sutures alone can't hold the skin edges together. The stitches will hold, but the tissue doesn't, and the nylon, steel, or whatever is used will pull right through the skin. However, if the suture material is run through buttons on each side of the cut, the pressure is taken by them and not the skin. The idea was not original with me. Buttons, gauze, surgical tubing, and all kinds of things have always been used in large wounds to keep sutures under tension from cutting through the skin.

Once I got busy with the job ahead of me, I calmed down somewhat and began injecting a local anesthetic along the wound edges. I kept my hand on the horse as I injected the local, so that my shaking hands wouldn't be as obvious. A typical horse wound will take somewhere between 10 and 20cc. I used over 300cc on Bob and would have used more, but that's all I had.

I had to stand on a plastic 5 gallon pail to reach the top of the incision. First I pulled the sliced muscles together as best as I could with absorbable suture. Almost three hours later I was tying the last of the skin sutures using heavy nylon. I had put in several drains, used up all of my suture material, dulled many needles, and used every one of those buttons. I stepped back to look at my handiwork. The three foot long incision was pulled together and lined on both sides with buttons of every description. There were coat buttons, pants buttons, and even a few dress buttons. I gave the horse some penicillin and a tetanus booster, and told Leonard not to let Bob lie down. He walked Bob into a straight stall and told me that it should be OK as he had never seen Bob lay down, "not once."

I drove back to the office feeling exhausted, but good. I walked in to tell my boss about how I had spent the afternoon. Before I got started, the phone rang. It was Leonard. "Remember I told you I had never seen that horse lay down. Well, he did, and all them buttons and everything just popped right out."

I asked my boss to drive back out with me. I couldn't face it alone. Sure enough, all those "buttons" and probably 10 pounds of muscle were hanging out of the wound. Things were a bigger mess than when I arrived at the farm hours before. When Bob lay down the strain on the skin line was too much and everything, including the buttons, had pulled through the skin. We cut through the tattered mess of skin, sutures and muscle to try to neaten things up. All this time I was thinking about how we could ever possibly bring the skin back together again. Before I could offer an opinion I heard my boss telling Leonard how to clean the wound out every day.

"Wait a minute," I exclaimed, "we can't leave Bob gaping open like this!"

"Well, we can," says my boss, "and what's more, that's just what we're going to do." I started to protest but he stared me down, and after things were cleaned up, we got back in the vehicle. As we drove back to the office, he said he probably wouldn't have sutured the wound in the first place.

I stopped and saw the horse regularly after that. It was a never to be forgotten lesson for me in how nature takes care of massive injuries. Within a few weeks, healing tissue had filled the gap of the wound. Three months later new skin was well on its way across the defect. In six months there was just a long raised scar. One year after the accident, you could feel the scar with your finger, but it was covered by skin and hair and not visible to the eye. Bob, totally healed, was back to pulling logs out of the woods.

I've attended many cut horses since, and now, decades later, have to agree with my old boss. There are some wounds in horses that are best left alone. In my experience huge tears over heavily muscled areas often heal best when left open. I still sometimes suture big wounds, and sometimes it works. However, there have also been times that I have had to go back and remove the sutures that couldn't hold a huge wound closed.

Some pastern and heel cuts also don't do well when sutured. This is true when wounds are in any area that is constantly flexing. Some wounds are too contaminated to suture. In others, the time lag is too long, and the edges just can't be pulled together.

I am not suggesting that you ignore these wounds. Take a picture of that laceration and send it to your vet. Don't be surprised if she tells you that this one may not need sutures. If a wound does need sutures, it is best to get it done within a few hours.

12

Buying Horses

———————— ♘ ————————

Buying horses can be a tricky business. At the time that I am writing this article, horse prices are down. Money wise, there hasn't been a better time to buy a horse for years. There are two market forces going on. One, of course, is the economy. The second force at work is that slaughter houses in the U.S. are closed. The slaughter or "killer price" has, in the past, always set the bottom line for horse prices. Both the economy and the no basement price mean that if you have the cash and the burn to own a horse, you may get a bargain.

Just because horse prices are down is no reason not to shop wisely. As a veterinarian I have witnessed many purchases that never, ever, should have happened. Here are a few pointers on protecting yourself.

First contact: Ask questions, ask questions, and then ask some more. The more time you spend on the phone, the more the owner will talk. If this is an internet contact, ask for the phone number and call the seller. Communication seems to be more honest on the phone than through e-mail. Time spent on the phone is an investment that may save you hours of driving or hundreds of dollars in shipping. Have a written list of questions ready. Here are some starters assuming that the horse is a gelding: When was he last vaccinated, with what and by whom? What has been the worming schedule? Do you have the horse's health records? Are there allergies, reactions to drugs? When was his last dental appointment? What is the date of his last Coggins test? How tall is he? Did you measure his height, or is that what you think he might be? Does he weave, crib, bite, or kick? How is he with men, the farrier, kids? Have there been any colic episodes? How much training does he have, and by whom? All these questions will give you hints as to the level of his care. Finally, "Is the price firm?"

First visit: If you aren't too far away, keep the checkbook at home. Arrive early so that the horse is still in the stall. Check out that stall for signs of vices. See if he will come over to you. A curious horse is a horse that loves training. Have his owner take him out. Pick up each foot. Tap on them. Check his eyes for haziness and for similar pupil diameter in each. Count the number of respirations per minute. They should be under 12 per minute at rest. Have him walked in hand, lunged, ridden or driven. Ask if you can "get behind the wheel." Now its time for some early dickering: "This horse is probably worth every penny you are asking, but it's more than I had budgeted," is not an insult and is understood.

Second visit: Bring a friend as another pair of eyes. Not a "yes man," but someone who is more knowledgeable than you. A trainer that you trust would be ideal. Don't waste their time taking them on the first visit, as you will may well turn down a few before finding the right one. It's sort of like shopping for houses where it's best to do a drive by before wasting the realtor's time.

Third visit: Ask your vet to do a thorough pre-purchase exam. Note: that the word is *your* vet, not the owner's. If you can't be present, make sure the vet can call you if he finds something very wrong early in the exam. Very often a professional exam will turn up something that makes the purchase riskier. It might be a risk you are willing to take, but it should drop the price. Assuming all is well, ask for a trial period at your place. If no other buyers are standing in line, the owner may let you take the horse. Ask for a month and settle for a couple of weeks. Expect to be asked to leave a deposit. Reach and *write* an agreement that clearly states who is responsible if the horse has an accident or gets sick while he is with you.

Here are a couple of tips from the used car business:

–A good coat of paint can hide a multitude of sins. (Flashy horse doesn't necessarily mean good horse.)

–Stay away from a vehicle that's been in a wreck. You should walk away from a lame horse, a horse with breathing or eye issues.

I know that all these suggestions will be ignored if you find the horse that makes you go all misty-eyed when you first meet. Try to remember that love at first sight doesn't always work out.

Good hunting. Make it fun!

13

Changes in Deworming Horses

———————— ♘ ————————

In my senior year at vet school we were told that 90% of all that we were being taught would be outdated within ten years. I didn't believe it, but it has proved to be true. In parasite control it is more like 100%.

We were taught how to administer wormers through a stomach tube that we slid through a horse's nose and down into the stomach. Understandably, it was a rare horse that didn't need to be twitched for the procedure. Tranquilizers at the time were not as safe or effective as today's. The liquid wormers that we pumped and poured in did the job, but they were harsh. Twelve hours of diarrhea or mild colic was quite common after deworming. Not one of those liquid wormers is still on the market, and tube worming is essentially a thing of the past. There were a couple of wormers that could be sprinkled on the feed, but most horses took one smell and said, "No thanks."

As you know, most of today's wormers are in paste form and available anywhere. Pastes made deworming safe and easy. It seemed like the equine parasite problem had been solved. Not true. Worms have co-existed with their hosts for thousands of generations and weren't fooled that easily. All available paste wormers fall under three or four general types based on their ingredients and how they act. Each of those types or classes of wormers is becoming less effective in killing equine parasites. Too frequent worming has meant that the resistance has grown to the point where some of the wormers are just not effective anymore.

In the past two or three years, new thoughts on the parasite problem have been evolving. Here is the current thinking. Most horses are able to co-exist with parasites. It has proved to be unrealistic to make our animals parasite free. So all horses carry some worms, but seem to have their own resistance to them. In other words, they have a natural immunity to the worms. However, there are some horses that don't. Parasites in those horses thrive. The adult worms living in their intestines produce thousands of eggs daily, and these pass out with the manure, making the pasture or paddock a sea of microscopic worm eggs. Several days in the warm sun and the eggs hatch into larvae which are picked up by grazing horses. The horses that carry this big burden of parasites are called "shedders," and are the most responsible for contaminating the ground with worm eggs. Parasitologists have shown us that in a herd of ten horses there is often one or two that are the culprits. It is those shedder horses that revised worming programs are targeting.

You can't tell by looking which of your horses is a shedder. It could be the healthiest looking horse in the herd. Fecal exams have to be done on all of your horses to identify who are the shedders. The exams are performed either by veterinarians in their office, or they might send the sample to a commercial lab. Shedders are identified by a very large number of eggs per gram of manure. Once identified, the shedders are the ones who get the intensive deworming attention, while others in the barn may need only once or twice a year worming. This system is called targeted worming. It is a program best guided by your veterinarian.

The object of targeted worming is to cut way back on the amount of worm medicine being used and so lessen the ability of the parasites to develop immunity to it. It's similar to human medicine where your doctor doesn't want to give you antibiotics for every little infection, knowing that it doesn't take bacteria many generations to develop immunity to drugs. At the moment there are no new wormers being developed, so resistance will become more and more of a problem.

It is tempting to throw the baby out with the bath water and say, "Well, if immunity to paste wormers is a problem, I'll just stay away from manufactured paste warmers and use *natural substances* for parasite control." The problem is that there have been no quality controlled studies showing effectiveness for any of these substances. One of the more controversial natural wormers is DE (diatomaceous earth) which is a fine powder made of exoskeletons of long dead tiny organisms. DE has lots of uses, but I am not convinced that it kills worms. The absolute highest number of worm eggs on any fecal exam I have ever done was on a horse that had been on DE for over a year.

Here's the bottom line. If you are currently worming all of your horses on an every other or every third month schedule, talk to your veterinarian about doing a targeted worming program. Even with the cost of the fecal lab tests, it should save money in the long run and will definitely slow down the resistance problem.

14

Deep Mud

(muddy paddocks)

U

The weather patterns in this past year have brought us some intense rainfall. If you have low spots in your paddock, barnyard, or pasture, you know first hand all about deep mud. It doesn't take long before the action of a horse's feet makes wet ground into a six-inch swamp. On a limited basis, mud can be a good thing for horse's hooves, but when horses are standing in it for days, feet get punky, and pasterns get irritated. When pasterns are exposed to moisture long enough, the annoying problem of "scratches" may result.

I have a client and long time friend who lives near by. She prefers to remain anonymous, so I will call her Kathy. She has a small barn that is located at the lower end of a very long slope of land. This means that water runoff is all towards the barn. The barn is a freestyle arrangement. Her three horses go in and out at will, through a wide, always open doorway. The animals like to hang out just outside the door, right where the run off from the paddock collects. For years, during snow melt, or after any soaking rain, her horses would end up fetlock deep in that muddy soup that lasted for days. This was thick, pull off your boots mud. Drains are an option in situations like this, but don't always work exactly as we would hope. Kathy came up with a plan that cost no money and was just as effective.

She was removing an old, thick 10 by 10 rug that had been in one of the rooms in her house. In a moment of genius she decided to lay it over the paddock area in front of the barn door to see what might happen. Problem solved! The old carpet has been outside, right in front of that door for over six years now, and the muddy area no longer exists. Kathy reasons that water on dirt doesn't make mud. It will either run off or just stay on top. But horses standing and milling around through that same area punch holes in the dirt and mix the water with the dirt, making mud. The rug acts as a mat to prevent the water from mixing with the dirt.

Walking through Kathy's paddock you would never know that you are walking on a carpet. Within two weeks the carpet got covered with dirt from the horse's feet and disappeared from view.

When Kathy saw that the rug was working, she put the word out and friends gave her some of their old rugs, so the total "carpeted area" is now about 20 by 20 square feet. The manure and debris is cleaned off the area with a fork, just like she would clean the paddock before the carpet was put down. I would have thought that only an outdoor carpet would be able to hold up this long, but the carpets were regular old, off-the-rack indoor carpeting. Three horses are standing and walking across that area every day, in sun, rain, snow, and ice. Kathy tells me that she uses the bucket on her tractor to lift and pull back the carpet about once a year so that she can level the ground underneath it. She has also carpeted a formerly muddy pathway to her riding arena, and that has worked as well. In addition, Kathy is now using old rugs to hold back areas of erosion on the sloping sides of the arena. I anticipate that by this fall those carpeted slopes will be covered with grass.

If you have a similar situation in a paddock or an especially muddy pathway, this idea might be worth a try. Kathy has used different kinds of carpets for these projects and tells me that the thicker the weave, the better it works. Companies that install new carpets have to pay to leave them at the dump and would probably welcome you taking some away.

15

Do the 22

If I were to ask you what you were short of these days, your first response might be, "That's easy, I could use some extra money!" With more reflection you might say, "Actually, I'm out straight, and could really use some extra time." My hope is that this idea will help make your time more productive.

About 30 years ago I got excited about veterinary acupuncture. I found a class that was starting in March and signed up. There were four sessions of four days each. The four sessions were a month apart. That meant four flights to North Carolina, which at the time was an all day trip because there were no direct flights from Portland. Two days of travel and four days of class meant almost a full week committed once a month. I didn't realize the full extent of what I had done until the first class began. There was a huge amount of material that had to be memorized. We were told that we would have to pass an oral and practical exam on the last day of the last session for certification. I had no idea how much work there was, and somehow I had to fit in all the studying during the spring, every equine vet's busy season. At the time I was working 10 to 12 hour days 6 days a week. There was no way I could study for an exam! I whined about the situation to a friend who told me that she had faced the same problem years before. She had to study for a major professional exam, but between raising young kids and working, there was no study time. I asked how she managed it. She said she owed it all to the 22-minute plan.

If you have something you want to learn or do but realize that it is going to take many concentrated hours that you don't have, consider the plan. Here's how it works. Every day, *no matter what*, you sit down for 22 minutes to study or do the job you've been putting off. You set the stage by telling your family that during that time you *cannot be interrupted for anything*. If the phone rings, you ignore it. If the Publisher's Clearing House gang rings the doorbell with their balloons and a big check, they will have to wait a bit until you are done. When you sit down to study, set a timer for 22 minutes, and that time is totally committed to the project at hand. Then, just as importantly, no matter where you are in your studying, no matter how interested you are, when the timer goes off, you *have to stop*. You can set another 22 minutes for some time later that day, but again, you must stop when the timer rings. This stops you from really getting into it, studying for over two hours and then saying, "Hey, I don't have to do anymore studying for six days!" The six will slip into seven, and the whole project will fold. Guaranteed.

Let's start with something simple as an example of how this might work for you. Let's say that your tack room is a mess. You know it's a mess, and you'd like to see it organized and cleaned up, but you just don't have the three hours it would take to sort out the stuff that needs heaving, put in shelves and hooks, and make the place look good. You may not have those three hours, but you *could* squeeze in 22 minutes. Set the timer on your cellphone for 22 minutes and start. As soon as the timer goes off, STOP. Don't pick up another thing. Go do the rest of your day. Then later that day, or the next day, do the 22 again. It's important that you stop whatever you are doing when the time is up. In just a few sessions, you are done!

If your horse sport is competitive dressage, at some point you will need to memorize a test. My suggestion would be to start the process long before you have to perform it for real. Sit down every day and study for 22 minutes. No interruptions allowed. 22 minutes. No more, no less. That way it's not panic cramming the night before, and the sessions are never so long that they are boring. The memorization work is intense for the 22 minutes. Don't stop or look at the time until the buzzer goes off.

Another example might be dissatisfaction with the way your horse's feet look, but you don't feel qualified to talk to your farrier about it. You would like to know more about how feet should look when the job is done right. Spend 22 minutes at a time. Again, no more no less, and start learning about feet. What should ideal angles be in front and behind? Where should the widest part of the foot be? What are the arguments for trimming out or not trimming out the frog? What's best, barefoot or shoes? What is laminitis anyway? A hundred questions that you will know the answers to when you sit down with the internet and start learning. A few weeks of 22 minutes on the subject, and you will be able to have an intelligent conversation with your farrier and share ideas. He or she will respect the fact that you are knowledgeable and understand what quality work looks like.

Maybe you own a mare that's a little too round. Are you feeding her based on what a friend told you or based on researched, true knowledge of the subject? There are hundreds of articles on feeding, and all the major feed companies have their own excellent information. Try to learn it all in one or two nights and you will just get confused. Spend 22 uninterrupted minutes every day, and you will soon become far more knowledgeable than 95% of horse owners. I have found that the first five or six minutes of each 22 minutes is best spent reviewing what you have learned in previous sessions.

Obviously, you can apply this study or work technique to anything outside the horse world as well. Do you like music and have always wanted to make some yourself? In that case I would recommend at least two 22 minute sessions a day because muscle memory is so important in playing an instrument. Maybe you already play, but would like to learn more about music theory. In 30 days of 22-minute sessions, you will have an understanding of what makes music, music which will improve both your appreciation and your own playing.

I use this 22 minutes every once in a while when my desk gets piled too high. I set the timer and get to work. The rule for this project is that every piece of paper that gets picked up gets filed, heaved, or acted upon. The next day it's another 22. This usually takes two, rarely three, sessions. It is relatively painless and very satisfying. It beats two straight hours of clearing your desk, which is brutal.

Because I had absolutely no free time in the four months that I was learning acupuncture, I decided that I would just get up ½ an hour earlier and get my 22 minutes in before the day started. Often I would get in another 22 minutes just before going to bed. I would be exhausted but did those late night 22's standing at my desk. Each time I traveled back for another acupuncture class, I heard my classmates complaining about not having enough time to get their studying done. I found that with my new studying habit I understood what the teachers were saying because I had taken the time to read ahead. I passed the exams to get certified with minimal hassle, with no cramming the night before.

I hope that something in the horse world is of enough interest for you to try the 22 minutes. I think you will be surprised at how much you can learn or do in an almost enjoyable way. Spend some 22s, learn or do something that will make you a better horse person, and enjoy a simpler life.

16

ESe

―――――――――― ♘ ――――――――――

This article is about a vitamin (E) and a mineral (selenium). In equine medicine the two things are usually talked about together because in combination they can really help performance horses. ESe (pronounced e see) is often far more effective for horses than joint supplements that cost 10x more.

First a disclaimer: I am writing about the needs of horses in New England. This information may not be useful, or can be totally wrong, in other areas of the country. For example, supplementing a horse with selenium in the southwest may be dangerous. The soil there contains huge amounts of selenium which is taken up by plants. One plant, locoweed, not only picks it up but picks it up in quantities that make it toxic to horses. Giving more selenium in that area is not a good idea.

The dirt in northern New England is selenium deficient, and as a result, plants that grow here can't pick it up. Selenium is important for healthy muscle function in horses. It is a small but critical part of some enzymes that clean up harmful free radicals in the horse. We think that selenium plays a part in the prevention of tying up, and veterinarians often recommend its use in horses with that issue. Although many grains list both E and selenium on their labels, the amounts are miniscule and of no real benefit.

Vitamin E is found naturally in green leafy plants. We do have E in our soil and plants, but when hay is stored its levels drop. E is an antioxidant which is important in the maintenance of healthy nerves. Lack of it can cause some serious neurologic problems in horses. One is a disease known as EMND (Equine Motor Neuron Disease). Horses with EMND become uncoordinated and lose muscle tone. Over months the muscles shrink, and horses get very skinny regardless of how much they eat. It is similar to Lou Gehrig's Disease in people.

Another disease in which lack of E seems to play a part is EDM (Equine Degenerative Myelopathy). With EDM the nerves of the spinal cord degenerate causing the horse to be ataxic. Like selenium, low Vitamin E plays a part in horses that tie up, and usually large amounts of E are used in treating that problem.

In my opinion, around here, every working horse should be on this supplement. I usually recommend 2000 IU (International Units) of E and 2 mg (milligrams) of selenium per day as a minimum for a 1000 lb horse. Some supplements have the two in that ratio, which makes dosing it very simple. If blood tests show that a horse is very low in E, I recommend one of the regular ESe supplements and then add more pure E to get the blood levels up to normal.

E and selenium supplementation is also important for brood mares throughout their pregnancy. Foals born with a deficiency because of low levels in their dams may never get to their feet after birth.

I can't tell you how many times I've watched a horse work that isn't really lame, but is just not moving well. Long before injecting or other therapy I ask if the horse is on E and Se. If not I will recommend it, and ask the owner to call in two weeks. Often within a week I hear back that the supplement has smoothed things out.

Vitamin preparations can be expensive and are sometimes worthless. ESe is one that is very cheap and often effective.

17

Fire!

—————————— ♘ ——————————

Some years ago I was asked by an insurance company to identify the bodies of some horses the morning after a very bad stable fire. A few upright studs, still smoking and charred were all that was left of the structure. Here and there on the still hot concrete floor of the aisle lay scattered nails and stall hardware. Two of the bodies were so badly burned that we had to rely on where the horses lay to figure out who they were.

Most Maine horse barns have the potential of burning completely to the ground less than 30 minutes after a fire starts. Our wooden barns were often built decades, sometimes hundreds of years ago. To save space we store our hay directly overhead. Hay is easily ignited, sometimes spontaneously if improperly cured. Firefighters will tell you that hay is considered almost explosive once ignited. Intensely burning hay causes rapid disintegration of the floor it is stored on, and horses below receive a literal rain of fire on their backs. In most cases the horses are not aware. They have already died of smoke inhalation. Barns burn so fast it is rare that a fire department can arrive in time to save the animals, or even any part of the barn. The rule of thumb is that barn fires can double in size with every passing minute. The devastation is often so complete that investigators cannot tell how the fire began.

It seems like every year we lose horses to barn fires here in the state. It's the disaster we all fear the most. I know I do. My wooden barn is around 150 years old, and the hay is overhead. One edge of the barn is two feet from my garage, which is attached to our 200-year-old house.

Barn fires are not always preventable, but there are some

preparations we should make as responsible horse owners. First, all commercial barns should invite the local fire department to come for an inspection. Firefighters usually welcome the opportunity to familiarize themselves with your layout. Ask them for recommendations about your wiring, type and placement of extinguishers, winter accessibility to the barn, and type and placement of smoke and heat detectors.

Work with the fire department to come up with a disaster plan. Get together with your family or boarders and make sure it is understood. Sketch out the barn with stall, tack room, and all exits. Ask yourself, "What would I do, and in what order, if I saw smoke coming from the barn." One of our clients who has been a firefighter for years tells me, "People underestimate the debilitating effect of smoke on their vision, breathing, and ability to function without becoming lost or disoriented. It is extremely perilous entering a burning structure." Once the building is involved, even a firefighter in turnout gear may only be able to save one or two horses. Always! Always! Call 911 before taking *any* other action.

Here are some quick cautions. Never store gas or diesel in the barn, and never, ever, allow an open flame. Beware of heat lamps, frayed extension cords, electric heaters in tack rooms without tip-over switches. Get rid of the cobwebs—they burn fast. If you use fans in summer, blow out the dust around the motor weekly. Fire trucks are wide and heavy. Your road to the barn should be solid and plowed in the winter. Allow at least a 12-foot clearance to get to structures.

The ideal barn would have every stall with its own door to the outside. If you are going to build a barn, use fire-retardant wood products. Store your hay in a separate structure, a good distance from the barn. Every stall door should have a halter with lead attached. The extra time it takes to go to the tack room for a halter could make the difference between life and death for that horse. Horses led out from a burning barn are apt to run back in if just let go. They associate the barn and their stall with safety. Think about a designated paddock or round pen far from the barn that will hold them safely.

Lightning rod protection and sprinkler systems are expensive, but a huge plus for peace of mind. Because most farms are not on town water, the sprinkler system would include a five-hundred to many-thousand-gallon tank, depending on barn square footage.

David A. Jefferson, DVM

Here's hoping you never have to deal with a barn fire. Because the potential is always there, have plans in place for this emergency and review them regularly.

* * *

My thanks to Chief Gary Sacco of the New Gloucester FD, and Dana Stewart, firefighter and CEO of Dean and Allyn, Inc, (Sprinkler Fire Protection Systems of Gray) for their willingness to review and help with this article.

18

Getting Sammy Up
(ice problems)

⊍

It was one of those calls that all equine vets dread in the winter months. It was Malinda. "Old Sammy is down in his paddock and has been trying to get up all afternoon, but can't. We almost got him up a couple of times but are totally frustrated!" As I drove the half hour to the farm, I ran through the possibilities in my mind. We had an ice storm two days before, and it had been misting all day. Dangerous conditions for a horse outside. Maybe Sammy slipped on the ice and was lying there with a broken leg. In our practice we see at least one leg fracture, due to ice, every winter. Perhaps he was down with a bad colic and was now exhausted and had run out of try.

Sammy is a 26-year-old Thoroughbred, and I hadn't seen him in over a year. Maybe this fall and winter he had gotten skinny and no longer had the strength to get up. Maybe he was dying. I was driving to Malinda's and thinking about Sammy when my cellphone started ringing. "Sammy just got up! But keep coming, I still want you to check him out." I told Malinda I was ten minutes away and would be there shortly.

I backed up to her barn and almost went down when I took my first step out of the truck. I have a pair of those slipover-your-boots ice grippers but had neglected to put them on before leaving. I hung onto the door handles and the back fender to keep from sliding as I worked my way to the back of the vehicle. The light rain had coated the ice, and it was like walking on greased ball bearings. Tiny steps took me to the back of the truck. I let down the tail gate and gathered what I needed for diagnostics. It was a slow shuffle as I worked my way the five feet to the barn. A few people from the neighborhood were standing just inside the barn door. They had been enlisted to help get Sammy up and now were hanging out with arms crossed to see what I was going to do.

Sammy was in his stall standing square on all four, with his head down, eating some hay off the floor. He turned to look at me when I walked into his stall, and his expression seemed to say, "What are you doing here? Nothing wrong with me!" I took a look under his blanket and was surprised to see that he wasn't skinny at all. Plenty of good cover over his ribs. I took his temperature, listened to his heart, checked for gut sounds, and watched him move around the stall. I concluded that Sammy was right. There really was nothing wrong with him. There were a few scrapes here and there from trying to get up, but essentially he was fine.

Malinda told me the story. She had found him around three that afternoon, lying on his side in the icy paddock. The neighbors had gathered to help. When he made an effort to get up, one neighbor pulled up on his tail, and two on each side pulled up on a nylon strap that was passed underneath his ribs. His hind feet kept sliding with nothing to grab. They had tried putting shavings under him, but it all slid away when he tried and almost made things worse. Each of his efforts was weaker, and then he just stopped trying altogether.

"OK, Malinda, so he is looking great, and it's for sure he'll be fine. How *did* you finally get him up?"

"We didn't. We weren't even trying when he got up. He did it himself!"

"What prompted him?"

"He had to pee."

"What?"

"No kidding. Just before you got here he started to moan and groan, and all of a sudden pulled all four of his legs together, and he just jumped to his feet. Then I swear he must have let about five gallons go. It just wouldn't stop coming!"

So, that's the story of Sammy, the horse that had to pee. I can relate. There are lots of mornings when I'd just as soon stay in bed, but my full bladder says, "Up you go!"

So what's to be learned from this incident?

First, if you have ever been involved in getting a horse up, you know that once they stop trying, you might as well too. Even with four big guys, 1000 pounds is way too much to lift, especially with ice underfoot. I can tell you from experience that it's not even easy with the help of an excavator and a horse sling.

Second, here is a suggestion on how to make a *completely* slip free area. This works when it is well below freezing. It is best done as a preventive measure to keep a horse from initially slipping on ice. However, it also is helpful when you have to get one up.

Most New England towns have free sand available in the winter for sanding walks and driveways. Get several buckets full. Before you spread it, take a pail of water or a hose and splash an area with it. Then quickly spread the sand right on top of the puddle. The sand will immediately freeze to the water you just put down and make an instant nonslip surface. That gritty area will last until the next big melt. The reason the shavings didn't work for Sammy is that there was nothing to bind them to the ice.

Borium welded on horse shoes for the winter is an excellent way of preventing winter slips, but many horses either never see shoes, or they are often pulled before winter. You can also buy Easy Boots with non-slip studs. If you are facing a period of deep freeze and icy paddocks, the sand on water trick will work. Wet an area, throw some sand on it, and your horses will be able to move around comfortably. If sand is not available, use the manure and shavings or sawdust from your stall cleaning after splashing the water down. A bit messier, but it is also effective. There are things that will always keep me rooted in New England. Ice underfoot isn't one. I never mind the snow, but I've gone down like a bowling pin just often enough that I am very leery of ice. On top of that are the horses that I have had to put down with broken legs. Stock up with sand to give your horses good footing no matter what. If you never use it that's okay. It has a forever shelf life. I keep my sand containers covered. My barn cat Annabelle thinks it has a better use.

19

Gravel

(foot abscesses)

───────────── ♘ ─────────────

Gravel is the unusual name for what is probably our most common cause of lameness. It would be rare for any equine vet not to be dealing with a case a week. A horse that is "graveled" might be three legged lame one day and completely sound the next. Many horses recover with no outside help. Even more remarkable is that usually, once a horse is over it, there are no after effects.

In order to understand this lameness and how to deal with it, we have to start with some basic knowledge of the horse's foot. Pick up your horse's foot and look at the bottom. The junction between the wall and the sole is called the white line. It's just like the junction between the wall and the floor in a room. It's not really a structure in itself. It's just a place where the wall and the sole meet. In a healthy foot, it's a faint line which is lighter in color than the wall or the sole. Have your farrier point it out the next time he/she is trimming.

The culprit is usually a piece of gravel that penetrates at that wall/sole junction. The small stone gets wedged in the white line and allows bacteria to enter. An infection may follow. If it is unable to drain out the bottom of the foot, the horse is on his way to becoming "graveled." Some people think the stone travels up the foot and causes the lameness. It doesn't. What does travel up, is the bacteria and the inflammation that they cause.

The abscess may just drain, or be drained by your vet or farrier, from the bottom of the foot. Often it works its way up the white line inside the hoof wall, following the path of least resistance. When the infection gets up to the sensitive areas of the foot, near the coronary band, the horse will become very lame, sometimes to the point of refusing to put the foot down. The lameness may not appear for days or even weeks after the original penetration. A graveled horse looks and acts like a horse with a broken leg. It hurts. The foot is often warm, and there is almost always a very strong digital pulse at the back of the pastern and low ankle. Pressure with hoof testers may cause more pain. If there is some doubt as to the diagnosis, X-rays may have to be taken, and sometimes (but not always) they show exactly where the abscess is.

If your farrier or vet cannot get a graveled foot to drain from the bottom, then there are two other ways that the issue is usually resolved. As the infection reaches the top of the wall at the coronary band, it may break open. The skin splits, and smelly watery pus will drain out. Relief comes quickly. To encourage this, soak the foot in a strong solution of Epsom salts. Place the foot in a corded, black-rubber feed tub and then slowly add water. Once the horse accepts that, add the Epsom salts until you see only a little bit undissolved on the bottom of the tub. There is nothing as soluble as Epsom salts, and the more concentrated the solution is, the more drawing power it has. Poultices can also help. Even with these aids, some graveled feet do not open up at the top, and then the third possibility will happen. In these stubborn cases, the abscess will slowly be absorbed, and the horse gradually becomes less lame.

Even though gravel is an infection, we usually advise not giving antibiotics. No matter how high the dosage, it is hard to get a therapeutic level. Abscesses tend to get walled off with fibrous tissue, and the medicine is unable to penetrate them. If possible it's best to avoid using anti-inflammatory medicines such as Bute or Banamine, which may make the animal more comfortable. These drugs do decrease the pain, but they also tend to slow down the possible release of the infection from the bottom of the foot or at the coronary band. Although rare, there are cases where the infection becomes very entrenched and severe, and these horses often have to be hospitalized and more specialized procedures done to alleviate the problem. Graveled horses should be current on their tetanus vaccination.

If you have a lame horse for no apparent reason, always check the digital pulse of the foot. A strong pulse as compared to the normal foot is often the best indication that your horse may have gravel. It seems to be a more consistent finding than heat in the foot. If you don't know how to find and assess the pulse, have your vet show you the next time he or she is in the barn. It is a skill that is easy to learn and one that every horse owner should master. I always ask owners who call about an acutely lame horse if there is a stronger pulse in that foot. If there is, the chances are good that the animal has that strange foot infection we call gravel.

20

Guilt Trip

Anyone who has used me as a vet over the past 10 years knows my technician, Erin. Before I hired Erin, I knew her as manager for two large barns and then as a client. She drives my truck and keeps our day running smoothly. Her intuitive nature and bodywork on clients' horses have become an integral part of my chiropractic work. Erin has superb horse-handling skills and a lot of common sense. As my right hand on thousands of farm calls in various situations, she has seen all kinds of problems. For this reason I was surprised when she told me that she experiences some lingering guilt over the decision to euthanize her pony.

Here is her story, which she has given me permission to tell you. Erin was eleven when her parents, with zero horse backgrounds, relented and made room for Spirit, a six-year-old gelding pony. Erin spent every minute she could riding and caring for him. Like all girls with a horse, she told him all her secrets. The years passed and Spirit didn't grow, but Erin did. Now it was Erin's daughter's turn to ride him. In his old age, Spirit began to choke. "Choke" is a condition in horses in which food gets stuck in the esophagus on the way to the stomach. As you can imagine, it is painful. Erin became vigilant about what she fed him. In his last couple of years even green grass would ball up in his throat and cause discomfort. If it didn't pass on its own, we would have to use a stomach tube to relieve the problem.

Toward the end, Spirit was choking on what was essentially a soup diet. Erin agonized over the situation, and in the end decided to put him down. I was there, and agreed with both her thought process and her decision. Now, a few years later, Erin has some remorse. "If I had only made his feed wetter earlier… If I had gotten him through this last episode it might have been the last one…"

That's Erin's story. Does it ring true for you? After decades of practice, farm vets get to know their clients pretty well. Over the years I have listened to owners confess their guilt over decisions that they have made about their animals and their care. Here are some of the things I have heard:

• I sometimes wonder if I made the decision to euthanize my old mare because it was convenient for me at the time.

• I often regret selling Charlie. I don't like everything I hear about how he is treated in his new place.

• I felt sorry for her in that paddock when all the others were out, heads down in the green grass. She never would have foundered if I had listened to you.

• I had a feeling I should have checked with someone first and not used that steroid ointment in his eye with the ulcer. Because of it he lost that eye.

• My horse trailer had been sitting for three years, and I didn't keep up with its maintenance. It wasn't in any shape to use, and I couldn't get anyone to trailer him that night. Surgery might have saved him.

• I fed the night hay, saw his halter on, and decided not to interrupt his meal to take it off. Found him in the morning, hanging by his halter from a hook in the wall. His neck was never right after that.

• I'm so busy. I really don't have time to ride her. I'm afraid that she is bored to death. It's all I can do to just to feed and clean her out. I haven't even brushed her in over a week!

• And many, many more.

Here is Erin who has been on hundreds of farms, seeing all kinds of management in the past ten years. She knows what good care and what poor care looks like. She is an excellent caretaker of all of her own animals, and yet there is that twinge of guilt that she hadn't done enough. I tell you her story because if Erin, with all her experience and expertise, is feeling some guilt, I'm sure that everyone reading this article feels some too. In my own case, I felt guilty skipping barn check three nights ago when we had the big snow storm.

Make no mistake, sometimes the guilt is warranted, but mostly we are all just trying to do our best. Our animals are dependent on us to put out the meals, clean out the water pails and clean up the poop. We blanket them, brush them, and even pay to have them massaged! They trust us to make decisions for them. Give yourself credit for taking on the responsibility of horse ownership. I believe that most of us don't have much to feel guilty about because we make our decisions based on what makes sense at the time.

On the other hand, I am thinking about one or two so-called rescues in our area where there are *way* too many horses kept in terrible conditions. Rather than "rescuing," these misguided folks are actually "collecting," with the conviction that no one can care for animals as well as they can. They usually don't read articles like this. Why bother? They have all the answers. I have been called as a witness in court cases involving a few marginal rescue farms. Typically they believe that their care is the very best. There is no guilt, only surprise that they are being singled out for abuse.

A little guilt is okay. It is one of the drivers that keeps us responsible. I have no solid advice for anyone with paralyzing remorse. In my experience, one thing that helps is a willingness to research what needs to be learned for the particular problems you are dealing with. Then it's just doing the best you can. Maybe that means getting on the heavy coat and boots and going out to do night check in a blizzard even though you don't feel like it. Then there is forgiveness. Forgiveness, especially of ourselves, is difficult, but it's good for mental health and moving on.

21

Hay Crisis

—————— ♘ ——————

Some years are great summers for ducks and umbrella sales, but not so good for making hay. Other years the hay-making season is way too dry. In either situation hay becomes less leafy and not as nutritious. Although the quality may be poor, lack of the product will make it more expensive. In those years we all look around for other sources of feed for our animals.

The Portland area equine veterinarians that share emergency duty got together the other day. Dr Rachel Flaherty of Back Cove Equine Veterinary Care gave us a presentation on hay-replacement options for horses. It was so well researched and timely that I am presenting some of its main points here.

There are a number of things that you can use to supplement hay, but it is wise to avoid them as *complete* substitutes. Good times or bad, day in and day out, most of the horse's diet should always be roughage. Down south that might mean pasture 24/7. In Maine it means pasture for one short season and roughage (hay) the rest of the year. Roughage has at least 18% fiber. Our GI tracts could never handle it, but the design of the horse's gut makes high fiber the perfect feed for them. It provides most of the digestible energy, proteins, vitamins, and minerals that horses need. It should be fed out at 1.5 to 2.0% of their body weight per day. This means that a 1000-pound horse will go through about ¾ of an average bale of hay a day. If you feed less, you can anticipate some health problems.

Issues always arise when people look for complete substitutes for hay. For example, particle size in feed is important. It should be at least one inch in length. Shorter particles may lead to colic and a tendency to chew on wood. Bagged *complete feeds* have that problem. They are eaten quickly, and if horses aren't spending time chewing, they tend to get bored and pick up unwanted behaviors. The complete feeds used as a total hay substitute increase the risk of colic and laminitis. They should be used only as a partial supplement in a poor hay year, not as a total substitute.

Hay stretcher pellets are not the correct particle size, and like complete feeds, should be considered only as a supplement and not be depended on for total roughage needs. These are mostly alfalfa meal with some peanut shells.

Hay cubes are often an alfalfa/timothy mix and are a good source of fiber. Their particle size is adequate, but they are richer than native hay and so should probably be avoided as a complete substitute. There is a risk of choke as the cubes are quite dry. Soaking for ten minutes before feeding is recommended.

Chopped hay is put through large commercial dryers after mowing and is packaged in air tight bags. It is pretty much dust and mold free. The particle size is generally over an inch so it makes an excellent supplement or substitute for native hay. The downside is the extra expense. Lucerne Farms of Aroostook County is the prime manufacturer in Maine and a good source.

Beet pulp is a good source of very digestible fiber, but has some vitamin deficiencies, and is extremely dry. Most of the cases of choke that we see in horses in our area are from feeding beet pulp that has not been well soaked for several hours before feeding. Like beet pulp, *rice bran* is often used to put weight on, and is a good source of fat and fiber, but shouldn't be a major substitute for roughage. *Wheat bran* is another good source of fiber, but because of a mineral imbalance, its use should be limited.

Straw has great fiber, of course, but is limited in nutrition value.

Lawn clippings are often thrown over the fence and, in limited quantities, would be okay with some warnings. The moisture content is high, so if left in a pile, the grass will rapidly mold. Generally, people mow their lawns once a week. A big once-a-week meal of grass clippings has the potential of causing colic, as the bacteria in the gut can die off with the unaccustomed feed, stopping the digestive process for a while.

Concentrates (bagged horse grains) are high in readily attainable energy and low in fiber relative to the volume. It would be a big mistake to feed more grain just because hay is scarce. Grain should always be considered as a supplement, and never the mainstay, of a horse's diet. There is plenty of evidence to show increased ulcer risk, potential metabolic syndromes, overweight issues, and all kinds of behavior problems from feeding too much grain.

To summarize: while expensive this year, hay is still the best feed. Chopped hay is a possible substitute. Hay cubes, hay stretcher pellets, beet pulp and rice bran are supplements, but not good substitutes for hay. Grain should be considered as a supplement and never a substitute for roughage.

22

Health Problems at Horse Shows

———————— ♘ ————————

"**W**arning: This show may be hazardous to your horse's health." If you had to pass under that sign on your way into a show, would it make you stop and think about going in? As a veterinarian I see problems every year that are directly related to horseshows. Whether or not your animal comes home with a problem largely depends on your preparation.

At least once a season I am called to tranquilize a horse that refuses to load. The frantic owner trying to get to a show has already spent two miserable hours trying to get that horse on the trailer. When you consider the horse's nature, getting into a confined, often dark and unstable space is not part of how they are wired. Initial loading takes time and patience and should be worked on long before any event. Horses that won't load can be very aggravating, so professional training is often money well spent. By the way, tranquilized horses don't necessarily load any better, and most shows don't want you showing a horse under the influence.

There are also those horses who, on the way to or back from a show, decide to kick out at the trailer walls, partitions, or ramp, injuring their legs, sometimes disastrously. Four full leg wraps, including the coronary band are a good precaution. The first time to put on a set of wraps is not when you are about to leave. Many horses, especially young ones, will kick repeatedly the first time wraps are put on. Train them to accept protective wraps well in advance of the day.

Respiratory disease is the biggest potential hazard at shows. First, there are all the bugs that may be new to your horse. Then there is the fact that the stress of showing lowers resistance to disease. If you don't have to stable overnight, your chances of coming home clean are better. While there, try not to let your horse socialize with others. If your horse does pick up a bug, you probably won't notice anything until you've been back home two to four days. That's when your animal may go off feed, run a fever, or start with a nasal discharge. Sometimes it means a cough that may persist for weeks. Best prevention is to follow your veterinarian's recommendation for vaccines. These ideally should be given weeks before the show. No vaccine is 100%, but they help. This is most important in young, unexposed horses.

If you plan to stable your horse at a show, be prepared with tools to correct any stall repairs at the grounds. There are facilities where broken boards, nails sticking into the stall, and uneven floors are common. Look around and correct any problems before leading your horse in.

Most people bring their own feed. This makes good sense. You are going to enjoy yourself and don't want to waste time looking for the hay guy, with his inflated prices, for a product that may be marginal. Even subtle feed changes are a common cause of colic.

While you are packing, don't forget a first aid kit to handle the common problems. Ask your veterinarian to supply you with what you might need. While it is true that horse show dangers exist, that is no reason not to go and have fun. Calmly think about what you might find, or what might happen, and be prepared.

23

High Tech Talk
(changing communications)

———————— ♘ ————————

I have been a veterinarian since 1969. Within a week of graduating from vet school, I was working in a general practice in a rural area of New Hampshire. Cellphones did not exist. Most vets had a wired-in Motorola radio mounted under the dashboard to talk with their office. An antenna with a spring base was mounted on a front fender. The base unit in the office was the size of a big bread box, and there was a 20-foot antenna, supported by cables, on the office roof. The office unit could communicate with its vets on the road, and vice versa, but not with anyone else. Each truck and the office had its own assigned call letters. There were FCC rules on proper procedure, such as how to sign in and out. A log was supposed to be kept on all conversations. That rule was mostly ignored. Talk was supposed to be limited to business, with no socializing. We didn't pay too much attention to that rule either. In my vehicle I would hear a burst of static, and then over my speaker:

"KCC323 this is KCB 434, come in please." KCC323. That was me. I reached down, picked up the microphone attached to the unit by a curly wire, pushed the switch, and held it down.

"KCB434 this is KCC323, come in." Release mic switch. More static, and then: "Elmer Loring has a lame horse over in Monroe, can you get there?"

Hit mic switch and hold it down. "OK. Tell him I'll be there late this afternoon. KCC 323 over and out." Release mic switch.

"KCB434 out."

Reception was spotty, and when you got a call, you often had to drive a few miles to find a high hilltop with minimal trees to call the office back. Transmission followed the rule of *line of sight*. If there were hills between you and the base station, you could only get static. There was a knob on the unit called the squelch, and if you turned it one way or the other, you could sometimes make the transmission clearer. Talking to a client directly meant driving to the next gas station with a pay phone in the lot. Today they are a rare sight, but back then there was at least one phone booth in every small town. I would pull up, and if I saw two or three teenagers crowded into the booth with all ears collected around the phone, I drove on, knowing this was going to be a long wait. I am still amazed by how easy it is to talk directly to a client these days while in my truck. The only downside I can see is the huge number of accidents attributed to cellphone use. After seeing so many people pay more attention to their phones than the road, I decided to never talk or text when driving.

Texting is a remarkable spin off of cellphones. It was teenage clients texting me, that forced me to learn how to do it. Of course, many prefer texting to talking. I think that misunderstandings are more apt to happen in texting, just like face-to-face conversations are probably better than phone ones. A few years ago, I was in a horse barn with an owner and two teenage girls. As I was talking to my client, I noticed that both of the girls were listening to our conversation but at the same time were each texting. I thought they might be texting each other and saying something they didn't want us adults in to hear, but no, they explained that they were texting two different people in two different locations. I still think that's a little nutty.

Having cellphones doesn't mean that communication is always what you would like it to be. Here's an example: Erin is driving the truck to our next call. My cellphone rings, and I pull it out of my pocket.

"This is Carol Green. My old gelding is sick. Can you stop by?"

"We could probably get there in about an hour. Is he running a fever?"

"I don't know; I can't find my thermometer."

"Are there any gut sounds, and is he restless like he might have colic?"

"Oh, I didn't think to listen, and I'm not sure he's restless, but he just doesn't seem normal..."

You probably can guess the rest of the questions and their non-answers. I wonder what amazing devices we will be communicating with in five years, but I'll bet some conversations won't get any better. About eight years ago, I saw my first cellphone with a built-in camera. It was a Nokia, and I said, "This will never catch on." Now, I find it a great help in practice and would never consider getting a cell if it couldn't take a picture or a video. Veterinarians often get calls about a horse with some lacerated body part. When I hear the question, "Do you need to come out and suture it?" My automatic response is always, "Grab your cellphone and send me some pictures." With these images we can usually tell whether a horse needs to be sewn up. Some wounds do, and some don't. It's awesome that we can take a very detailed picture and send it through the air to someone else miles away, all in less than a minute.

Two weeks ago I was asked to look at a horse with a perplexing lameness. We took digital X-rays and noticed an unusual area in the coffin bone that made me wonder if it was the problem. We sent the X-rays by phone to a referral hospital for some advice. What a cool thing that is! Up until a few years ago I would have taken flat films, brought them home to be developed, and then sent them via the U.S. mail for that second opinion. The referring vet would get them two or three days later instead of the minutes that it took. That day we had an expert opinion for the owner before we left her farm.

My wife Bonnie and I just got back from a Florida vacation. One day we had been on the beach and had enough sun. We agreed that an ice-cream cone would taste good. I got behind the wheel and started driving. Within minutes Bonnie said, "You missed your turn; you should have gone left back there." I knew she was wrong, so I pretended I didn't hear her and kept on going.

"David, are you listening? You are on the wrong road." I insisted that we were going the right way and kept driving. It got a little testy in the car. I pulled up to the ice-cream stand a few minutes later. Bonnie said, "I thought we were going to Larry's ice cream." I replied, "Oh, I assumed we were going to Super Scoops."

There we were, in the same car, talking live, not texting, and still had a communication issue. In the years I have been in practice, there have been huge advances in our ability to communicate with each other. Yet, misunderstandings still happen, and perhaps even more so when we talk via high tech. Is it because it's so easy to get in touch that we don't take the time to think first?

If you have a problem with your horse, I have a few suggestions before you call, text, or email your vet. First, calm down and assess the situation. Temperature, pulse, and respiration are always great information. If it looks like colic, check gut sounds and the color of the gums. If it's a breathing problem, count the respirations per minute. If your horse has been cut, be ready to describe exactly where is it, how deep, and if it's bleeding. If you have a smartphone, take a picture of it. If there are discharges, be ready to describe them. If you don't supply this information, I guarantee you that you will be asked to go back to your horse and get it. We have these incredible instruments at our fingertips. See if you can be as smart as your phone.

24

Hopeless Fractures

---------- U ----------

Would you consider skiing down a mountain knowing that if you broke your leg that would be the end of you? Me either. Hundreds of skiers suffer fractured legs every year in the U.S., and within six months most are walking without a limp. Yet we have all heard about horses that had to be put down because of a broken leg. What's the story? Are veterinarians so far behind that they have to have to kill the problems they can't fix?

In order to answer this question, let's go back to the ski slope. Mary, trying to avoid a small child, veers off course, hits a patch of ice, and is thrown into a tree. She struggles to get up, but can't bear any weight on one leg. Within minutes the ski patrol has arrived, splinted the leg, and soon Mary is sledded down to an ambulance and is on her way to the hospital. All the way from the slope and into the hospital, care is taken to insure that there is no leg movement. Within an hour of the accident, X-rays are taken and show a complete mid-shaft fracture of the femur. Complete means that the bone is broken in half. This is much more serious than just a crack through the bone. It is a bone in two pieces.

Muscles around a complete fracture go into spasm, which makes it hard to get the two ends into alignment. That's the doctor's first job. This requires muscle-relaxing drugs to ease those powerful leg muscles. Appliances will be used to pull the bones into place. That process will take hours, perhaps days with Mary confined with her leg elevated by a system of cables and pulleys. Once the two ends are in alignment, a fixation system will be applied, which in this case will include hardware like rods, screws, and plates, and then, often, a full length cast. At this point the fracture is not really "fixed." The bones have just been brought back into position and kept from moving so that the body can begin the true repair. If the blood supply is not too severely damaged, and the reduction and fixation are successful, the fracture should heal, and Mary will be ambulatory.

Let's compare Mary's fractured femur with what happens to a horse with a fractured femur. The ones I have seen have happened in the winter or on slick mud. The horse slips and falls with one leg too far under the body. As the huge weight of the body is driven down onto that leg, the leg snaps. I have been called out in the morning more than once to check on a horse that has been down all night with a fractured hind leg. Often the owner and friends have been trying to get the horse up for hours before calling for a vet. The horse is usually found lying on the fractured leg. It takes at least three people to roll a 1000 pound horse over to the other side. Then, once the injured leg is on top, it becomes obvious if the fracture is complete as the leg will bend in the middle like it never should.

If we suspect a fracture, but aren't sure, X-rays will be necessary. Most equine vets carry an X-ray machine, but there is the problem of getting power out to the horse. Then there is the fact that the immense muscle of the quadriceps scatters the X-rays enough that a good radiograph with a portable machine is often not diagnostic. Machines strong enough to get through that mass don't fit in a truck. With or without X-rays, the animal still has to be transported to the nearest major equine hospital. This is no easy job if a horse can't get up. If it is a complete fracture, we are faced with reducing the break. As with Mary's broken leg, this would mean making sure that the animal remains still for hours while the muscles are stretched out to get the ends back in position. I'm sure you get the point. All this can and has been done, with horses less than a year old, but when I see a full grown horse with a complete fracture of the femur, I recommend immediate humane euthanasia. There is a somewhat better chance in dealing with the humerus of the front leg, but it would still be very challenging. I suppose if a 1000 pound horse fractured one of these big bones while in the operating room of an equine hospital, there might be a chance. Even so it would be a very difficult repair, with a guarded prognosis. Fortunately, big bone fractures of horses are rare. Successful repairs to date have been mostly limited to youngsters.

On the bright side, there has been a tremendous amount of progress made in the last 20 years on bone fractures in horses. Cannon bones, and occasionally tibia repairs, are successful with advanced orthopedic equipment in the hands of skilled surgeons. Horses with fractured pasterns that used to be considered hopeless now have at least a chance of being mobile again. Fractured coffin bones will usually heal in six months, but new techniques may have a race horse returning to work in half that time. Of course, part of the consideration will always be the inevitable huge cost on an uninsured animal.

Small-animal orthopedic surgeons often repair every conceivable type of fracture in dogs or cats hit by cars. Dealing with horses is completely different. The size and temperament of horses makes repairs of big bone fractures impractical and often impossible, and so, yes, often we have no choice but to put these unfortunate animals down.

25

Horse Journaling

It was my first visit to Barbara's barn. I had just finished a routine physical exam and vaccinations on her 12-year-old mare, Ginger. I asked Barbara if she had any concerns, and she replied, "Yes, there is something. Ginger occasionally gets belly aches. Why would that be?" I questioned Barbara about the barn feeding schedule, amount and type of hay and grain, and anything I could think of that might give us a clue. I did learn that the episodes came just every so often, and that an oral dose of Banamine made her comfortable every time. Barbara had made some feed changes but couldn't remember there being any connection with the colic episodes. She also couldn't recall any special relationship to weather, time of day, or the season. After 10 minutes of conversation I was stumped as well and suggested that she consider keeping a daily journal on Ginger.

After many years of practice, I have found very few owners who keep daily records on their horses. Those that do have a wealth of information at their fingertips, and when mysteries like Ginger's colics come up, a pattern often emerges that can give you an answer.

Here is what I suggest. First, get an inexpensive notebook. Just a simple spiral one works fine. Enter the date in the left margin. After that, write in your entry. It's that simple, and should be kept simple. When the pages start to fill, you have something very powerful. Keep one book for each horse, and keep the journals in the barn where they belong. Resist the temptation to put the entries on your smartphone or in your computer. If you are like me, you'll forget to put the entry into your computer when you get back inside the house. There are smart phone apps for this, but they are still not as good as a notebook. You may not have the phone in the barn, and if you are away, no one else has access to the information.

Here's a sample of what a typical page on a made-up horse might look like:

3/1/14 Spring vaccines (EWE-Tet on left side of neck, rabies on right). Vet says teeth OK for now. Cataract in left eye about the same. Still not enough to cause any significant vision problems. Taped for weight. 1050 pounds.

3/2 Doesn't want to put head down. Sore to touch right side of the neck. Called vet. Advised hot packs, who said, if no better call back. Hot packed 2x before going to bed. Eating ok. Temp 100.5.

3/5 Neck OK. Can get head down now. Vet here to check boarder's horse. Felt neck and said next time we should spread shots out. Maybe give the rabies in hind quarter instead of the neck.

3/7 Lunged for 20 minutes. Moving well.

4/2 Up to 45 minutes of work. At end of ride resists going right. Legs not swollen. Foot seems OK.

4/3 Walks OK, but lame RF at trot on lunge. Called vet. Told me to check pulse RF and check bottom of foot. Pulse stronger than LF. Abscess? Vet said could come out tomorrow if still a mystery. Soaked with Epsom salts for 20 minutes tonight.

4/5 3-legged lame this AM. John the farrier was in barn and he checked. Foot sensitive with testers over 2nd nail hole on inside of RF foot. Found tract and opened it to drain. Told me to soak for 2 more days and to keep a boot on that foot. Soaked once tonight.

Some of the entries may quite ordinary, but they are packed with information. Writing down where the vaccines were given is always useful in case a horse does get a reaction. Noting which leg was lame and what was done becomes a permanent record. We think we'll never forget, but without it being entered, we probably won't even remember which leg it was months later.

Wondering about Barbara and her mare Ginger? Barb did start keeping a journal and made an entry every time the mare got colicky. She made note of weather conditions and any changes in her management. The colics continued, off and on, for several months. The next time I was in the barn was almost a year later, and I asked to see her journal. When we looked at it together, we found the pattern! All along I had been thinking that her colic was intestinal and somehow diet related. But when we read the entries, we saw that Ginger's colicky episodes were always toward the end of her heat cycles. It seemed like her colics were from ovary pain when she was about to ovulate. The clincher was that the record showed that Ginger never colicked from October until January. Those are the months that most mares do not come into heat. Without the journal entries we would still be trying to figure it out. I did an ultrasound exam of her reproductive tract. Everything looked normal. The recurring colics (the word just means abdominal pain) were from the pain she felt close to ovulation. The one dose of Banamine that Barbara was using was an appropriate drug for what was going on, and there was no need to investigate further. In time Barbara put the mare on an herbal remedy designed to lesson painful ovulation and smooth out heat cycles. The mare has not colicked since.

I keep the journals for my two donkeys in separate spiral notebooks right in the feed trunk in my tack room. Each has a ballpoint pen clipped to the cover so that I don't have to go back to the house for one. Vaccinations, dental work, and other medical stuff are all entered. Comments by the farrier are noted. If one of my guys is off feed, I enter pulse, temperature, and respiration. I also note any severe weather or other changes that might be going on that day.

Keeping a separate horse journal for each of your animals is a good equine management tool and important in becoming more aware of what is going on with your horses (and of course, your small animals). It is invaluable when you are looking for answers. It doesn't take many months of journaling for patterns to become evident.

26

Horse Poor

$\bigcup$

Just this morning I visited a farm where the owners told me that they were considering stopping their rescue operation. Increasing expenses have made it hard for them to continue providing just the basic daily care for the animals they have saved.

The times are hard financially. It's especially difficult for horse owners who pay out more each month for hay, grain, and everything else that comes by truck. The price of bedding skyrockets as mills use their shavings and sawdust as fuel.

In spite of the costs, we continue to keep our horses, sacrificing in other ways to stay afloat. Horses are part of our lives, and for most people whose farms I visit, an empty barn is not an option. However, I do think there is a limit on how many horses one should have. That number is different for everyone. It's all about the size of the pocketbook.

Here is how to do the math, taken one step at a time. Let's keep it simple and say that you have just one horse, and it is kept at home. One of the biggest expenses is simple care and feeding. An average 1000 pound horse will eat about ¾ of a bale of hay per day. That's about 23 bales per month, times the number of months that you feed out hay, times the price per bale. Do the same arithmetic for the bags of grain and supplements that you feed per year, times the price per bag or container. Now calculate bedding cost. If you board your animals out the math is simpler, but, of course, a lot higher. Multiply out the board bill per month times 12 for the year, or fraction of the year that you are boarding.

Work out the numbers for the farrier bills for shoeing or trimming for the year. Take old receipts from your vet for the past two years and average those out for routine care like shots and dental work. Add in the worm medicine for the year. Multiply by the number of horses, and you have a pretty good idea of what your horses cost you per year. Because of the increasing cost for everything, I'd budget an additional 10%. Are you beginning to understand why you might be a little short each month?

Here is the problem from the point of view of an equine veterinarian who is on horse farms in Maine year round. At least twice a month, I will visit a farm and find a situation that requires hospitalization. Let's say the chances of recovery are good, but the bill is estimated at $2000. If your horse numbers are such that you might be able to afford this, perhaps with some stretching, then you are apt to go for it. If your horse population is so high that you struggle each month just to provide the basics, a bill of $2000 might be completely out of the question, and it will be the horse that suffers.

Bottom line: Horses are expensive to keep. My recommendation is that your horse numbers be kept to a point where basic care is absolutely guaranteed, even in today's economy. Our animals should be eating well, have plenty of bedding, regular dental and foot care, and good preventive veterinary care. I know of many horses that were purchased or taken in because someone felt sorry for them and just wanted to get them out of a bad situation. I have a donkey myself that I bought for that very reason. Accept too many "free" animals and you'll find yourself skimping on good health essentials because you can't afford it. Ignoring good basic care doesn't pay in the long run. Have the horses that you can afford to care for. Give them a good life.

27

Horse Talk

(old horse sayings)

———————— ♘ ————————

We have the most amazing horse heritage in this country. Do you realize that back in the early 1900s there was one horse for every four people! Every day saw gridlock on the streets of big cities like Boston and New York where thousands of carts and wagons were pulled by horses. In their amazing book, *The Horse in the City,* authors McShane and Tarr display photographs of the horse crowded streets. They describe horses at the time as "indispensable…providing the muscle for vehicles that moved freight, transported passengers, fought fires and were the power in breweries, mills, foundries, and machine shops." Horses were called "living machines," and sadly, were often treated as such.

Our equine heritage continues today, although we use them differently and abuse them less. Most people now see horses as living beings and not machines. The ratio of horses to people has changed. There is now one equine for every thirty-four of us, but there are actually more horses in the U.S. today than in 1900. In fact, the United States in 2009 had more horses than any country on earth!

It's no wonder that horse sayings are so much a part of our culture. Here are a few examples, with backgrounds on each.

Horsepower: When steam engines were first invented, they were used as pumps to pull the water out of deep coal mines. In the 1800s a Scottish inventor by the name of James Watt made that engine much more efficient. Then, to increase sales, he coined the term horsepower. He watched horses work and calculated that a fit horse was capable of pulling a load of 330 pounds of coal up from a mine through a pulley system at the rate of 100 feet per minute. He called that one-horsepower. Imagine a machine that could replace 10, 100, or if large enough, even 1000 horses! Businesses of the day with stables of many working animals were quick to change to mechanical power. Today the capacity for work in everything from garden tractors to aircraft carriers and the planes they carry is still measured in terms of horsepower. Incidentally, a fit human can produce a steady 1/10 horse power.

Vetting: This term was originally used in horseracing. Every horse was checked or "vetted" by a veterinarian to see if it was healthy and sound before being allowed to race. The word is often used in politics. A political party will thoroughly "vet" or investigate candidates for office to make sure that they are competent and don't have a history that might later prove embarrassing. Businesses should be thoroughly vetted before one buys their stock or relies on their guarantees. In today's horse world the term is shorthand for a pre-purchase exam before the sale. In the buying of horses, as in politics and business, sometimes things don't show up on the vetting, and that's when things get interesting.

Hungry as a horse: Go by any horse pasture and you'll see the heads down. It's no surprise to horse owners that their animals spend a significant amount of time eating. The horse stomach is relatively small and is usually trouble free, if there is some roughage in there to work on 24/7. If you deprive a horse of fiber for even a couple of hours, the stomach acids start to irritate the stomach lining. This is one of the primary causes of ulcers and has become a big problem today when horses are left at home alone all day and run out of roughage.

"I have to pee like a race horse": Right after a horse wins a race, he is taken to the "urine stall," where his or her urine is collected and analyzed for drugs. Its midnight, long after the last race, and the horse and groom would like to go home, but are required to stay until the collection is done. That's the reason that racehorses are trained, from the time they are quite young, to urinate "on demand." This is done by grooms whistling and shaking the bedding in their stalls whenever they see a youngster take position to urinate. The training takes, and after a while the race horse will urinate when prompted. So, the term comes from racehorses that seem to be able to "pee" anytime they are asked. Today many horses legally race on the drug Lasix, which is a potent diuretic that has been shown to markedly decrease lung bleeders on the

track. A side result of that is that after the race these horses may be more than ready to urinate.

Long in the tooth: An old time phrase applied to someone getting on in years. A young adult horse has teeth that are about four inches long. Most of that length is below the gum line where you can't see it. As horses age, more of the tooth emerges from the gums, in both the upper and lower jaws. The incisors in horses past 25 are noticeably long and give rise to the expression, long in the tooth.

Don't look a gift horse in the mouth: This is sort of related to the long-toothed horse. It means that if someone gives you a gift, don't critically examine it because, after all, the price was right! The gift horse may be very old, and the way to check is by opening his mouth and checking the teeth to estimate age. How to age a horse by inspection of their teeth is in another chapter, *How Old.* Gift horses often have problems that in the end don't make them the bargain they seemed to be.

Saddlebags: You need things on that long ride you are taking, and the saddle has always been a handy place to hang bags and pouches. When those containers are full, it makes the saddle bulge out to the sides. It became common to apply the term to someone (usually women) whose thighs have a bit of extra off to their sides.

Founder: This is a word that goes back to the days of wooden sailing ships. Ships getting too close to shore were always in danger of a sudden wind driving them onto the rocks. The ships would break apart and were said to have foundered. Founder in horses can also mean disaster. A horse with the inflammatory disease of the feet, called laminitis, may reach a point in which the coffin bone rotates within the hoof capsule. This is founder. It is very painful, and even with advanced treatments and surgery, some horses, like the old sailing ships, become irreparable. Founder was the end of two Kentucky Derby champions, Secretariat, some 20 years ago, and just a few years ago, the colt Barbaro, who foundered weeks after his fractured leg was repaired and healing.

Take the bit between your teeth: Most everyone with time in the saddle has at one time or another had the scary surprise of having a horse take off and pay no attention to the bit. I've checked with three excellent professional riders from different disciplines, and they all agree that the horse doesn't literally take the bit in his teeth. But they can set their jaws and pay no attention to you or the bit. The phrase used in every day talk means someone who has cut off all restraints and goes full speed straight ahead on a headlong course. An example would be, "She ignored everyone's advice, took the bit in her teeth and ran with the project." I found a song with the title, *Take that Bit Between your Teeth* by the European rock group, Electrane. The lyrics have nothing to do with horses, bits, teeth, or taking charge. I guess the group just likes the phrase.

The old gray mare, she ain't what she used to be: We sometimes hear this phrase, taken from a very old song, and it is usually refers to a woman who might be getting "long in the tooth." One interesting fact about gray horses, of either sex, is that as they get older, they tend to get melanomas, tumors of the melanin cells that produce the pigment that makes gray horses that color. Melanomas are so common in grays that you can pretty much count on an older one getting them eventually. They are often round and tend to grow in bunches. Melanomas in horses are usually benign. In people they are often malignant.

There is no question that horse terminology has enriched our language.

28

Horses Raising Kids

———————— U ————————

My wife and I were on vacation in Florida this winter. We reconnected with a former client who now lives in St Augustine. When I was attending her horse in Maine over 20 years ago, she was a teenager at a very active stable, with an emphasis on kids. She has become successful in business and rides competitively in Florida. During our visit we talked about the people and horses we knew from "the old days." At one point someone listening in asked how we knew each other, and she said that we go way back. She shared that I used to work on her grandfather's horses. That was true. Her grandfather Tom loved Standardbreds and raced them at the old Lewiston Maine Fairgrounds. Just to put things in perspective, at that time Tom had retired and I was a very green vet, but her remark did make me feel like an old timer. Our conversation started me thinking about the generations of youngsters I have known that had the good fortune to be brought up around horses or cattle. I am convinced, through many examples, that this exposure is an incredible education for kids.

A few years ago another lady, who was also a youngster in that same stable, told me that it was the responsibility of caring for horses that saved her life. I asked her how, and she told me that as a teenager she had started hanging around with the wrong crowd from school and eventually stopped showing up at the stable. She slid into the drug scene for a time, but it was the emptiness of that life as compared with caring for and riding horses alongside quality friends and mentors that brought her back to horses and responsible living. She has since had a variety of animals, including horses, on her own farm. I know that her own daughter is better for it.

At the age when kids start getting rebellious, there is something grounding about the responsibility of caring for animals. It doesn't matter who you are mad at, or how you feel the world is either mistreating or ignoring you, those animals out in the barn have to be fed, mucked out, and taken care of every day. What the weather is that day or how you feel doesn't matter. There is also the healing aspect. At a time when the family is intolerable, the barn is a great place to go. You pick up a curry comb and brush and start telling your problems to your animals. As a client once told me, "They just listen and listen and never, ever give you any advice." Teenagers all go through that stage of seeing themselves as the center of the world. When they take on caring for another life, it's an attitude changer.

All of this hasn't got a thing to do with my being a large animal vet, but it makes me feel like I'm part of something bigger than just making animals well. When the kids are still young enough to think the vet is cool, it's fun to motion them a little closer, put my stethoscope in their ears and ask, "Would you like to hear your horse's heart?"

I never tire of being present at the birth of a horse. Only one thing is better, and that's observing kids as they watch a horse or cow give birth and then a few minutes later get to see the newborn's first wobbly steps. It's a wise parent that pulls them out of bed at 2 AM to share in the wonder.

Whatever you can do to get your kids, grandkids, or neighbors kids caring for another life, do it. It's a sound investment in all of our futures.

29

How Old

(aging by teeth)

⸺⸺⸺⸺⸺ ♘ ⸺⸺⸺⸺⸺

A few years back my wife and I were on a flight and noticed a young girl sitting across the aisle. She was very chatty and had an incredible smile. Later, I asked Bonnie how old she thought the girl was. Without hesitation she said, "Eight." I asked her how she knew that. I hadn't remembered it coming up in our conversation with the youngster. She said, "That's easy, I could tell by her teeth." Her teeth? You have to understand that for many years Bonnie taught second grade. Every day she would see the mouths of the children in her school. Without even trying, she learned that the children in her grade were losing baby teeth and getting adult teeth in a very predictable way. I got a big kick out of the whole episode, because I am often asked to "age" a horse. I had never given any thought to having this work with kids.

So, how accurate is aging a horse by his teeth? Actually, up to the time that a horse is eight, this is a pretty good measure of age. After that, age estimation isn't as accurate because it depends somewhat on a horse's diet and the anatomy of each horse's skull and jaw. As they become teenagers, it is really more of an art than a science, and even two experts can differ by two or three years on just how old a certain horse is.

Here are the fundamentals from three to eight years old that, with some practice, can make you a pretty good estimator. First of all, the teeth to focus on are the incisors. If you are going to be bitten by a horse, it's the incisors that will get you. Gently roll your horse's upper and lower lip back and you will see 12 incisors, six uppers and six lowers. Both lower and upper incisors come in pairs. There are the central two, the intermediate or middle two, and the corner two, top and bottom.

When a horse reaches his third (actual) birthday, the permanent centrals will have come in. These four permanent or adult teeth will be quite a bit bigger than the intermediate and corner baby teeth. By the fourth birthday the four intermediates will have erupted. Now the incisors will show four large adult teeth and the tiny baby teeth on the corners. At five years the horse will have a "full mouth," which means that all of the incisors will be the larger permanent teeth. It's that easy, right about the third, fourth, and then fifth birthdays, the centers, middles and corners become adult teeth.

There is also something that happens right around the six, seven and eight-year birthdays. Focus just on the bottom jaw and look at those incisors. Right on the flat, biting surface, look for a dark oblong depression, or "cup," right in the middle of each. Just as the teeth erupt at definite times, the cups disappear on a timetable. At six years, the center cup disappears, at seven, the middle cup, and at eight, the cups are gone from all the incisors. So the time table is: three, four, and five years for eruption of the permanent teeth, and six, seven, and eight years old for the cups to leave.

If this is of interest to you, start learning this skill by checking horses in the barn whose age you know, and then see if what you are seeing checks out. It's a great skill and with a little practice will be yours.

30

I should have. . .

(mistakes made, lessons learned)

U

Christmas surprised me again this year, and I found myself saying once more, "I should have done my shopping earlier." This article is a small collection of regrets that I have heard from people in our horse community. Perhaps the new year is a good time to get some stuff taken care of now, and then you'll be able to say, "I'm glad I. . ."

"I should have either gotten rid of it or fenced this side of it," Charlie said. His horse's legs were snagged by barbed wire. The old wire circled his property long before he bought it 20 years ago. It rusts, but it doesn't rust away. It took us a half an hour with rugged wire cutters to completely unwind Charlie's gelding. All four legs were a tattered mess. Barbed wire was a great invention, but it was invented with cows in mind. It fenced in the Wild West and made cattle drives a thing of the past. Bovines literally have a thicker skin than horses and aren't quite as "goosey." When they push up against barbed wire they tend to slowly back away. In the same situation, horses may panic and once trapped, things tend to escalate. It's just a fact. Barbed wire and horses don't mix.

"I should have cleared around it after the storm." In my part of Maine at least 90% of horse trailers are outside year round. When we get a good snow storm and the plow truck does its thing, there are mounds of snow all around that trailer. A little rain comes next, and you have a horse conveyance locked in by several hundred pounds of ice. Pulling the trailer out means a lot of ice chipping to free the locked in wheels. What if yours is iced in right now and you get a colicky horse that needs surgery tonight? I have been part of a couple of emergency trailer dig-out parties at midnight. Not so much fun when the wind is blowing, it's near zero, and the horse should have been in the trailer an hour ago.

"I should have ordered that hay before the storm." While weather forecasting isn't 100%, it's really pretty darn good. If you are like me, you have only so much room to store hay. Maybe you, too, have a convenient hay supplier who will bring you what you need even on short notice. When you hear about a three-day storm coming, it's time to count bales and get on the phone. Wait, and you'll be borrowing a few bales from a neighbor because your hay guy may be in Florida. Those of us that were around for the big ice storm years ago learned another lesson about making plans to have water available. One of my neighbors was without power for 10 days. Every day was a drive to the fire station to haul water back in two 50 gallon drums for her four horses and the house needs. It was a good lesson in how much water one horse drinks. After that Ann always made sure she had plenty of drawn and stored water when it looked like power might be out. It's just another situation where our New England weather forces us to plan way ahead or say, "I should have. . ."

"I guess I should have had that taken down." As I drive around, it amazes me how many big, really big, trees I see that are hanging over barns, sheds, and homes, leaning toward the roof. It might make sense to stand back, way back, once a year, and assess your trees. If a strong wind came from the right direction, would that one go through the roof, or maybe through that fence? Go ahead and cut it down. You or a neighbor could probably use the wood in the stove.

"I should never have left it on him. . ." Right on the door to your horse's stall or within easy reach, hang that animal's halter, with lead attached. In my opinion halters should never be left on stalled horses. They can and do get caught on just about anything, and it is the nature of horses, when trapped, to pull back hard and fast. I have known of instances where horses have been hung up for hours when their halter got snagged by a hook when no one was in the barn to hear the ruckus. Sometimes the injuries that result are not always fixable. I have heard the argument that "I use break away halters," but they don't always break away, and certainly there are times during training when you don't want them to. I like to see halters either hung on the door or just beside it, so if there is a barn emergency that halter is always at hand ready to grab and put on. A lead should be attached to each and every one so that there needn't be a hunt for one.

This list could go on, and I know that you must have said "I should have. . ." many times yourself, and you could add to the list. When you notice something that, unless fixed, may affect your horse's health or safety, fix it. *Now.* Then you'll be able to say, "I'm glad I. . ."

31

Inherent Risks

U

"**B**y your presence on these grounds, you have indicated that you have accepted the limits of liability resulting from inherent risks of equine activities."

You have seen this notice posted at every public stable. The word *inherent* means that horses are, by their nature, potentially dangerous. The person who hangs the sign is saying: "You have been told, so you can't sue us if you get hurt."

The fact is that horses really *are,* just by their nature, dangerous. This is especially true if you ride or drive. If you personally have never spent time in an emergency room after a horse accident, you certainly know people who have. Statistics show that horse activities are in the same inherently dangerous category as motorcycles. Motorcycle accidents result in injury or death 80% of the time. In an automobile accident, you will be injured or die 20% of the time. We don't know those statistics for horses, because after most of our falls or kicks we get up and dust ourselves off. However, 70,000 people *are* treated in emergency rooms in the U.S. for horse-related accidents every year! I know a lot of them. You do too. Maybe you have been one!

The difference between motorcycles and horses is that motorcycles aren't at all dangerous when we aren't riding them. Horses are. The fact is that people are hurt every day just being around them. Walking them, grooming, picking out feet, even approaching them should be done in a careful and mindful manner. In most cases hospital visits caused by horse injuries can be prevented. The workers' comp premium for techs on the road, in my veterinary practice, is many times that of our office personnel. Insurance companies know exactly what the statistics are and charge their premiums accordingly.

I used to get beat up a lot by horses before I learned some hard lessons. My leg was broken when a horse fell on me while he was recovering after surgery. I have been kicked and bitten an embarrassing number of times. It took a full force kick to the crotch about 30 years ago for me to learn not to be so macho in handling horses. In looking back, almost every one of my run-ins was because I was not paying attention or was just being stupid. Horses outweigh us many times and have very fast reflexes. They are wired to bolt and run when scared. If we are in the wrong place, and doing dumb things, it's easy to get hurt. If you are naïve about a horse's ability to inflict damage, go to You Tube and enter just two words: "horse kick." It is amazing how many people are asking to get hurt. One thing we can learn from these videos is to never, ever surprise a horse when approaching them from behind. Their reflexes are far too fast for you to be able to react to their lightning reaction time. There have been some videos posted of riders, in the saddle, pouring ice water over them and their horse for the ALS challenge. Did they not expect the horse to take off and dump them?

When techs comes to work for us, I always insist that they use a lead when handling a horse. I tell them that even if it takes an extra minute to find a lead, they should take that minute. If a horse gets startled and you are holding his halter by hand, he will pull you with him. Our tendency is to hang on, and that's when shoulder injuries happen. I have a shoulder issue today because I used to try to restrain horses by pulling on their halters without a lead. The lead gives you a few feet of slack and an extra moment of time to control the horse that may have "checked out" mentally for a few seconds.

I admire horse owners who will not permit their animals to run in and out of their stalls. If your horse tends to bolt into his stall, train him to stop and wait for you to lead him in at your pace. Go with him, turn him around in the stall and release the lead when you are back at the door, facing your horse. Don't just release him at the door. Horses will fracture their pelvis rushing through a doorway. If you are in the way, you will get knocked down too.

Crossties are handy to park a horse when he is in the aisle. However, ties can be deadly when a horse panics and pulls back. The chain or strap is instantly under hundreds of pounds of pressure, and when it breaks it becomes a flying whip with hardware on the end. Don't rely on the quick release feature of some snaps. Crosstie accidents usually happen in seconds, and trying to release a snap under pressure may put you in harm's way. I know at least one horse that was blinded in one eye when hit by a flying snap. A veterinarian in our office had several teeth fractured when she was just walking past a horse who got scared at something, reared back, and the crosstie broke. If you are in a situation where a startled horse pulls back on the ties, turn away and duck. I never work on horses that are crosstied and always ask the owner or trainer to hold the animal with a lead, standing on the same side as I am. *More about that in the chapter, You Gotta Know How to Hold 'em.*

I don't understand it when people with rude horses say, "I apologize for his barn manners, but he is bombproof under saddle." That never made sense to me. If he is unmanageable with you on the ground, how you could *ever* trust him up there on his back, several feet away from the hard ground. If he does not obey you willingly in everything you ask for on the ground, then it is time for some elementary training. If you aren't up to that job, hire a trainer that will teach your horse and you. Any horse can be taught good manners. Horses with good stable manners are a joy to be around and are as safe as horses can be.

We value them for their strength and speed. Respect these same qualities as you move around them to keep yourself safe.

32

Intensive Care
(commitment of keeping horses)

———————— ♘ ————————

I was thinking about how much attention and care our horses need. I tried to come up with the exact opposite, some living thing that would require almost no care at all. Tortoises came to mind. A quick check online showed me that they are kept as pets. An enclosure the size of your horse's paddock might be about the right size. I learned that a two-block-high cinder wall is all you need to keep one in. Tortoises won't try to dig under the wall if you provide a cool shelter for them to get relief from the summer sun. Here in Maine we would have to provide these cold blooded reptiles some sort of an insulated box with a heat lamp against the winter cold. A slow drip of water over a hefty ceramic bowl sunk in the ground would supply all the water needs. From what I read, with a little planning, you could grow enough food right in their own enclosure to supply most of their nutrition. Apparently they are quite fond of dandelions. You might throw in some table scraps for a little variety. Total cost, including all the second-hand cinder blocks, probably less than $200. Just think. $200 spent just once. Wow, you could leave for a month, come back, and that big boy would be just fine.

Imagine! No training, grooming or mucking. No blankets, ropes, snaps, saddles, bits or bridles. No farrier or veterinary visits. If you have one big enough to ride, there would be no visits to the emergency room when you fell off. You'd be at most three feet off the ground, and going real slow. Think of all the time and money you have spent educating yourself, learning about horse care and training. With just two hours of study, you could become the most knowledgeable person for miles around about the care of your pet. Best of all, there would be no dread of that day when you would lose your friend. That tortoise would probably outlive you, your kids, and maybe your grandchildren.

Even after you have considered all the savings of time and money, I'm guessing that you still wouldn't trade your horse for a big turtle, and I'm not trying to talk you into it. So, why do we keep horses? I can't think of another animal that requires the degree of intensive care and money spent that horses do. To answer my own question, I personally have received far more from my own horses than I have invested in time or money. I have used them for riding, driving, and as just good company. I have kept some at home and boarded some out. In the past 48 years as an equine vet, I have been part of the care of thousands more. Perhaps you agree with me, just having one around is special.

Unfortunately, in my daily work, I see horses that are not looked after. I'm thinking of owners who don't care enough to vaccinate, worm, or even groom them, not to mention proper nutrition. I'm thinking of owners who don't replace the barbed wire fencing on their place for something safer. My ongoing hope is that these owners either recognize and correct their own deficiencies or let someone else take their animals. Horse care certainly teaches us discipline and responsibility. I am often asked if putting very old horses down is the worst part of my job. It's not, really. What is hardest for me is seeing some horses abused by someone not caring enough.

What's the point? I think that every once in a while it is a good thing to think hard and take stock of what your horse means to you. Ask yourself if the benefits for you outweigh the responsibilities. If you, like me, feel that the return is well worth the effort, then make sure that the care you give is the best. If you are starting to begrudge care to your horses, then maybe it's time to reconsider their ownership. I'm hoping that you feel that it's a blessing to have horses and a privilege to care for them.

33

Invasion
(biting stable flies)

U

I am writing this article on a warm Sunday afternoon early in September. Everything is peaceful on my farm right now, except for the bang! bang! bang! coming from the barn. I know the sound well. I have heard it every day for the last few weeks. It's Shamus and Shiloh, my two mini donkeys slamming their feet on the wooden floor of their stall. They have free access to the outside, but these warm days they prefer the stall where the stable flies aren't quite as bad.

I've been a New Englander for 45 years, a Mainer for 42, and I have never seen a summer like this for stable flies! I know it's not just on my place. As an equine vet, I spend my days on other farms, and it seems like everyone's horses (and cows) are being attacked. More than annoying—these flies hurt! I have learned not to wear shorts in the barn. They prefer horses, but if there are enough of them, and my legs are available, I get bitten. Where do these flies come from, and what makes them bite?

First of all, I love their scientific name: *Stomoxys calcitrans.* Translated from the Latin, the first word means, "sharp mouth" and the last word, "kicking." They do have a sharp mouth, and they sure cause kicking. They are in the same family as the house fly, but are ½ to ¾ their size. Unlike house flies they have very sharp teeth and a specialized mouth part that acts like a hypodermic needle to draw in blood. Both male and female flies bite and take blood for their nutrition. The male dies soon after breeding, while the female takes off on her mission. She lands on animal legs, bites, and takes in their blood. I don't know who does research on things like this, but she has to have at least three separate blood meals before she will lay any eggs. Breaks are taken by landing on a fence, a stall wall, or anything nearby. She does some digesting and returns for more blood. Now, engorged with blood, she flies sluggishly to a pile of rotting vegetation or manure and lays bunches of eggs. Without the blood meal, the eggs will not mature. Ten or eleven egg-laying periods occur during this last part of the life of the female.

As with many insects, the eggs hatch in a day or two and become larvae (maggots) who eat the rotting vegetation or manure around them. During the next 15 days or so, the larvae go through some further stages and then become pupae (like a cocoon). This is the stage that is susceptible to fly predators (parasitoids) that many of us buy to stop the development from pupa to adult fly. Unimpeded, the fly will hatch out from the pupa in about 15 days and then head directly for a warm blooded animal. Some adult flies live a few days, others as long as four-six weeks.

You might be asking, doesn't this vet have the sense to spray some insecticide on his equines. I have, and nothing that I have tried lasts more than an hour. I hung a three-foot-diameter fan in the stall which the donkeys can stand in front of, but those determined flies still zoom in and bite. Mosquitoes can't fly against that wind, but it doesn't deter the tiny stable flies.

Why the stable fly invasion this particular year? I'm not sure, and neither is Dr Kathy Murray, an entomologist at the Maine Department of Agriculture, Conservation and Forestry. She told me that the stable fly can travel long distances from their breeding ground. That means that if you are using the fly predators in your compost pile, they may be ineffective against the stable fly that can leave your neighbor's compost and fly right over yours to reach your horse.

I think that the 80-degree days we have had for most of the summer must play a part as well. In Maine this was the hottest August ever. The heat makes compost break down quicker. The adult fly is also more active on hot days. I have noticed that when the temperature drops below 65 degrees, my donkeys stop kicking, and their legs and bellies are free of flies.

A few years ago Damariscotta Lake State Park was shut down for the afternoon, and everyone's admission price refunded because the beach goers were so viciously attacked by stable flies. The massive fly attack was the result of piles of pond weeds that had washed up onto the beach. The rotting vegetation was the perfect place for the fly to lay its eggs. After they hatched, they headed for all the beach goers.

So, what can we do about these pests? Your first line of defense is good housekeeping. Keep your stable, paddocks and pastures clean and dry. Mow grass low around the perimeter of these areas. Clean up feed spills promptly. Create good drainage and keep composting bedding, manure, and other potential fly breeding habitats as far away from animals as possible. If you get your manure picked up regularly, you are ahead of the game. Spreading manure so that it dries makes it unsuitable for fly breeding. You can keep the female from laying eggs by covering the pile with a tarp. Keep its edges well secured with something heavy such as rocks, boards, or the side walls of old tires. (If you use whole tires, drill holes in them so they don't collect water where mosquitoes can breed.) Fewer eggs hatched mean fewer flies.

Dr Murray suggests additional measures. Put up bird boxes. Cultivate some types of flowering plants to attract nature's hit squad. That would include natural enemies such as beneficial insects, birds, spiders, and frogs. If you are considering the tiny predatory wasps, do your homework and choose a reputable supplier. Ask the company's technical staff which species' mix is best for your situation.

The final line of defense would be the use of stable fly traps to capture the adults. Some that get good reviews are the "Starbar Bite Free," the "Olson Biting Fly Trap," and the "Knight Stick by Bugjammer." Each has a sticky coating which must be cleaned and replaced periodically. They have to be set in the right locations and at the correct height to work effectively. A downside is that occasionally small birds are trapped. Hanging the simple fly strips can help. I hung six in my barn when the stable flies first appeared this summer, and they have trapped hundreds, but it didn't get them all. Dozens more are still landing on my donkeys' legs. Dr Murray tells me that bug zappers that attract and electrocute are not a good idea. They tend to kill more beneficial insects than pests.

I've been thinking that leg wraps might help when the fly population is intense. Perhaps then the flies would all go for the belly. There are fly sheets that have a broad bellyband, but the stable fly is so small and determined that I'm not sure how well they would work.

Besides being an extreme annoyance, any biting insect that draws blood can carry disease. Of special concern is Equine Infectious Anemia (EIA) which is usually fatal. We monitor for this disease by using the Coggins test. Any biting insect, including the stable fly, has the potential of carrying the EIA virus.

We will always have stable flies, just like we will always have worms in horses and fleas on dogs. Awareness, good management, and wise choices in their control should make the situation livable, even in extreme years like this one.

34

It's the Law

(bone remodeling)

———————— ♡ ————————

Several months ago I was asked to look at a two year old gelding who was wearing a big ugly bump on his skull. He had banged his forehead full force, just above the eyes. The injury was the result of rearing. With the exception of the Spanish Riding School and circuses, rearing is not a good thing. It can get a horse in trouble, especially when there is something hard overhead. This youngster had gone up while being wormed. If it hadn't been for the overhead beam, he might have gone over. The owner said that his forehead, from poll to eyes, was very swollen and sore for several days. I saw him a few weeks after the collision. The swelling and pain were gone, but now the gelding was wearing that hard bony knot on his forehead. It stuck up nearly an inch. His owner was concerned that the bump might never go away.

Everyone trained in the medical profession learns about Wolff's law. This law says that bone is deposited and reabsorbed according to the stresses placed upon it. We tend to think of bones as being hard, dry, and not as alive as other tissues. The fact is that bones are very active, have an excellent blood supply, and are constantly undergoing changes. When a bone is stressed by one big insult or many small repeated ones, the bone changes its structure.

This gelding had cracked his head as hard as if had been hit with a heavy hammer. The skin and connective tissue over the skull responded with the swelling that we call edema. Within a few hours the injured bone also responded. Cells in the bones called osteoblasts started to lay down new bone, and when I saw him, he was wearing that big mass of new bone. So the initial "stress," the bang on the head, caused the new bone to be laid down in response.

As things calmed down, the bump began to remodel again, this time by the action of another type of specialized bone cell, called an osteoclast. These cells are active in the process of getting the bone back to its normal size. There is another law, which I don't think has a name that says, "Use it or lose it." If you've ever had a leg or an arm in a cast, you know that when a muscle isn't being used, it atrophies (shrinks). Soon after the cast is off and the muscles are back in use, they regain their size and strength. The same process happens with the underlying bone. It's the bone obeying Wolff's law.

An example of this in people is found in the sport of tennis. Compare the two arms of an active pro. You would expect the "active" arm to have bigger and stronger muscles, but the bone itself on that side, because of the constant use, will be denser and noticeably larger.

We see Wolff's law in action with "splints" in youngsters in early training. The ligaments that connect the cannon bone to the splint bone are inflamed and are partially pulled off the bone. The bone reacts by becoming larger and thicker, which is what we see as a splint high under the inside of the knee. Ease off the training and the splint (bony reaction) gets smaller. I'm not sure that Wolff's law works 100%, because with severe skull trauma or big splints, the increased bone never seems to go totally away. The gelding that cracked his head will probably have a slightly raised area years from now.

35

Learn from the Pupil
(telltale eye structure)

It's always scary. You walk into the barn and right away sense that something is wrong. The horse that is usually at his door is way back in the stall. As soon as you enter the stall he comes over, seeking comfort and relief. Even in the dim light you can see that one eye is shut tight. There are tears running down his cheek. You speak softly and very gently try to pry his eyelids open, but he won't let you. You know he's in pain, and you are in a panic.

Veterinarians get calls like this quite often. All we know from your phone call is that you have a horse with a painful eye. It could be anything from conjunctivitis to a punctured eyeball. As you know, eyes are sensitive, and many things can cause the kind of pain that will make a horse keep his eye shut. As a veterinarian I ask myself: *Should I cancel another call to get to your farm right now, or can it wait a bit when I will be a half hour closer to you?*

My tendency in most cases is to give you some first aid measures over the phone, which will enable us both to better assess the situation within a couple of hours. The first thing I would probably tell you is to give your horse a systemic anti-inflammatory medicine. Banamine or Butazolidin (Bute) are quick acting and very effective. The homeopathic remedy, Arnica, is also helpful. Next I advise cold water soaks. Throw some ice cubes into a pail with some cold water. Make a pad of a folded hand towel and dip it into the water. Wring out the excess and very gently place the pad over the horse's eye. He will probably flinch at first, but once he feels the coolness, it will be welcome. Hold the pad gently on the shut eye for a few minutes, then wet it again and reapply. Keep this going for about an hour, and in most cases the eye will begin to open for you.

Before going further we need a quick anatomy lesson. The colored part of the eye is the iris. The iris is muscle. Its opening or closing lets more or less light into the inner eye. The pupil isn't really a structure; it is the dark opening that is regulated by the iris. Think of it as the doorway to the inner eye. When the iris constricts, as in bright sunlight, the pupil is smaller. In the dark the iris pulls back, and the pupil gets larger.

You can evaluate the overall seriousness of most eye conditions by checking the relative size of the pupil. Nothing tells more about the overall health and condition of an eye than the diameter of that pupil.

Severe eye inflammations cause a spasm of the iris and make it constrict even more than it does in bright sunlight. It constricts so much that the pupil is hardly visible at all. All you can see is the colored iris with the pupil as a tiny dot in the middle. Compare one eye to the other. If the painful eye has a small pupil as compared to the other side, it means a serious problem. This is important information for your vet and his or her decision as to how soon to see your horse.

Tonight, after dark, take a strong flashlight out to the barn and look at some horses' eyes. Watch the pupil constrict as you shine the light directly into the eye. Compare both sides. Having done this you will be in a good position to let the pupil be your teacher should you ever have an equine eye problem.

36

Let It Be, Let It Be

(warts)

──────────── ♆ ────────────

The virus known as papilloma affects just about every species of animal. It usually causes skin eruptions, and in people 100 different subtypes of the virus have been identified. One type causes genital warts in young women. These usually disappear in time. Another type of the virus can cause the very serious problem of cervical cancer.

The horse's head is a target for two types of the papilloma virus. One causes a mass of warty growths all around the muzzle in yearlings and youngsters up to about three years old. There are ointments that are designed to make them go away. Another treatment is to remove a few of the warts by cutting them at their base. The idea behind this is that when you snip them off, they bleed and some of the virus gets into the blood stream. The immune system then produces a response to make the rest disappear. I have tried both the ointments and the surgery, and my experience is that neither the ointments nor the snipping of the warts speeds up their disappearance. With time, they always go away on their own. Muzzle warts don't bother horses, but they may bring a lower price at yearling auction barns. They are most often seen in racing stock, because the youngsters on brood farms are usually running together, and the virus is spread from one to another by nose contact. Because they are contagious, your vet may not be able to fill out a shipping health certificate for affected youngsters with warts. The interesting thing about them is that one day the muzzle will be peppered with warts, and a few months later, they are all gone.

The other common papilloma of the horse's head causes a far more irritating problem called aural plaques. The word aural means ear, and the word plaque refers to its raised appearance. The virus causes a huge skin overgrowth on the inside of the ear. The mass may stick out a good ¾ of an inch above the level of the skin of the inside of the ear. It looks like a fungus growing out of the bark of a tree. Google *aural plaques horse* for typical photographs. The growths are pink or gray in color, and the dead skin on the surface is continually flaking off. Insects are thought to spread this form of the virus, which in northern New England means our friend, the black fly.

It is tempting to want to scrub out the ear of a horse with aural plaques. I used to do that. They hate it, so my procedure was to tranquilize the affected horse quite heavily. I then used a damp gauze pad and diligently scrubbed out the messy plaques right down to the normal skin level. After that I applied the latest salve, and had the owner follow up doing the same. The problem was that often, after this aggressive treatment, the owners couldn't get near those ears, sometimes for months afterwards. By the way, the plaques always came back.

The latest treatment being used for aural plaques is Aldera, which is an expensive human ointment used to treat papilloma genital warts in teenagers. One research study showed that it is effective for aural plaques, but the report also says that ointment itself can be irritating, and I'm not sure that the horses in the study wouldn't have gotten better on their own.

Having dealt with many cases of both muzzle warts and aural plaques, I am now convinced that both should just be left alone to heal. For each, nothing I've used so far seems to help either problem. While aural plaques are ugly, most horses are not bothered by them. However, if you aggressively scrape them out, the ears become painful, and horses become highly sensitive to their ears being touched in any way. I have known a few horses that after ear cleaning would not even permit a bridle to be slipped over their ears. Instead, the owners had to approach the horse with the bridle in pieces and put it on very carefully, piece by piece, to avoid touching the ear. Most horses eventually get better, and while the lesions don't totally disappear, they do subside with time and become less noticeable. Take the Beatle's words of wisdom from the song and for aural plaques and muzzle warts, "Let it be, let it be."

37

Let the Body Heal
(the importance of inflammation)

⎯⎯⎯⎯⎯⎯⎯⎯⎯ ♘ ⎯⎯⎯⎯⎯⎯⎯⎯⎯

It is one of those cases that I will never forget. I was working at the old Lewiston Raceway and was going to be there all morning. A horse owner that I didn't know called my office and told my office manager that she had to see me right away as her horse needed attention. Cindy told her that I was at the track and was going to be there all day working on Standardbreds, but if she wanted to trailer her gelding to the track, I would see her there. Two hours later the owner unloaded her horse at the paddock, and I got word that she was there waiting for me.

I hardly had a chance to introduce myself to Becky when she started telling me her story. Three days before, she was working her dressage horse in a sand arena. After a few minutes Becky noticed that her gelding was a little off, but thinking that he would warm out of it, kept him going. Ten minutes later the horse started to limp. Becky stopped, dismounted, looked at his legs, and saw that he wasn't putting full weight on his right fore. Right before her eyes, she thought she could see the leg start to swell. She hand walked him back to the barn and wrapped his leg snugly from pastern to knee with a polo wrap. She kept him in his stall for three days. Twice a day she unwrapped the leg, and each time she did, it immediately started to swell. She then quickly wrapped it again to prevent more swelling. This went on twice a day for those three days. Unwrap the leg, note the leg filling, and quickly wrap it back up again to keep the leg from getting bigger.

I asked Becky to unwrap the leg so that I could take a look. She hesitated for a minute and then said, "Look, Doctor, if I take the wraps off, it will start swelling, I just know it will, and I really don't want to see that leg get big." I told her that there was no way that I could begin to diagnose the problem with the wrap on. Very reluctantly she undid the leg. Sure enough, before our eyes the leg started to swell from just below the knee down to the fetlock. It was actually quite impressive how fast it happened. "Quick, quick," she cried, "let me wrap it back up!" Understand, I had never met Becky before, and there had been no chance to build up any trust. Clearly, she thought that I was wrong in not agreeing with her.

"Becky, listen to me. I need to get my hands on that leg of his so that I can know what to do about it." I almost had to physically restrain her as we watched the leg swell before our eyes. "Oh, no!" she cried! "Look what's happening! We have to get that wrap back on right away." I had to be a little firm. "Becky, I have to tell you that wrapping that leg to get the swelling down is probably exactly what is keeping it from healing." I could tell from her face that she thought I was the biggest quack ever, but she did stand back and sobbed softly as the leg continued to get bigger. I watched it for a few minutes and noted that although the whole leg was rapidly filling, the swelling was concentrated mostly in the back of the leg, right over the flexor tendons. Within a few minutes, it was as big as it was going to get, and it really was big!

I picked the leg up with my left hand supporting the cannon bone and ran the fingers of my right hand down to palpate the tendons. This was over 30 years ago, and ultrasounds were just being introduced in vet schools. I certainly didn't have one. However, I did have a mostly racetrack practice at the time, and I sure knew a bowed tendon when I saw one. I told Becky that bowed tendons are relatively rare in saddle horses and, in my experience, were usually the result of working horses in deep footing. I then told her that the great majority of "bows" healed in time. Now, I faced the more difficult task of explaining why she should not wrap that leg.

Becky listened as I explained how inflammation after an injury is really a good thing. The signs of inflammation are familiar to all of us from our own experience. Think of the last time you got your toe stepped on by a horse, twisted an ankle, or had a car door shut on a finger. The result for you was pain, swelling, heat, redness, and loss of function. These are all the classic signs of inflammation that every doctor and nurse knows. The only one of those signs not usually seen in horses is the redness, which is only visible in very light-skinned animals. The swelling and heat are the result of the local blood vessels "leaking" out the healing white cells and serum into the injured area. That influx of fluid and blood cells is responsible for the almost immediate swelling and the heat. It is what brings healing. Without it, injuries don't heal. I explained to Becky that the swelling simply had to happen and that initially the best thing for her to have done was just cold hosing, and perhaps the use an anti-inflammatory drug to smooth out the acute inflammation. Rather than helping, her three days of tight wraps were arresting the healing process.

Another common mistake is to wet down a recently injured leg with liniments. Liniments have their time, which is later, once the leg has cooled down. Using liniments during the early stages of inflammation is like throwing gasoline on a fire. When in doubt about how to handle any acute injury, snap a picture of it the injury and send it by phone to your veterinarian.

Use good sense and let the process of inflammation happen. You might have to cool it somewhat by cold water and or medication, but to some extent it has to happen. It's healing.

My wife proofreads what I write. After she read this one, she said, "Well, don't leave me and everyone else hanging! What happened to Becky's horse?" I'm happy to report that after a few months of rehab, he went on to compete and lived out a happy life, sound as a dollar.

38

Liniments

———————————— ♢ ————————————

I'm betting that you probably have at least one bottle of liniment in your tack trunk. That's good. Liniments are one aid to keeping horses sound. However, they can do more harm than good if used at the wrong time.

In order to use liniments wisely, you have to understand the basics of what happens when a leg is injured. Injury to any living tissue always results in inflammation, and from your own personal experience you know what that means: redness, heat, swelling, and pain. The redness and heat are due to the sudden increase of blood to the area. The swelling is caused by blood and fluids moving into the injured area. The blood that gathers at the injury site is rich in white blood cells and healing proteins. The increased pressure from the fluids affects nerve endings, and causes pain. The pain is important to insure that the limb is favored and rested. The redness will only be seen in horses if they are light colored and the hair has been clipped or shaved. Inflammation seems like a setback, but it's a good thing. Without it, healing doesn't happen.

For a real life scenario, let's assume that a youngster that you have been working comes up lame. You check out his legs, and right under the knee, on the inside of one leg he flinches when you squeeze. He probably has a splint, and within a short period of time the area will show all those signs of inflammation. It is then that many horse owners make the mistake. Because they want to do something, *anything*, to stop the swelling and lameness, they reach for that bottle of liniment and start sloshing it on the sore leg. Not good.

The dark red color of most liniments is from iodine in the solution.

Iodine is an irritant. When rubbed on a leg it increases blood supply to the area. If the liniment is strong enough, it will also cause swelling and pain to the point of blistering the skin. In other words, the liniment itself is causing inflammation! Remember that the body's response to injury is inflammation, and it really doesn't need any help doing that. By causing further inflammation we are aggravating the situation. It's like throwing gasoline on a fire that you are trying to put out.

At the beginning of this chapter I said that liniments are good, and they are, but only if used at the proper time. The rule of thumb is always, always cool an acute condition and apply heat to a chronic one. When a leg has been recently injured, keep the liniment in your tack trunk. The first aid is to use cold therapy. Sit on a lawn chair, let your horse nibble grass, and cold hose that injury. A very fine spray is all you need. Hose the area for 10 to 15 minutes and repeat several times through the day. There are all kinds of strap-on flexible boots that hold ice that also work, but they are expensive and require a lot of fussy adjusting. Cooling a leg out requires days, and sometimes weeks of attention. Anti-inflammatory medicines like Banamine, Butazolidine, or Previcox are also helpful in calming things down, but are not a substitute for cold therapy.

After leg injuries have been cooled down, they often reach a static phase. The heat is mostly gone, but the pain and some swelling persist. Now is the time that liniments are helpful. They increase the blood supply to the area and really do speed up healing.

Using a liniment too soon aggravates the injury and makes pinpointing the injured area more difficult. I am reminded of June, a new horse owner whose mare had come up lame. June had a large economy bottle of Absorbine liniment in her trunk and started to rub it on the mare's right front leg. She wasn't sure just what hurt, so she rubbed it in from the shoulder right down to the foot. Then she stood back and thought, "Well, I'm not exactly sure where this soreness is coming from. Maybe it's the other leg, so I'll rub some there too." June used up the entire bottle. This particular mare is a chestnut, who, in general, seems to have more sensitive skin than other colored horses. Within a few hours both legs started to swell, and I was called out. By the time I got there the mare was miserable. Both massively swollen front legs had a crusty covering of dried liniment over the irritated skin. There was no way to tell where the initial lameness was coming from because she was sore all over. It took another two weeks before we could even begin to deal with the initial issue.

Another problem with using liniments before a diagnosis is that after the liniment dries, the iodine takes on its natural crystalline form which shows up on X-rays as a cloudy area. This makes reading through it difficult, and sometimes impossible.

If you have an injured leg, do your horse and your vet a favor by staying away from liniments *until* the problem has been diagnosed and cooled out. Then, and only then are they helpful.

39

Long Nylon Fibers

U

I was doing a search on the internet and came across a website for "repurposed materials." The term is used by industry to describe materials that are highly engineered and ruggedly made but are now too worn for their original use. The items might end up in a landfill somewhere, but many are now being recycled and sold for entirely different purposes. This is about industrial strength recycling. An interesting example is the huge street-sweeper brush mounted underneath city trucks. After they have swept hundreds of miles of streets, the bristles get worn and finally become too short to be effective. They are sold or donated to a repurpose business. The repurpose yards sell them to zoos and livestock farmers. They are mounted on upright or slanted poles for the big animals to use as scratching posts. One of the repurposing yards proudly tells of two brushes sold to the Bronx Zoo for their rhinos to rub against.

On this same site, one of the listed materials made my eyes get wide, and I said out loud, "Uh-oh, here we go again!" That material was conveyor belts. Most conveyor belts are made of very tough rubber, reinforced with an internal matting of long nylon fibers. The fibers give strength and durability. It is just like the nylon belting in vehicle tires. Conveyor belts give years of service before needing replacing. The longest ones (sometimes miles in length) are used in the mining industry to carry ore long distances from mines to processing areas. All of us have personal experience with the conveyor belts at airports where they carry our checked baggage to the plane and our carry-ons through the X-ray tunnel. You yourself probably have been "the product" moved at a large airport on a conveyor belt.

In northern New England, paper mills use thousands of feet

of heavy-duty conveyor belts. Over 30 years ago, the old belts were discarded in town dumps. Enterprising horse people at the time picked up the belts and cut them into long strips a few inches wide. The strips were nailed or screwed to fence posts to replace the horizontal wood planks. The rubber was free and lasted years longer than wood. No more rotting or splintering. It seemed like a great idea. However, it wasn't too long before the problems started. Vets began to see a mysterious type of colic which was often fatal. It wasn't until a few surgeries and post mortems were done that it became clear what was going on.

When a conveyor belt is cut into smaller widths, little tags of the internal nylon fibers can be seen at the cut edges. Horses fenced in by the rubber strips seem to be fascinated by those little strings poking out. A horse will nibble and then pull, and the persistent ones are rewarded by a one or two foot long strand of nylon fiber. For some, the game ended there. For others, it was "Hey, maybe I could eat this." Nylon is indigestible. A long strand can get stuck between the many turns of the gut. The gut moves, the nylon doesn't, and it saws away at the intestine's lining. In other cases concentrated masses of the fibers can cause a blockage that can only be removed by surgery. Equine veterinarians who were practicing at the time will remember these horses. Most of them died. Word got out, and I haven't seen a fence made out of the recycled conveyor-belt rubber in years. This was a generation or two ago, and the problem of long nylon fibers and horses has mostly been forgotten. In an internet search, I could only find one reference to the problem.

When I saw the websites for repurposed materials, I immediately thought, *this is apt to happen again.* Horse people are quick to jump on "new" ideas, and I'm sure that some will come up with the same idea of using the conveyor material for fencing. I'm afraid that we might see another rash of this problem soon. At least one site suggests livestock fencing as a possible use for the old conveyor belts. Another one offers to do the hard job of cutting them to the width you want. Buy enough and maybe you can get free shipping! Don't be tempted. I can assure you that, given the curious nature and the sometimes strange appetite of horses, the fencing idea is not a good one.

On the other hand, the old conveyor belts do have plenty of other uses around the farm. For example, I have been in a number of barns where they are used as inexpensive rubber matting for the floor. You can run two or three strips four-feet wide for the barn aisle far cheaper than buying standard rubber floor mats. They also work well as trailer- and wash-stall mats. I have never known any horse to bend his head down and start pulling out the nylon fibers from the rubber underneath their feet. There must be something about it being at eye level that makes horses want to tease out the fibers from the edge of the strips.

Old conveyor belt strips are ideal for round pen fencing. The sometimes crazy, green colts will bounce off them as opposed to smashing into wooden planks. I would recommend this only if the round pen is not used as a paddock on occasion, and, of course, most are. If the horses are left alone for a long time with access to the rubber strips, bored or curious horses will start to pull on those nylon fibers poking out from the cut edges of the belting. If they decide to make a meal of them, be prepared for a serious problem.

I took the phone number from one of the repurposing sites that showed a photo of fencing made from the belting. The salesman who answered the phone said that he had heard about the problem with horses and promised to ask any horse people, who wanted to buy belting material, what they would be using it for. He said he would discourage its use as horse fencing. Hope he does.

The take home is that the repurposing sites have some great items for sale for reasonable prices that can be used around your place. Use your imagination, but, before you buy, do some thinking about potential problems with the material in question. Committed vets never mind questions like, "Did you ever have any problems with..."

40

Looking and Seeing

L ast week I was on my way to an evening church activity with a friend. The roads were icy, and he drove slowly. We noticed a police cruiser facing us at an intersection a few hundred yards from the church. We turned left, and then as we started into the church lot, those blue lights came on and followed us in. While we were waiting for the officer to approach the car, we looked at each other and wondered why we had been targeted. My friend definitely wasn't speeding; he had made a full stop and had signaled his turn. After the usual license and registration checks, the policeman told my friend that he had noticed that his registration sticker had expired six months before.

It was totally dark out, the windshield of our car was visible for maybe five seconds, and yet he was able to spot the outdated sticker! He knew what to look for and focused on it, probably totally unconsciously because of his training. He not only looked, he saw.

I went to vet school knowing that my career was in cows. I had plenty of experience on dairy farms and even ran one for a while. However, as I worked my way through vet school, I found myself drawn to horses, even though my experience with the species was slim. The fact is, I had ridden exactly one horse, several years before, and although I didn't admit it at the time, the experience was terrifying. I had never groomed a horse or mucked out a stall and had no idea how to put on a halter. But despite all that, the horses I saw at the vet school clinic were getting to me. I felt stupid about the species, but I wanted to learn. I started to hang out with students who had horse backgrounds. I watched closely how they handled horses in the clinic.

I remember the first time I was exposed to the importance of conformation in horses. I could see it in cows, but up to that point I was just looking at, but not seeing, horses. I learned how to evaluate all the parts in relation to the rest of the horse. It took a while, but finally I could see the hind end that was weak and the "upside down neck."

You may have just bought your first horse, and maybe you are just as bewildered as I was in knowing much about them. Perhaps you've been around horses a long time, but you feel that there are some gaps in your knowledge. I have found that if you ask the right questions of the right people, you can become quite knowledgeable. Let's say for example that you would like to learn better how to evaluate a horse's foot. Your farrier might be the best place to start. Ask him or her: "What do you look for in a good foot?" Listen carefully, take that answer and build on it with other resources. Make use of trainers, clinics, books, magazines, videos, and of course the internet. Compare what you have learned to what you are looking at, and soon you will start to see. You will know far more than someone who never asks. You have learned to do this in other aspects of your own life. It's the same with horse knowledge.

We have all "not asked" at times, because it means we are clueless. I think that people who would embarrass you because you don't know something are a bit insecure in who *they* are. If you would like to know more about any aspect of horses, just admit that you are ignorant in that area and would like to learn. The horse world is full of incredible people who would love to help you see.

41

Lower Leg Wounds

—————— ⊍ ——————

Some 20 years ago I was paged early on a Sunday morning by a client who used to live right in my town. Her colt was cut on a front leg. "Do you want to come out now, or can this wait until tomorrow morning?" I told her I'd drive right over.

I pulled into Meg's yard a half hour later. She brought the young gelding out of his stall and onto the barn floor. His left front was done up from foot to knee. I held him as Meg took off the leg wraps. She explained that when the colt was playing with another youngster, he ran full tilt into a drainage ditch and right into the end of an exposed steel culvert. She apologized for getting me out on a Sunday morning, but said she would just feel better if I could suture him up today.

I wasn't prepared for what I saw when the wrap was removed. The sharp edge of the culvert had slashed through the skin, leaving an eight inch gash down the front of the leg, starting just under the knee. The skin edges had pulled back from each other, leaving a large gaping wound. The extensor tendon and the bone underneath were both visible.

The big gap and the fact that there was no fresh blood told me that the accident hadn't happened that morning. "Oh, no, it happened yesterday evening, but I didn't want to call you out on a Saturday night, so I cleaned him up and managed to stop the bleeding with a sterile gauze and a leg wrap. I knew that he wouldn't die or anything, so I waited until today to call you."

Well, Meg was right. There was no chance that the colt was going to die. However, for every minute I would have spent that Saturday night suturing the wound, I ended up spending ten in trying to keep the scar to a minimum. Had she called me as soon as it happened, I would have sutured the leg, and within a few weeks he'd have been back playing with his buddy. Because Meg delayed calling for help, the colt had to put up with months of therapy and daily leg wrappings.

This is an extreme example of something that happens to every equine veterinarian from time to time. Well-meaning clients, trying not to be a bother, put off calling about a problem until they figure that the timing would be more convenient for their veterinarian. Some horse owners wait to avoid an after-hours emergency fee. Both are reasons why most veterinarians always expect a full Monday. But, after all, emergencies are just that and need immediate attention. Early colics, eye problems, and respiratory diseases are often more effectively treated if they are caught early on. However, in lower leg wounds the earlier the better is always the rule.

As soon as a horse is cut the skin edges start to pull back or retract from each other. This is a natural process that has kept horses together for thousands of years, long before anyone ever thought of running a needle through skin. When the edges of the skin retract from each other, it causes a gap, wider at the skin than in the depths of the wound. This allows drainage and healing from the inside out. Ideally, once the defect fills in, skin will grow across it, and the two edges will be joined by a strong scar.

The skin that covers the shoulder, neck, and most of the upper body of the horse is quite loose. You can easily grab a handful. In those areas there isn't such a rush to get wounds sutured. Even though the wound edges have retracted, there is plenty of loose skin to "borrow" to pull the edges together. Below the knee and hock, it's a different story. There is no extra skin in the lower leg, and when a wound retracts (within a few hours), it becomes impossible to pull the two edges back together. Within days connective tissue starts to fill in the gap. On the lower legs when that connective tissue reaches the level of the skin, it often keeps growing. That mass of very vascular tissue is called proud flesh and can become another problem. The reason is that while skin will grow across defects, it can't grow up over the mound of proud flesh. Unless it is removed either chemically or surgically, it will remain there and keep the wound from closing, sometimes for months.

In summary, there are good reasons to call right away when a horse gets any kind of a wound, on the lower leg or anywhere on the body. If you are unsure, call anyway, no matter what time or what day it is. Early treatment can make a huge difference in outcome.

Offer to send a digital photo of the wound by email. These are really helpful in determining whether a horse needs that immediate attention.

42

Never Never Land
(avoiding trouble)

U

There are many things that you should never do as a horse owner. This article is a list of a few of those that the staff at MEA has brainstormed. You might think of more. If so, email me at *dajdvm@maine.rr.com*, and it may well make the next edition.

• Never make abrupt feed changes. Horses, being herbivores, depend on bacteria for healthy digestion. Each bacterium has a narrow range of conditions in which it lives and functions. When you have been feeding a certain grain or hay, and then the next meal you change the feed to something entirely different, huge numbers of bacteria in the intestine will die. The lag time between the die-off and a new type of beneficial bacteria taking over is not immediate. This can mean undigested food and potential colic. Introducing a new grain? Some horse nutrition experts suggest a change of about 10% a day for a smooth transition. Going from first to second cut hay? Just a little bit of second cut the first time, and then slowly replace the first cut.

• "My horse's eye looks a little cloudy. Maybe I'll wait a few days to see if it clears on its own." It might, but then again, it may get worse. Horses are only issued two eyes, and waiting those few days before having your vet come out could mean the loss of one. Call your vet and describe the eye or text a photo of it. Most eye problems, if noticed early on, can be corrected. Never use the eye ointment you have in the barn from the last horse. It may not help, and it might be the wrong medicine and cause a bigger problem.

• Let's say you are lunging your horse. You want him out there at the end of your line on the circle, but he keeps coming in. You realize that you need a lunge whip, and there is no one around to bring you one. You reason, "Well, he already has the lunge line snapped on to his halter. I'll just tie the other end of the line to that fence post and he can graze while I go get the whip." Don't do it. It doesn't take long for a tethered horse to get a lunge line wrapped around a pastern. As the horse moves, the line tightens, and he may start kicking or running to get free. A nylon lunge line can saw through skin right down to the bone in just a few minutes. I have seen a number of leg wounds from people staking out or tethering their horses. The tissue is often such a mess that the wound can't be sutured. Healing time is typically months. Never tie a horse with a long line to anything and walk away for even a few minutes.

• After the summer barbeque, resist the urge to throw corn cobs to your horse. Horses enjoy them, and after they pick off the remaining kernels, some will try to eat the cob itself. We were called out to see a horse that had choked because he didn't chew the cob well and swallowed one of those short cobs. The two-inch long cob wedged so tightly halfway down his throat that there was no way we could budge it. In this case surgery was not an option, and after a very frustrating attempt to move the cob, we had to put him down.

• Never let a horse go into a stall, paddock, or pasture without removing his halter. Halters can and do get snagged when horses scratch their heads or necks on hooks or fence posts. In the panic that follows, necks can get broken. It takes five seconds to take a halter off and ten to put it back on. Take the time.

• Buy the horse. Never buy the story. A seller anxious for the sale will exaggerate the good qualities and forget to tell you the bad ones. Take all horse histories with skepticism. There is an old story about the horse dealer who sold a horse to a first-time horse buyer. The horse was returned to the dealer a few days later. "You didn't tell me he was blind!" The dealer answered, "Well, I *did* tell you he didn't look so good." Your best plan is to take the horse on trial and see for yourself what is true and what isn't. This may require a big deposit and you buying interim insurance. Great investment! I also strongly recommend an equine veterinary pre-purchase exam. It's not all about price, but vets often find problems that can markedly drop the price of a horse.

• Never think that there is a fortune to be made in boarding horses. Board horses because you love to have a barn full, and your boarders share your ideas on feed, turn out, and other management issues. Sit down with a pencil and paper and run the numbers, *all* the numbers it takes to run a barn. If you include everything, you will see that boarding is not and has never been, an easy way to make money. It's also tough when you'd like to take a vacation.

• This is an old one, and I have written about it several times, but here it is again. Never turn horses out into paddocks or pastures where there is any barbwire, either strung or just sitting around in a roll. Barbwire was designed for cows and works well to keep them in. Many have found that keeping horses in with barbwire is a mistake. Getting caught up in it and then trying to kick free can produce some terrible wounds.

• Last one. Never fail to control your tongue. It's easy to gossip, and, for sure, it can be fascinating to listen to. I visit hundreds of barns every year, and am amazed at how quickly rumors spread and then remain as gospel. Our horse community is small, and careless talk spreads like wildfire. As much as possible, keep your conversation focused on your shared interest, the horse. I believe that the damage done by careless talk to impress others causes as much damage and pain as Lyme disease.

43

Night Check

―――――――――― ♘ ――――――――――

I have never felt right about going to bed without taking that last trip to the barn for a night check on my animals. I grump a bit pulling on my boots and shrugging on a coat on a cold night, but once there, I have never regretted going out. For your horse's health it's an important thing to do.

Besides the very real connection with your animals before you go to bed, there are practical aspects to doing a nightly bed check. You are really going out to throw everyone some more hay, but you notice things when you are there. It might be the feed door that wasn't properly closed, or a light that has been left on. If you are like me, you say "Hi" to your animals and maybe scratch them behind the ears when they poke their heads out. It's a special time, but you can also make it a conscious time to check on your animals.

Here's a quick review of what to look for, which shouldn't take you any longer than two minutes. It's really about being aware. Make it a point to visually check each horse. Look at them head on to see if both eyes are wide open. Are they standing square, with weight on all four legs? They will probably move some as you greet them. Are they walking OK? Is there anything unusual about their attitude tonight? No one knows better than you how your animals act and react. Is the horse who usually greets you at the stall door hanging back? Is the one who usually hangs back wild eyed tonight?

You want to be sensitive to anything that looks or feels different. If an animal doesn't seem just right, get a halter on him or her and check the animal's temperature, pulse, and respiration. Listen for gut sounds. Check the manure in the stall. Is there more or less than you would expect? Is it too loose or too hard? Is it just this one horse that doesn't seem right? Do all the other animals look OK?

If something is amiss, you will have to decide whether to call your veterinarian or let the situation go until morning. If you do call, have your observations written down. If you haven't taken the sick horse's temperature before you get on the phone, you will be asked to go back out and get it. Listen for gut sounds on both sides behind the rib cage and be ready to report if they are present or not, and on which side. If it's a sick horse, note the heart rate. If an eye is half shut, use a flashlight to look closely at the cornea to see if there is a puncture or an ulcer. Check the pupil size of the injured eye and compare it to the other eye. If the horse is standing off one leg, take a few minutes to pick out the foot, looking for a loose shoe or a possible nail in the sole. Run your hand down the leg to check for swelling or tenderness.

Some situations you may encounter can wait until morning; others can't. Give your vet enough information to make that decision. I can tell you from years of experience, we'd much rather come to your barn at 10 PM than 2 AM.

For me, late night barn check is that last, quiet connection with my animals each day. Heading back to the house I know I'll sleep better. Make night check a quick health check and you will as well.

44

One of these Things

(ponies vs horses)

⚓

Remember that song from Sesame Street? "One of these things is not like the other, one of these things is not the same."

Think about that catchy little verse when you are contemplating getting a Shetland pony to sort of round out your stable. There are over a hundred breeds of ponies, but Shetlands are the most common here in the U.S. It's the breed you probably image when you think pony. Shetlands look more like horses than anything else, but if you treat them like a small horse, there will be problems. Their conformation, attitude, and metabolism are not the same as horses.' The differences are great enough that it's actually smart to think of and treat them as a separate species.

In order to understand what a Shetland is all about, you have to know something of their origin. The group of Shetland Islands is located over 100 miles north of the northern most part of Scotland and 300 miles due west of Norway. The Islands are located exactly where the cold North Sea meets the Atlantic. Here on the Islands, the climate is severe and the land mostly barren. No spot on the Islands is more than a four-mile walk from the sea. Archeologists say that ponies have lived here for thousands of years. It is thought that their ancestors, larger in size, came over on an ice bridge from northern Europe. Obviously, only the strong survived the wild conditions. Those smaller, chunkier equines, that we call Shetlands, are the survivors. Animals with that conformation will typically do better in cold and windy conditions. Their characteristics have been passed down: small stature, dense hair coat, and tough nature. They were used in the United Kingdom as "pit ponies" to pull loaded ore cars on tracks far below the earth's surface from the coal seams to the shaft. Some were exported to America and were used in the Appalachians for the same purpose. Short, muscular necks, strong legs with short cannon bones, and deep barrels all add up to strength and endurance. Pound for pound, no horse is stronger than a Shetland.

It's part of the nature of survivors of harsh conditions to carry a little attitude. Many, but not all, Shetlands are impatient and a bit un-cooperative. I am always pleasantly surprised by those that take vaccinations in stride and permit dentistry without sedation. It is not unusual to have them rear or strike when they don't agree with some procedure.

The biggest mistake we make with these ponies is in treating them like horses at mealtime. Thousands of years of genetic selection means that grain and green grass are close to poison for these animals who can survive on next to nothing. It is common for equine veterinarians to be called out in the spring to attend to a pony that has been pastured on rich green grass. Their systems simply can't handle unlimited grass. Centuries of selection has made their metabolism amazingly efficient. As we say in New England, "They can get fat on snowballs."

If a Shetland's diet has too much of the carbohydrates found in grass or grain, the result will be more than just a belly ache. The rich diet starts an internal process that often doesn't end well. High carbs in the diet mean high blood sugar. Insulin is produced and secreted to try to get the sugar from the blood to the cells. After a while the body reaches a point of insulin resistance, which means that the system finally stops reacting to it. The result is large fat deposits that ironically start to develop at the same time that the ponies get "ribby." Shetlands often develop the syndrome called Cushing's disease, and the extremely painful foot condition of laminitis often follows.

Ponies should be kept in relatively grass free paddocks until the grass turns brown in the fall. When everyone else in the barn is getting scoops of grain, give your pony a handful of hay stretcher. When feeding hay, avoid the rich second cut. Even very leafy first cut hay can cause a problem, and sometimes it's necessary to soak the hay in water to leach out the starch and sugars.

Despite the problems associated with "too good care," nothing makes us smile more than a blocky little Shetland standing tall and proud as if he were a Budweiser Clydesdale in a beer commercial. They are smart and trainable. For a kid's first mount, they are ideal and are perfectly suited for driving. If fed properly and exercised regularly, Shetlands are as hardy as they come. If you keep that song running through your head when dealing with them, having a Shetland around should give you decades of pleasure.

45

Panic

(evaluating calmly)

───────── ♘ ─────────

It happens a few times every year. A horse owner goes out to the barn for night check and discovers one of her horses with sawdust all over him. He is up and down, and when up he is kicking at his belly. The owner has never seen colic, but, "I guess this must be it!" She pulls out her cell, calls my number and gets the emergency information. She hurriedly enters that. My pager starts beeping. I check the screen and see a phone number with five digits instead of the necessary seven. I can't return the call. This has happened often enough that my next move is to start changing and gathering what I will need to head out. Hopefully within the next 15 or 20 minutes she will call again, that is, if she has calmed down enough to put in her complete phone number. It doesn't matter if it's our spouse, kids, house pets, or horses. When we see them in serious trouble, we tend to panic. It's a natural reaction. It doesn't matter how many emergencies you have dealt with, when it's one of our own in in trouble, we can feel it coming on and moving in.

If you have had me as a veterinarian in the last ten years, you know my technician, Erin. Long before she started working for Maine Equine Associates, she had a world of experience working in and running stables. She has always had horses of her own at home. Erin is my driver, trots out all the lame horses we see, and assists on all of our surgeries. She has seen horses with choke, severely bleeding wounds, and sadly, many horses put down. She has heard me talk to clients in thousands of situations. Yet, despite all this experience, when Erin calls me from her own farm with her own emergency, I can hear that edge in her voice. The last one was a couple of years ago.

"Prophet isn't eating and keeps looking at his side. There has been no manure since this afternoon." Erin's voice is tight.

When I talk to anxious clients I purposely start talking slow. "OK, Erin, have you taken his temp?"

"Oh, no, I didn't do that."

"Gut sounds?"

"Oops, no, forgot to do that."

If Erin, with all of her years of experience in seeing emergencies, tends to get flustered when one of her own is in trouble, I anticipate that you will too. Here are some steps you can take to minimize the panic.

• First, accept that if you keep horses you *will* run into situations that make your pulse run and your brain fog. Now is the time to prepare, not when things are falling apart.

• Keep enough horses, long enough, and you will have a colicky one. *Before* it happens, know how to evaluate what is going on. Next time your vet is out, ask for some training.

• Keep a notebook in the barn with a list for each situation. For example, you might head one page: *Colic.* List the common symptoms such as restlessness, tail wringing, up and down behavior, looking at side, etc. On a separate page list the things to check for before calling your vet: Temperature, Pulse, Respiration (TPR), presence of gut sounds behind ribs on both sides, how long since the horse has made manure, color of membranes in mouth and blood vessels of eye, odor from the mouth. Then write it all down before you call. Your vet will ask you at least some of these questions.

• Evaluate each of your horses annually. Ask yourself: "If this horse were to colic and surgery were the only option, would I send him or her to the hospital?" It is wise to make this thoughtful decision for each animal before there is an immediate need, and your emotions take over. The quote on colic surgery and aftercare today is often around $10,000.

• Have on hand a first aid kit, which should include Banamine paste and the basic diagnostic instruments: thermometer, flashlight, and stethoscope.

• If a horse has a wound, take a couple of pictures. A view from a few feet away, and a close up or two. Contact your vet and text him or her the images to see if it needs suturing. Many don't, and we can often tell from a good photo.

• If you really feel momentarily unable to make good decisions, call an experienced friend.

• Be prepared for eye issues by knowing how to judge the size of the pupil as compared to the other eye. Photos can be helpful here too.

• If you have an acute lameness, it is very helpful to know how to take a horse's pulse at the artery going to the foot. Ask your vet to show you how the next time he or she is in the barn. Don't ask for an explanation on how to do this when you are faced with a lame horse. I have found it impossible to describe over the phone. You have to be shown. It is a great skill and takes just five minutes to learn.

• Before you push "send" on your phone, make sure you have seven digits on the screen.

• When we are in a state of panic, we are out of control. Thinking seems to stop. Not a good place to be making decisions from. The Boy Scout motto is "Be Prepared." Being prepared means thinking about what might happen, and then taking steps *ahead* of time so that you can deal with the unexpected more effectively. As an example, if your horse needed to be transported to a surgical facility tonight, is your trailer ready for that? In the winter is it always plowed out? If you are relying on someone else to truck your horse, have you asked two or three friends in advance if they would?

• When faced with an emergency, take a deep breath and calm yourself as much as you can before you call. I will never forget the caller, whose voice I didn't recognize, shout into the phone, "I have a bad colic! Get right over here!" and then she hung up. She was panicked. I was frustrated. I have often wondered since, whether she expected me to drive in ever increasing circles until I found her sick horse. When I tried to call her back I got the recorded message, "I'm sorry; the person you are trying to reach has a full mailbox at this time." I hope she got some help. Panic just doesn't pay.

46

Porcupines and Equines

♘

Porcupines are peculiar animals. Along with beavers, they are the largest rodents in the U.S. Beavers are busy and social. Porcupines move slowly and are shy. They don't even interact with each other very much. They do get together in the fall for a short breeding season, and otherwise, they travel alone. There is a riddle that asks, "How do porcupines make love?" The answer is, "Very carefully." The truth is that during mating the quills flatten out so no one gets hurt.

The porcupine's preferred habitat is high up in the top of mature hemlock trees, eating the tree buds and bark. They do climb down to vary their strictly vegetarian diet. They prefer to mind their own business, and interaction with other animals usually leaves the other party in pain. Whether a domestic or wild animal gets a nose full of those sharp quills depends more on the nature of the animal receiving the quills than on any aggression on the part of the porcupine.

My first two years out of vet school, I worked in a general practice, treating both small and large animals. It would be a rare week that we weren't pulling quills from somebody's dog. Dogs see porcupines as intruders and try to bite them, sometimes repeatedly. I have always been amazed by dogs that don't learn their lesson and bite more than once, or go on to attack other porcupines later. I owned a dog like that myself. She would tangle with both, skunks and porcupines, and when she saw one, she would seem to say: "I'll get him back for that last time!" In our vet hospital, unless the dog had just three or four quills, we generally gave a short-acting general anesthetic, so that we could pull the quills with no distress to the dog. We used to count quills as we pulled them, and it wasn't unusual to have well over 100, most in the tender nose and mouth. I don't remember ever seeing a cat with quills. It's just not in a cat's nature to be investigating wild life as big as a mature 30 to 40 pound porcupine.

Horses also tend to shy away from porcupines who might wander into their pasture. However, in New England and Canada rural equine vets will get an occasional call. It's not horse aggression toward the porcupine that causes the interaction; it's the horse's curiosity. If a horse's nose comes too close, the porcupine tail connects, and the horse will jump back with some deeply imbedded quills. Usually there are less than a dozen, because horses, unlike dogs, would never consider a second helping. I have never had to pull quills from a horse more than once. Because there are so few quills, you may be able to pull them yourself without calling your vet.

You can pull quills with your fingers, but you have to grab them firmly and then pull straight out. They go in easy but come out surprisingly hard. I have found that needle nose pliers work best. The long thin jaws enable you to grab a few quills at a time. Back the horse into a corner and grab the quills firmly as close to the skin as possible. People always ask, "How hard should I pull?" You don't have to worry about that. As soon as you close on the quills, just squeeze hard and hang on. The horse will do the pulling. Take your time, try to settle the horse, and then grab a few more. Since horses don't bite porcupines, it is rare to see any in a horse's mouth. We will occasionally see quills in a lower leg, and I always assumed that perhaps that horse may have tried to kick the porcupine. When you have pulled all you can see, gently rub your hand over the nose, as some may have penetrated deep and all you feel may just be the stub end. Fine forceps may be necessary for these.

Most of the length of the quill is yellow and feels soft because they are hollow. There is a belief that by snipping them short, they will collapse and be easier to pull out. They do deflate, but what actually holds them tight in the skin are hundreds of microscopic barbs at the black tip. Each little barb acts like a fish hook. The black tip is very sharp and slides into the skin easily. It comes out hard because of the backward facing barbs. After the quills are pulled, there is often a drop or two of blood. When you find them, don't delay trying to pull them out. As time goes on, the quills tend to work in deeper. If a horse has many deep quills and is very swollen, a dose of Banamine or Butazolidin may make him more comfortable after the quills have been pulled. Some horses will absolutely not let you near their face when they have quills. Then it's time to call your vet who will heavily sedate your horse for the procedure.

We don't see porcupines much in the winter in New England. Some authorities claim that they hibernate, and others say no, but in any event, they aren't out and about much. You can spot them 40 or 50 feet up in the branches of tall pines and hemlocks, close to the trunk. In the spring and summer they venture out a bit, and we start to see the evidence of their travels sticking out of our animals' noses.

47

Probe

When my wife Bonnie first brought up the idea of two fruit trees for the backyard, I was in. It seemed like a good Memorial Day weekend project. The two cherry trees we picked out were seven footers with their roots encased in big plastic containers full of potting soil. The struggle began in trying to get both into the back of our vehicle. Back home we picked a spot for the first tree. The label on the trees said the hole needed to be about two feet deep. Luckily, we had just had a good amount of rain, and I easily removed the grass and two inches of top soil to form a circle three feet in diameter. The first 14 inches were relatively easy going. Then I hit the rock. Hoping that it wasn't too big, I whacked away with a pickaxe, but it extended way beyond the edges of my hole. I was a half hour into the project and had to admit that the tree was not going in that hole without a good big backhoe to tackle that boulder. I sighed, shoveled the dirt back in, and tamped the grass back down.

It was a warm day. I was hot and feeling cranky, knowing that the next two holes I dug might well turn up more surprises. Our old Maine farm has plenty of stone walls, made of thousands of rocks that all came out of this dirt. Then I remembered my pinch bar. It's a five-foot long solid iron rod. It has a pointed end and weighs twelve pounds. It's heavy enough that when you hold the point a few feet over the ground and drive it straight down, it sinks in pretty far. We picked a new site, and I probed with that bar until I knew I was safe. There would be an occasional clank as I hit a rock, but probing an area several inches away, it would slide in without that clank of iron hitting stone. I knew that any rocks that I was going to find would be removable. Using the bar I was able to locate a good spot for both trees, and they were soon part of our landscape.

Using that pinch bar as a probe made me think about ways that horse owners often come home from horse shopping with a different horse than the one they were looking for, because they weren't probing. I can't tell you how many times I've run into this situation. Here is an especially crazy example. I was called out to look at a horse that a dad wanted to buy his daughter. Melissa was 14 and wanted an event horse. If you aren't familiar with the sport, eventers have to be pretty tough and all around athletic. I was surprised to hear that the mare that Melissa had picked out was on a farm that I knew had mostly Saddlebreds. Sure enough, when I arrived at the farm, the farm owner brought out a very attractive and good size gelding with all of the style and high stepping action that gives the breed the reputation of being the peacocks of the horse world. Perhaps a few Saddlebreds have been successful at eventing, but for sure this would be rare. It would just be an inappropriate animal for the dressage, cross country and jumping required for the sport.

Before I even pulled out my stethoscope I tried to talk to Dad. He wasn't hearing it. "But this is the horse my daughter is interested in. She loves him, and look, they've already bonded." I tried to explain that while the horse was quite handsome and really did have an engaging personality, the chances were that he would never be an eventer. I used myself as an example of someone who at 160 pounds would not make it as a center on a football team. Dad insisted that I go ahead and examine the youngster. I never tried so hard to find something wrong with a horse. However, after an hour and 15 minutes I had to admit that this animal was easy to like and very sound. I filled out all the paperwork, and before I left, I had Dad sign a statement that I wrote on the invoice. It stated that the animal, while sound and quite fit, would be a very long shot as a horse that would be comfortable eventing. That was probably 15 years ago, and I've always wondered what ever happened to Melissa and her purchase. I hope she changed her mind about a career choice for him.

It is very easy to get caught up when a horse lays his head on your shoulder. It's called love. So, this is where my iron probe comes in. Start probing for those things that would *not* make this horse fit for what you want to do. If you are interested in a particular equine sport, get informed about what type of horse does that best, in a natural way. Continue your probing by finding someone who excels in the sport.

Learn from them what you should look for in a horse for the planned activity. Have them look at and try the horse before you get emotionally attached. Get on the internet and find out what kind of horses do your sport well. Commit to finding what its ideal conformation would be. Your last probe is to have a pre-purchase exam done by a vet who knows what would be expected of a horse in your area of interest. If it seems like the horse you have been checking out isn't the right fit, you've found a big stone in that hole, and it's time to dig around for a new one.

When I was digging those holes to put trees in, I wasn't falling in love with a particular hole. That pinch bar is unemotional. But it's great for finding rocks. When you are seriously looking for a horse for a particular sport, know the attributes and start the probing process. Many a horse is standing around in the paddock all day that was an inappropriate purchase for what was planned. Until you find the horse that fits the bill, try not to fall in love. You and your horse will both be happier.

48

Put Away that Chain Saw

(maple leaf poisoning)

U

Samantha called me at noon on a bright day in mid-September. She said her ten-year-old mare Trixie hadn't eaten any grain or hay that morning and now was acting "dumpy." Banamine paste had not changed anything. I told Samantha that I would finish up at the farm that I was on and rearrange my day to see Trixie next. I arrived at her farm around two o'clock.

Trixie was standing along the back wall of her stall. Her head was down, and she didn't react when I walked in. Normally this mare is quite social. From the stall door I could see her breathing pattern. It was rapid and very shallow. Her heart was racing at 85-beats/minute, which was twice normal for her. When I rolled back her upper lip, I was surprised to see that her gums were dark brown instead of pink. I was sure that she must have a twisted intestine that had ruptured. This would mean intestinal contents spilling into the abdomen and a guaranteed peritonitis, with certain death within a few hours. However, when I listened for gut sounds they were still there, faint but present. Usually when an intestine ruptures, all abdominal sounds stop. I knew she was in serious trouble but was baffled as to why. I pulled on a rectal sleeve and was lubing up my arm when Trixie humped up her back and urinated. The urine was pure black. We see that with "tied up" horses, but it only happens when a horse has been worked hard, and that was not the case. This left me with the only possible cause that I could think of.

I turned to Samantha and said, "Let's take a walk around the farm." She looked puzzled, but followed me. We walked out of the barn, through the wooden gate and along the north edge of the pasture. Sure enough, we hadn't walked 100 feet when I spotted what I was looking for. A large limb had split off a red maple. It was hanging across the old stone wall and into the pasture. A wind and rain storm had passed through the week before and must have taken the big branch down. We could see where leaves had been eaten off the branch. I told her that this was probably the cause of Trixie's sickness. Samantha blamed herself. She didn't know that the downed limb could be a problem and had put off cleaning it out of the pasture until she had more time. I called the nearest equine hospital and told them that we had a probable case of red maple leaf poisoning. We got Trixie loaded and on her way within 20 minutes. Despite some heroic work, including blood transfusions, Trixie died early the next morning. Blood tests and a post mortem confirmed the diagnosis.

Plant poisonings in northern New England are rare when compared to the rest of the country. The big exception is horses poisoned by eating the wilted leaves of red maples. This tree is also called swamp maple and is common in our area. Under the right conditions, just a few mouthfuls of its leaves can mean death to horses. What is unusual is that horses can eat the leaves right off of a *live* red maple and not get sick, because those leaves haven't gone through the wilting process. Horses can also walk through a pasture in the fall, plowing through fallen leaves up to their fetlocks without harm. I have never seen or heard of a horse getting sick from those leaves that fall off in autumn.

From my experience and other vets I have questioned, it seems that the leaves are only poisonous when they are eaten off a downed branch or a whole tree uprooted. The downed tree or branch can't provide sustenance to the leaves, and they wilt, still attached. These wilted leaves are somehow attractive to horses. When they eat as little as a pound, they get very sick. Even with immediate hospitalization and intensive care, most don't survive.

Researchers have found gallic acid to be the toxic element in the wilted leaves. When a horse eats the leaves, the toxin enters the horse's circulation and destroys the body's red blood cells. To compound things further, the dying red cells release hemoglobin. Hemoglobin is the compound that is carried on red blood cells. It binds with oxygen in the lungs and carries it to every living cell. When the hemoglobin is released, the red cells are no longer capable of carrying oxygen. All of the body's cells become oxygen starved. The released free hemoglobin *itself* acts like a poison and damages the kidneys, rapidly destroying them. So the horse is not only deprived of oxygen, it is also experiencing renal (kidney) failure. This explains the rapid breathing and the black urine.

All the cases I have seen, heard about, or researched seem to happen only when horses eat the wilted red maple leaves off a downed tree or split-off branch. The leaves that turn colors and come off in the fall do not seem to be an issue. Maybe that's because those dried leaves don't taste good. Perhaps it's like buttercup. All the books talk about buttercup being poisonous, but I've never seen any horse eat it. My two donkeys are chest deep in buttercup every summer. I used to whack the buttercup down but gave up when I found that it doesn't get eaten.

So, here is my take-home about red maple poisoning. Google red maple and what its leaves look like. Walk around and see if you have any on your property. You may not be able to identify the tree itself, but the leaves are distinctive. If you do have red maple, take note, but don't go running for the chain saw. I hate to see perfectly good trees cut down that are not a problem as they stand. It would be prudent to check after storms to see if any are uprooted or if branches are down where a horse can munch on the leaves. The wood is perfectly safe; it's just those leaves wilting on the branches that are so toxic. They remain dangerous for a month after the tree or branch is down. If a red maple is down where horses can get to it, it's time to get busy with a chain saw and remove any branches with leaves on. If it happens in the winter, and there are no leaves, there is no danger, and you can cut that excellent fire wood after the snow melts. Those crunchy and colorful underfoot maple leaves that drop in the fall do not seem to be a concern. If they make you nervous, go ahead and rake them up. I'm leaving mine right where they are. Be aware, and enjoy your horses *and* your trees.

49

Raw Exposure

(kids and horses)

———————— ♘ ————————

A few years back I arrived at a farm to geld a colt. One of the owner's children and another from the neighborhood were hanging around, obviously curious. I guess they were somewhere around six years old. I was surprised when their parents told them to go somewhere else to play. Apparently the surgery wasn't something the parents wanted them to witness. After the kids reluctantly left, I asked the parents if they might not want to reconsider. I explained that, in my experience, youngsters exposed to all aspects of daily farm life grew up with pretty healthy attitudes. The questions that come from young kids are both amazing and pointed, and can be a great learning experience about life with its sometimes raw moments that suburban kids never see.

The episode reminded me of an incident in our own family's life. Our son was about the age of those two boys when I was called to out to see a sick horse late one afternoon. I thought Jim might like to go with me to see what his dad did every day. This was to be his first farm call with me. I knew it would just be the one stop and wouldn't take long. Bonnie gave her OK when I said that we'd be back in plenty of time for supper.

After you've been doctoring horses for a while, the ones that won't make it are obvious. To the owners, he just seemed sick. One look told me that he was going to die. After checking all of his vital signs, doing a rectal exam, and a belly tap, I told the owners that it looked as though he had suffered a twisted gut, that his intestine had ruptured, and that he was beyond any help, including surgery. They were devastated, but agreed that he had to be put down to spare him a long and painful death.

My son Jim is now six foot five, but at the time wasn't up to my hip. He had never seen a horse euthanized, but there we were. He watched as I injected the IV solution and saw the horse sink to the ground and let go of his last breath. I was cleaning up to go when the owners insisted on having an autopsy done.

I don't know if you've ever seen a horse autopsy, but it's no small job, is a very messy procedure, and takes a solid hour. I was a little concerned about my son's reaction. A few minutes before, this horse was alive. Now Jim was about to see all the horse's insides on the outside. It was starting to get dark, and the backhoe was on its way, and, well, there we were. As I made the initial incision, I tried to explain to Jim what he was seeing so that it would hopefully become an anatomy lesson and not just a memory of a big stinking mess.

"Now here's the heart, see how big it is? Every time it squeezes, blood is pushed up into this big artery called the aorta. Look! I think it must be two or three times as big as our garden hose. What do you think? See how the big pink lungs sort of cradle the heart? Over here is the stomach, and look, way up here are the kidneys. See how this small tube runs from each kidney down to the bladder?"

I thought that things might get a bit too much when we got to the intestines, but, as I said, there we were. I had to pull yards of gut out and onto the grass to find the point of rupture, and there it was, way back in the large intestine. I pointed out where one section had turned blue black, and finally had split. All this time I was worried that Jim would be totally grossed out and maybe never be the same again, but he seemed pretty interested. From the corner of my eye, I noticed that the owners were slowly backing away. They were probably wondering how all that stuff could fit in one body. Jim and I were late for supper that night.

Jim never seriously considered being a vet and instead became a boat captain. As he grew up, he'd go on occasional calls with me and watch wounds get sutured, stallions neutered, and mares bred. Questions came up and were answered on the spot. I don't think it hurt him a bit. A few years ago it all came back around when Bonnie and I joined Jim on one of his Alaskan ecology cruises. We caught some halibut and salmon, and our son was the crew member who was by far the handiest at gutting and cleaning the fish.

I sometimes wonder if my daughter, Tally, more hardwired for this kind of thing, got her start in the healing arts by riding on calls with me. She never really went through the "Oh. Yuk!" stage because of what she saw at an early age. Although I don't remember it, she tells me that she also watched me do an autopsy when she was five and was left with a sense of wonder about the body.

I think that the healthiest place a boy or girl can grow up is in the country. Don't deny your kids the chance to experience it all, from birthing through all the messes that our animals get into, and finally, when the time is right, to be there for euthanasia at life's end. It can all be an incredible education for them.

50

Red Snow

(bloody urine?)

U

Ihad been out of vet school just seven months. I was working in a general practice in northern New Hampshire that had hired me right out of vet school. It was a busy practice, and in those several months I had seen a fair number of horses. I was just barely getting over being totally anxious every time I drove onto a farm. When the phone rang that morning, it was a client who sounded even more nervous than me. There had been a winter storm the night before. In the bright morning light, she saw where her gelding had urinated on the snow. What startled her was the fact that the snow was colored red. She assumed that there was blood in his urine, and to be truthful, I bought right into it.

I went to her farm that day and agreed that the color of the urine soaked snow was a little alarming. The horse himself was bright and alert, feeling just fine. I did all the diagnostic things that I had been trained to do. I took blood. I poked. I prodded. His temperature, pulse and respiration were all normal. I tranquilized him, examined his penis, and even did a rectal to see how the bladder felt. His urinary system from bladder all the way up to his left kidney was perfectly normal. There was no straining.

That winter I ran into the same situation once or twice more. Each time it was right after a fresh snow. I finally realized that in each case, the caller was either a new horse owner or one who had moved to the area from the south. I should tell you that I wasn't brought up with horses, and that this red-colored snow was not something that I had learned about in vet school.

Every winter since, when it first snows, I get the "red snow calls." We had our first snow of the season on December 26 of last year.

It took just 24 hours before I got the call. The owner had moved her horse home from a boarding barn. That meant that she was really caring for him for the first time. I asked if the horse was feeling OK, and she said that he was. I told her that, almost for sure, there was no need for a farm call. I let her know that she was the first caller of this winter season with the concern, and that I anticipated a few more before March.

If you were brought up with horses in snow country, you have probably seen the deep orange to red stains on the snow from time to time after your horse has urinated. However, if you have never had your horses in snow, it is a surprise the first time you see it, and it looks alarming. What's it all about, anyway?

The medical term for blood in the urine is *hematuria*. Pure blood or blood clots in the urine are not normal, and there can be a number of reasons. Horses can get bladder stones, and when these pass, the lining of the urethra may get abraded and bleed. Inflammation and cancer anywhere in the urinary system may also cause bloody urine. These bleeding issues are almost always accompanied by other symptoms such as pain or straining. When quantities of blood are passed, you will actually see blood clots in the urine. Horses that have tied up will pass very dark urine which results from the breakdown of muscle. There is also a rare and peculiar bleeding syndrome seen in Quarter Horse males in which the lining of the urethra gets torn as it turns around an arch of the pelvis. All of these problems cause very real bleeding and are, of course, of concern and require veterinary attention.

However, the huge majority of cases of deep orange to red coloration on the white snow are usually the result of the uniqueness of the equine urinary system and not due to blood at all. Horses, from time to time, will normally pass mucus and minerals in the urine. This will thicken and darken the fluid. Horses also occasionally normally pass red blood cells in the urine. A certain amount is considered normal.

There are also some proteins in the urine which oxidize when exposed to air, much the same way that a sliced apple quickly turns brown. We all know what yellow snow is, and why we tell kids it's not for eating. With horses, sometimes it's yellow, and at other times it can be a deep orange to red color. You don't notice the dark color until it is against the white snow. Usually, if your horse is feeling fine in every other way, you can generally assume that the dark stained snow is just another demonstration of how special horses are.

On December 28, I got my second red snow call.

51

Reflections on Lyme Disease

The headline on the first page of the March 30, 2014, Lewiston, Maine, *Sun Journal* shouted "TICKED OFF." What followed was a full three-page article about Lyme disease in people. I knew that we had a severe problem here in New England but was unaware that New Hampshire has the highest rate of Lyme disease in the U.S., with Maine coming in second. It is not a reportable disease in horses, so we don't have numbers, but every equine veterinarian in New England sees more cases every year. There is never a time in our practice when we are not treating at least one horse with Lyme disease. There are seasons when we will be treating a number of them at any given time. In the winter the ticks do just fine, as long as there is snow cover, and become active again once the temperature hits 40 degrees. I know veterinarians out west who have never seen a horse with the problem. In the same way, I've never seen a horse with a rattlesnake bite. Ticks thrive in woodlands and bushy fields; rattlesnakes like the desert.

I wrote an article about Lyme disease three years ago for the *Horse's Maine*. It was a brief summary of what we know about the problem in horses. The article was factual: what causes the disease, its prevention, and treatment. Since that time I have seen many more cases and thought it might be helpful to share my own experience and thoughts about Lyme disease in horses that I have seen in Maine. I want to be clear that these are my opinions about Lyme and may not be shared by other equine veterinarians.

I have noticed that there are certain towns in Maine that consistently have a high incidence of Lyme in horses—and probably in people. One such town is Cape Elizabeth, just south of Portland.

Perhaps the high rate of infection is due to the local restrictions on deer hunting. In any area where the deer population is high, Lyme will be more common, because deer are one of the hosts for part of the life cycle of the ticks that carry the disease. In towns like these, I always include Lyme disease in my differential diagnosis for almost any equine problem. There are also towns in Maine where I have never seen a case.

It's a good idea to routinely check your horses for ticks when you bring them in. You'll have to look carefully. The nymph stage of the ticks that carry the bacteria that cause the disease are tiny, about the size of the tip of a pencil. We find most underneath the lower jaw, at the tail head, on the underside of the tail, and beneath the mane. Ticks like dark places. As you have probably heard, they have to be on a horse, or you and me, at least 24 hours for the bacteria to pass from the tick to the host.

The most common symptom of Lyme disease that I see is extreme skin sensitivity. Even horses that normally love to be brushed and fussed over just don't want to be touched. Many articles will talk about a shifting lameness (in this leg today, in that leg tomorrow) as a common symptom of Lyme. I haven't noticed that so much. I do see Lyme horses that move stiffly as though they are sore all over. There can be a variety of other symptoms, depending where in the body the bacteria that causes Lyme takes up residence. Our practice has seen Lyme horses with neurologic problems, vision issues, and GI symptoms among other things. When vets see a horse that is showing many of the common symptoms, we refer to them as being "Lymie."

Last year an older gelding in Oxford County kept losing weight. I did the usual dentistry and ran all the normal blood tests and fecals, but everything came up normal. I couldn't figure out what was wrong and chalked it up to old age. I didn't suspect Lyme, but to humor his owner I took a Lyme test, and when he tested strongly positive, we put him on the usual antibiotic, and he promptly gained all his weight back. The next horse we saw with the same perplexing symptoms, a year later, turned out to have Lyme disease as well and also responded with treatment, gaining 60 pounds back quickly.

Most veterinarians in New England will send their blood samples for Lyme testing to either the University of Connecticut or to Cornell. These are different tests. Both are valid, and each has its fans. There is also a "snap" test, the same one that your dog gets with his annual physical. We run that identical test on horses, right in the barn and get a yes or no answer within ten minutes. It doesn't give numbers, but if a horse seems "Lymie," we sometimes use it so that we can begin treatment right away.

The antibiotic Doxycycline is the usual treatment for Lyme in horses. The pills have become prohibitively expensive, so many veterinarians are using compounding pharmacies to make the powder. Some veterinarians believe that IV treatment is much more effective than oral, and one limited research paper from years ago did show that. I personally have not found that to be the case. I treat with oral Doxycyline for six weeks. My recommendation is that horses being treated this length of time be on a probiotic. If an animal is still not right after that long antibiotic treatment, I often recommend an herbal mix that a local certified herbalist puts together.

There are numerous articles and even books about people with Lyme who don't test positive on the lab tests. There are also many people for whom the antibiotic is not effective. You may know someone with Lyme disease who can't shake it and is living a miserable life. I think that the blood tests and our treatment for the problem in horses are usually effective because we are testing and treating earlier in the course of the disease. When an owner has an animal that isn't right, she looks for help quickly, whereas when we ourselves are feeling off, we tend to dismiss our symptoms, thinking it's because we are overtired or stressed. Some MDs are skeptical of Lyme and as a result diagnostics and treatment may be put off for months or years. When the organism is in the body for a long time, it can hide in joints and seems to be able to mutate and become resistant to the usual treatments. Chronic Lyme is very debilitating. Again, I think the success in diagnosis and treatment of horses is because we know there is such a thing as Lyme, and we get at it quickly.

An interesting side note to Lyme is the disease that we are now calling Anaplasmosis. It is carried by ticks as well, and it is often characterized by a persistent fever and legs that stock up. These horses often look neurologic. Labs usually test for this along with Lyme, and it is included in the snap test. Treatment is the same as for Lyme.

I am not a believer in testing all horses in a barn for this disease.

155

Many horses (probably most in Maine and New Hampshire) have been exposed and are carrying antibodies that will show in a blood test. It is just like you or me carrying antibodies for measles, which might only mean that we have been exposed and have immunity against it. I think it is important to test for horses that are showing symptoms, but personally I consider it a waste of money and time to test non-symptomatic horses. This is one of many aspects of Lyme disease that is controversial, and these are my personal opinions and may prove to be wrong.

Lyme disease has only been recognized in New England for about 40 years, but it looks like it's here to stay, and we'll just have to learn from each other how to best live and deal with it.

52

Regularly Irregular
(scheduling barn chores)

U

Sammy was a pretty gray mare. Pretty to look at, and pretty darn smart. I was on the farm that day to vaccinate everyone, and when she was brought out of the stall, I noticed her big right knee. I asked her owner what was going on, and she said, "Oh, it's my fault, and I feel awful about it. I got up later than usual two days ago, and before I even got to the barn, I heard her banging on the stall door. Whenever I'm late, or if I grain someone else first, she either starts kicking the walls, or banging the stall door with her knee." I think this owner *should* feel awful about the situation, because she caused it. Not by being late, but by letting herself be trained by her horse instead of the other way around. Good job, Sammy.

Horses have the most amazing internal clocks. Feed them for three days in a row at 7AM, and at 6:58 on day four they're looking for you. With horses like Sammy the anticipation becomes physical. Do the same 45-minute workout with your horse every day, and then go a few minutes over, and you may well notice a sudden lack of motivation from your animal. Sounds a little like us when quitting time comes.

If you stick to a regular schedule, your animals very quickly learn your timing, all without the benefit of clocks. Here is a suggestion. Instead of always being on schedule as you do chores around the barn, vary the time that you show up. Be regularly irregular. For example, if you usually feed up at 7 AM, show up tomorrow at 6:45 or 7:15. If your horse is used to a one-hour work out, make it 50 minutes next time and maybe the next day an hour and 15. If you always show up after a workday at say, 5:30, run some errands first and be late. Vary your schedule enough and, as ironic as it seems, your animals will feel more secure as they learn that eventually you will show up, and that there is no sense in getting in a tizzy because you aren't punctual.

An excellent trainer once told me that if he is heading home from a ride and his horse begins to jig a little faster when the driveway to the farm comes in sight, he just rides right on by and goes another five or ten minutes past his place. Then he turns his horse and heads back home again. If the horse starts to get anxious to turn in from that direction, the trainer again just rides on by. He told me that he will keep this up, no matter how long it takes, until the horse finally will walk by the drive without speeding up. When they arrive at the barn, he praises the horse and puts him up. Next time the acceptance comes quicker. This wise trainer told me that every minute spent with a horse is a teaching opportunity. He said he has been late to more than one family dinner to make a point with the animal he is working with. "Throw away your clock and your own schedule when a particular issue needs to be resolved."

Understand, I'm a veterinarian, not a trainer, but it's not unusual for me to come into contact with at least one horse every day who decides what will happen, and when. This was taken to an all-time low about ten years ago when I arrived at a farm just as my client was coming in from a trail ride. I asked her where she went for her ride, and she replied, "Not too far today, he only wanted to go for 15 minutes, and then he turned and headed for home. He decides where we are going and how long we are going to be gone." No surprise that this horse is very difficult for the farrier and me to work on. Just picking up a foot is a project. The decisions concerning all your animals should be well thought out and should, of course, include their welfare, but *you* should always be the leader.

53

Respect

U

I love to hang over the fence and watch broodmares with their foals in the spring. It's fun to see the interaction among the youngsters as they play. I especially like the way mares teach their babies. It has always struck me how respect is taught so well and at such a young age. It doesn't take long for a youngster to learn that running around is OK, but slamming into Mom isn't. Nip your friends, sure, but try it with one of the grownups and punishment is fast and appropriate. The babies pick up pretty quick on "the look" from their elders who say, "Careful now, keep it up and you will wish you hadn't." This learning of respect is one of the reasons I don't like to see youngsters separated from their moms much before six months. There is a lot to learn, and mares are by far the best teachers. Many orphaned babies have behavior problems all their lives.

There is a hierarchy that gets established anytime two or more horses are together. There is always the top dog, and the one who defers to everyone else. One of the techniques of good trainers is putting a spoiled horse in with an established herd. Manners are learned fast and well in this situation. All of this is good, because it keeps order in the herd.

Over the past several years I have been watching some new horse owners who weren't brought up on farms. They have fallen in love with the idea of having a horse and are often able to open their wallets and buy their dream. I always hope that they will watch and learn from experienced horse people in addition to what they read or see on videos. I wish they would take some time to watch the mares and foals. That's the best way to learn how things work in a bunch of horses and how each animal finds its own place in the herd.

All too often I see some of these owners treat their horses as though the barnyard is a democracy. It's not. Each horse you come in contact with sizes you up and is hardwired to try to figure out who is boss in this relationship. It is great to love your animals, but in my opinion, if you don't establish your leadership, you are creating a great deal of anxiety in your animal. Behavior issues are usually caused by owners who have no idea how the mind of a horse works. If a horse is confused about who's who, he may feel the need to challenge you. They know there has to be a leader, and some owners may never have established themselves in that role.

You must, absolutely must, be the dominant being in your relationship with your horse. You respect their incredible ability and nature, and they have to respect your leadership. Do it correctly and not cruelly, just like their mommas do. Do it right and your animal will own that sense of security. This is also about your own safety. They outweigh us by five or ten to one and are lightning fast. You must draw the line over what is acceptable, and what isn't. As a simple example, you should be able to touch your horse anywhere, and it should be welcomed. It's OK for you to touch them, not OK for them to come into your space uninvited. A gentle push on their shoulder or rump, and they should step over for you. Haltering, bitting, saddling, and loading should be readily accepted.

If you are having behavior issues with your animal, it's time to contact a trainer. The good ones, the *really* good ones, will have as their main goal, educating you to be the leader in your relationship with your animal.

54

Safe and Effective Fencing

A few months ago I got an email from Beth Carlson of Bath, Maine. Her email inspired me to write this article. She and a student of hers had been barn shopping and saw some beautiful facilities, but were surprised by inadequate fencing on some of the farms visited. Beth wrote: *"Accidents waiting to happen, I'm sure. I've known of barn owners that would spend money on cross country jumps, etc. while their fencing was in terrible condition. Boarding stables need to know well educated horse people will not board at their facility when they see these scary situations. The sad thing is, I think many potential boarders are afraid of hurting the barn owner's feelings so walk off without offering some constructive criticism in a kind way."*

I totally agree with Beth. Good fencing keeps horses safe. It should contain them and never be a source of injury. The first job of our fences is to keep animals confined so that they don't wander off. My suggestion is to walk your fence line every spring before pasture turnout. Tug on every post. Replace the rotten ones. Make sure that the boards are secure and will take the weight of a horse leaning into them. The rails should be fastened on the horse side of the posts. Not as pleasing to the eye as rails on the outside, but they won't pop out if leaned on. Electric fences are a real advance in fencing. You can fence a field almost as fast as you can walk. We forget that electric fences also need maintenance. Electric fencing without a charge running through it is really no fence at all. In every herd of horses there is one who will test the fence every so often. If he finds it dead, he will push against it to get to that green grass on the other side. Most electric fence posts are no contest for a hungry horse. Weed whack regularly to keep the wire clear, and use a fence tester to make sure that your electric fence is delivering adequate charge. My suggestion is to turn off the fence once a week before you let the horses out and walk the line, straightening things out as you go. Then, most importantly, turn it back on again.

The second important aspect of our fences is that they not cause injuries. The biggest offender is barbed wire. It has no place on horse farms. Horses tend to panic when trapped, and your vet can probably tell you what a mess barbed wire can make of a horse that gets tangled in it.

I sometimes run into situations where people use fencing that I can only describe as ornamental. The most striking example of this for me happened over 20 years ago. The call was from a client named Chet, who asked me to drop everything and get over to his farm.

"Better get over here, Doc, there's a board sticking out of my old mare!" I asked him where the board was sticking out from and if he had tried to pull it out. I knew Chet as an excitable guy and was thinking that the "board" was probably just a stick.

"It's coming out of her chest, and nope, I ain't pulling on it. It's a 2x4! If I pull it, I'm afraid she's gonna bleed to death. Just get over here!" The drive to Chet's farm normally takes 15 minutes. I was there in 10. When I drove up, I saw Chet and some of the neighborhood folks in the paddock next to the barn. They were in a circle around the old mare. Her head was down, and she was standing very still. The crowd parted when I walked up. This was long before cellphone cameras, and I remember wishing I had a camera in the truck because I was sure no one would believe what I was seeing.

There was a two-foot length of 2x4 that *did* look like it was coming out of her chest. When I got closer, I could see that it was actually sticking out from that space between the shoulder blade and the chest. I walked around to her side and saw the *other* end of the board coming out from the behind the shoulder blade and lying along the outside of the rib cage. This meant that there was about 18 inches of a 2x4 buried in the mare's muscle between ribs and shoulder. To complicate things, the front end of the board, coming out from the mare, had a few big nails sticking out of it. I had never run into anything even approaching this much trauma with a horse that was still on its feet. I had to fight the growing panic that arose, because I had absolutely no idea what to do

162

about this. I forced myself to think about what had to be done and how to prepare for each step. I grabbed everything I thought we might need from my truck and talked the situation over with everyone present. They were all eager to help.

I gave the mare a strong IV tranquillizer. Within two minutes her head dropped, and she got wobbly. We tried pulling the board out from in front, but it was stuck fast, and she got uneasy. Next best was to pull the board from the back of the shoulder, but we had to get rid of the nails sticking out in front first so that they wouldn't tear through the heavy muscles as the board passed through. Chet got a hammer and used the claw end to pull on the nails, but even tranquilized, the mare felt every move. It was obvious that we had to put the mare completely out. I gave her an IV general anesthetic, and with everyone's help, we laid the horse down gently so that the 2x4 was on the up side. I knew that we had, at most, 20 minutes to get rid of that board. It still seemed to make sense to push the board from the front to the back, the way it went in, but we still had those nails to contend with. Chet tried to pull the nails again, but they were badly bent, and he couldn't get a strong pull on them without severely twisting the 2x4.

Someone suggested a skill saw to cut off the front end of the board to get rid of the nails. Chet ran an extension cord from the barn, plugged in his skill saw, and whacked off the first six inches of the board. I had two of the neighbors pull straight up on the leg to ease the weight of the leg on the board. One man pulled the board from the back as another pushed from the front, and it slowly slid out! I was able to get my hand into the gaping wound from both the front and the back, behind the shoulder blade, to check for splinters and possible broken ribs. It was clean as a whistle. I flushed the gaping wound, gave the horse antibiotics, some IV Bute, a tetanus shot and said a quick prayer.

After the horse was back on her feet, I asked Chet to show me how the mare had managed to impale herself on that board. At the side of the barn was a steep wooden ramp that ran from the barn down to the paddock. Chet had made a railing along the side of the ramp by nailing two 2x4s as uprights to the side of the ramp. Another five-foot 2x4 was nailed alongside their tops to serve as a hand rail. That afternoon Chet had been sitting on his back porch when he heard a commotion in the barn, some horses squealing, and then the thunder of horses tearing down the wooden ramp. There was a brief silence, then crashing and the sound of wood splintering. We figured that one of the horses had run out the door at an odd angle and crashed into Chet's railing, snapping off one end. The mare must have followed, and she ran into the broken end at full speed, driving the 2x4 into her body between the shoulder and the ribs. In her struggle to get free she broke off the railing supports, leaving those nails at the front end of the board. Chet had put together the assembly for people going up or down that steep ramp, but it was definitely not horse proof.

Lesson learned: Expect interaction between horses and anticipate all the things that can happen. Anything you build with wood has to be able to withstand the weight of a horse slamming into it. Use big dimension, solid lumber that is firmly secured. Power driven screws are stronger than nails, and bolts trump screws. The episode had a happy ending, as amazingly, the old mare never went off feed and stayed sound.

Several years ago I was called to remove what was left of the right eye in a Quarter-horse gelding. His owner actually saw this accident happen. The horse was playing with another one in the pasture, running back and forth at a full tilt. At one point they were running near the fence line. The gelding got very close to it, perhaps felt trapped, went up on his hind legs and came down full force with his head sort of sideways, like goats at play will do. He slipped and dove right into the top end of a steel T-post with his left eye. I have seen T-posts, which have not been maintained, lean into pastures, leaving the raw steel end to penetrate legs or bodies. T-posts have a history of trauma to livestock, which is why plastic shields are made to place over that dangerous top end. If you use T-posts, buy an equal number of shields, and when the posts have been pounded in, jam those shields on top. Old tennis balls can also be used to cap them. T-posts without the top shielded are dangerous.

Have you ever seen a spring gate? It is a large diameter spring that looks like a long slinky. It connects on either end to the electric fence and is made to stretch out across gateways that may be 12 to 15 feet wide. When hooked over the wire at both ends, it carries the same charge as the electric fence. They had always seemed handy to me as an easy gate…until I had a run-in with one. I was helping a client catch her horses to bring into the barn for vaccinations. She led her mare, and

I had the 17 hand, 3 year old, mostly unbroken gelding. Mary unhooked one end of the spring gate, and as she and the mare passed through, she handed me the insulated handle. I held the handle with one hand and guided the colt through the opening by pulling on his lead. After he passed through I hooked the handle back onto the fence, completing the electric circuit. The spring gate was now carrying a full charge. Can you see where this is going?

As I turned to walk the colt to the barn, he backed into the gate, got a shock, and went airborne. I was trying to control him, when his long tail got caught in the coils of the spring gate. In trying to free his tail, his butt touched the spring, and he received a *second* shock and took off at a gallop. His shoulder knocked me down, and I was dragged a few feet before I had the sense to let go of his lead. Off he went, and one end of the spring gate disconnected. The coil quickly stretched out to make a nearly straight wire, which allowed the release of his tail. What a cluster! I have not been a fan of spring gates since. I saw one in a catalogue made of bungee cord that must have wire woven into it to carry the juice. Sounds like a better option than the coils, but I'll take a well-constructed steel, aluminum or wooden gate any day.

You can anticipate that whatever kind of fence or gate you use *will be* leaned on, scratched against, run into, legs stuck under, and sometimes successfully, sometimes not, leaped over. Anticipate all of the crazy things that horses do, and plan or improve your fencing accordingly.

55

Scratches

———————— ⊍ ————————

Maybe it's called scratches because even a minor scrape in the skin of the pastern can start this annoying and hard to treat problem. In some parts of the country it is called grease heel, and in others, mud fever. Both of those names are descriptive. The official name is "pastern dermatitis." It is usually seen on the hind legs of horses with thick leg hair and most often in wet weather. The moisture trapped by the hair is the perfect breeding ground for a mixed bag of bacteria and fungi. With even the smallest break in the skin, microbes enter, and the problem begins. Abscesses erupt at the back of the pasterns and ooze serum. The serum is sticky and dry. It hardens like glue, adhering tightly to skin and hair. If you aren't familiar with what this looks like, Google "scratches horses" and check out the photos.

I never write about subjects that I don't have plenty of personal experience with. It would be fine with me if I never saw another case of scratches, but I can tell you that I will, for sure, before the month is out. I always check the books and do online searches before writing to see if there is something beyond my experience that I have been missing. My research on the subject of scratches tells me that not much has changed over the past 50 years. It has always been a problem, and will continue to be.

The condition is more common in horses with that magnificent long hair that extends from just below the hocks and knees all the way to and covering a bit of the foot. Any veterinarian will tell you that white legs are especially susceptible. So those long white "feathers" make horses of the Clydesdale breed ideal candidates for the problem. Get any two owners of Clydes together, and eventually the talk will turn to how they are dealing with scratches.

Cleaning the area is hard to do and painful for the horse. Just clipping the hair to get down to the skin becomes a real challenge. Even when you declare victory, it often reoccurs. Horses that get scratches are apt to be repeaters, so daily inspection of legs by owner or trainer is important. There is some thought that horses with weak immune systems are more likely to get the problem. Medications that stimulate the immune system are sometimes used with the idea of speeding up the healing process.

My own experience with the problem has taught me a couple of things I'd like to pass on. First, if there are multiple draining abscesses and your horse resists your trying to pick or scrub them off, let ichthammol do the work. This is an old time ointment that is available at any horse supply. Use a tongue depressor and smear it onto the leg as thick as you would chocolate frosting on a cake. Over the ichthammol use sheet cottons or a quilt, secure with a leg wrap, and keep the leg done up for two to three days. If the scabs don't come off easily after that, repeat. This ointment does an outstanding job of loosening caked-on skin eruptions and in soothing the irritated skin. When it's time to remove the wraps, scrape off any excess ichthammol and wash the leg gently with betadine or some other antibacterial scrub. Let the foamy soap sit on the leg for 15 minutes, then rinse well and pat completely dry with a Turkish towel. At this point you may be able to clip the leg if necessary. Finally, it is time to apply your vet's favorite "scratches remedy." These are ointments made up of combinations of two or more ingredients. We all have one.

The second important aspect of treating scratches is to refrain from washing the area every day. Remember the bugs love that moisture. Once you have done the initial ichthammol treatment and cleaned up, apply a light coat of the remedy daily, and resist the temptation to wash the leg again. Some cases will need appropriate antibiotic therapy. Horses with white legs that are continuously affected should probably not be in sunlight for long stretches. White skin is more easily irritated by ultraviolet rays. Horses with liver problems may be even more susceptible to the damaging sunlight. Keep animals prone to scratches out of muddy pastures and paddocks. If the lesions get worse and large bunches of them coalesce, the condition is called "grapes," which is a real mess, and surgery may be indicated.

Vets are usually called to look at scratches as a last resort after a lot of strange potions have been applied to the leg. If not treated effectively and soon, scratches tend to creep up the leg. Long-term scratches can lead to a cellulitis which in some cases means a leg that never returns to normal size. My recommendation is to call in your vet at the first sign of any dermatitis of the pastern.

56

Sheaths and Beans

U

What could I possibly add to a topic that has been written about in every horse magazine ever published? Is regular cleaning of a gelding's sheath important for his health, or just a waste of time? This article is my perspective on the topic, with some situations that I have run into over the years.

First, here is a one-paragraph anatomy and physiology lesson. The sheath is a thick double fold of tissue whose function is to protect the penis. It is like a collapsible telescope. When the penis is extended, the folds of the sheath disappear and become part of the penis. The sheath has some glands in its lining that produce a waxy secretion. When mixed with dirt and old dead cells, it's called smegma. It smells about the way it sounds. At the end of the penis, close to the urethral opening that carries urine out, is a small cavity that you can just get the tip of your finger in. Its official name is the urethral diverticulum. It doesn't have a common name that I am aware of, so let's call it the bean pocket. Smegma tends to collect and compact in that pocket, and like play dough, it takes the shape of that space. The smegma dries over time and when you get the tip of a finger in that cavity and work the smegma out, it looks like a bean, which is what it is called. Part of cleaning the inside of the sheath is the removal or "popping" of that bean. Cleaning the sheath without removing the bean is not really completing the job and can lead to problems down the road.

One early morning this spring I was called out to examine an 18-year-old gelding who hadn't eaten breakfast and was mildly painful. The owner had given him Banamine paste over an hour before, and although he seemed better, there was a concern because he still wasn't right. I already had a full day, but agreed to come out right away and had Lizzy call our scheduled clients to say that we would be late.

When I got to the farm, the horse had just made manure, but still seemed distracted. His temperature, pulse, and respirations were all normal, and there were good gut sounds on both sides. Everything was checking out OK, so I didn't understand why he seemed restless. I did a rectal exam, but couldn't get very far in because his bladder was so big. I gave him an IV diuretic so that he would urinate. He soon became even antsier and acted just like a person who has to pee but knows that the nearest McDonald's is still five minutes down the road. Finally, his urine came out in a huge stream, and his relief was immediate. I did another rectal and found all the intestines in place and nothing distended. We watched him for a bit, and then I left to drive to my first scheduled call. About two hours later his owner called my cell.

"Hey, I know what was bothering that gelding."

"Go ahead, tell me."

"I called my wife at work, and she said that since we've had him, he has never had his sheath cleaned, so we did that and found a monster bean. Hey, this thing was the size of a walnut, and we had to break it up to get it out. He's been 100% ever since."

I hadn't made the connection between that full bladder and the real reason for it. I suspect that the huge bean distended the end of his penis enough that he didn't really *want* to urinate, but the diuretic in his system finally gave him no choice.

Several years ago I ran into a peculiar lameness that made no sense. The horse had been off for several weeks before I was called. On examination I could see that the horse was off behind, but his gait didn't fit any of the usual patterns. We decided to do a more extensive workup in a week, but before I left we gave the horse his annual vaccines and cleaned his sheath at the owner's request. He had a bean that was good sized and quite hard. She called the next day and said that he was totally sound. Was it the bean? I'm pretty sure it wasn't the vaccines, and there were no other changes, so yes, I think so. This isn't a common cause of lameness, but I have had this happen just enough over the years to believe that a large bean can cause discomfort which can be expressed in different ways.

One of the most interesting cases we ran into last year was a horse who was having some behavior issues when his owner took him on a trail ride. He wouldn't obey, kept wanting to head for home, and was getting quite cranky about it. As part of his examination we checked his sheath. My technician, Erin, does all of our sheath cleanings, and in his case she found something very unusual. The pocket that collects the smegma had a membrane running through it, making more than one compartment out of the space. Erin is nimble and very thorough, but it still took her quite a few minutes to completely remove several very hard beans from this gelding. The next day the owner reported perfect behavior on her ride, and he has been fine since. His owner now makes sure that our annual visit always includes cleaning his sheath and checking that pocket for, in his case, beans.

It's an unpleasant job, but when asked to clean a sheath I know that it will give us a chance to do a good exam of both the penis and sheath. There are some types of cancer that are found at these locations. Early detection and treatment is always best. Horses vary in the amount of smegma produced. There are horses that never need cleaning, and some that produce so much smegma that it oozes out and collects on the inside of their hind legs. We commonly find beans the size of lima beans, and some horses never collect enough smegma to be called a bean.

Before sitting down to write this article I did an online search on sheath cleaning and bean removal. A few mentioned the use of a garden hose run up into the sheath to remove the smegma. This had to have been submitted by an arm-chair horseperson. Straight water just won't work. It would be like rinsing a breakfast plate with yesterday's egg stuck on it, hoping water pressure alone will remove the dried yolk. You need a non-irritating liquid soap, an old washcloth, cotton, even an old sock worn over your hand, to gently scrub the smegma off. There are products which are smeared inside the sheath that are designed to loosen the smegma. After applying them you have to give them time to work. Even so, there is still manual work to be done. I recommend disposable gloves, unless you don't mind the smell of the smegma when you sit down to lunch. Without gloves that odor just has to wear off.

Some horses will tolerate a sheath cleaning well without tranquilization. Others will object, and a tranquilizer should be used for everyone's safety. Tranquilizers have the added benefit of relaxing the muscle that draws the penis into the sheath, so it hangs out for easy access. If you have never cleaned a sheath and popped the bean, and would like to do this job yourself, my suggestion is to have your veterinarian train you rather than going to an online source like You Tube. I see scary videos with owners standing in places that almost guarantee getting kicked. Your veterinarian has had plenty of experience to share with you on how to gently, effectively and efficiently clean a sheath and pop that bean. If it's a job that you just can't wrap your mind around, have your veterinarian do it annually.

57

Shipshape
(barn cleanliness)

U

Ihad a very interesting conversation with a businessman the other day. He owns several rental houses. I asked him if he has tenant problems. He said that this is now rare for him. He has found a way of telling how a prospective renter would be likely to treat his properties. I asked him if it was by checking references. He replied that he does call references, but mostly he relies on checking out their car. I asked him what he meant. Is it the year of the vehicle, or its outside appearance? The answer might surprise you. When he has made an appointment to show a house, he always arrives early. He walks to the applicant's car to greet them as they drive up and makes a point of taking a quick look inside the vehicle. He has learned through many experiences that if the inside is a total mess (old candy wrappers, older soda cans, and assorted junk around everyone's feet) that this is pretty much the way his house will be treated.

As an equine vet I am in hundreds of barns every year. Most are a pleasure to walk in. A few others are always a mess. I'm thinking of a client who has since moved out of state. This was an extreme situation, but the barn was exactly like I am about to describe. The floor always looked like the inside of one of those messy cars. Mixed in among the old hay on the floor would be empty paste wormer syringes, a cardboard box or two, and even empty feed bags that had never been thrown away. If I picked up a horse's foot, there would always be a five-minute hunt for them to locate a hoof pick. Rakes, shovels, and brooms were left wherever they were last used. Seeing this mess on every visit bothered both my tech and me. The only way we were finally able to work effectively was by us first sweeping a 12 by 12 foot area near the door.

We would then ask to have all the horses that needed attention brought to our little oasis of sanity. I explained to the owner that I have a hard time working in clutter. She never really got the message.

I like to write about things that affect a horse's health. Is there any reason to think that an unkempt barn might influence that? I think so.

If you have ever spent any time on a sailboat or sailing ship, you know that one of the rules is, "a place for everything, and everything in its place." All lines are neatly coiled, and that piece of gear goes on that hook right over there—and nowhere else. It isn't neatness for the sake of it. Things are put away because lives depend on it. On a dark windy night, with the rain coming sideways, all hands must be able to locate what is needed and to not trip over what isn't. A barn isn't a boat, but there are so many tools and so much tack that goes with barns and horses that if things aren't shipshape, it starts to look like a twister just set down.

Most horse owners truly love their animals. To quote one owner, "My horses are more than a hobby, they are my life." If that is true, then why wouldn't we want to keep them in as safe an environment as possible? Barns with hay not swept up and years of cobwebs hanging from every rafter are more than a mess, they are a fire hazard. It seems to me if your surroundings are always messy, it is a reflection of your thinking. If you suspect that your thinking might be cluttered, one avenue of correction is to straighten out the messes around you. Don't you feel better mentally when you have finally cleaned up clutter that has been sitting there for months, and everything is where it should be? If nothing else, squared away barns are timesavers. Rakes, pitchforks, and shovels hung in the same place after every use never have to be hunted for. I have found that when my desk gets too deep in papers, I have to take the time to straighten it or I can't be productive. Are the horses happier in clean barns? Probably not, but I have noticed in most cases when the barn is a mess, the horses don't get groomed very often. It all seems to go together.

58

Slippery

(horse saliva)

———————— ♘ ————————

Sandra moved to Maine four years ago with her two horses. On my first visit to her farm she told me that her older gelding, Benny, had a history of belly aches. I asked what he was getting to eat. She said he gets about ¾ of a bale of hay and 2 pounds of low carb grain a day. That seemed about right for this 900 lb. Morgan. Our conversation was taking place as we stood outside Benny's stall. Sandra moved a little closer to me and said in an awed whisper, "The thing is, Benny likes to eat." She paused, and then, "He *really* likes to eat!" I questioned what she meant.

"I mean he plows right into it and his head doesn't come up until he has eaten every little scrid! I start with hay so he won't choke on the grain, but, I kid you not, hay and grain are all done within 20 minutes. He just scarfs it down! He seems fine, I leave for work, and more than a few times I've found him colicky when I get home. Do you think it could be worms?"

I told Sandra that Benny's problem was probably not worms. Morgans do like to eat, and Benny was more than true to the breed. I thought that the real problem was that most of the day he *wasn't* eating. Sandra would leave for work, and there was Benny in an empty stall or paddock with nothing to eat. He had already had enough, but not in a healthy way. Part of the reason for the colics was his lack of saliva. How did I come up with that? Would learning about saliva change anything that Sandra or that you might be doing? Estimates on how much saliva horses secrete run between 3 and 15 gallons per day for a 1000 pound horse. That's quite a range. That's because the amount is dependent on *how* they are fed. What does that mean?

In all animals saliva moistens and softens the food and then eases its passage down the esophagus and into the stomach. Most of saliva (99% +) is water. It also contains some buffering compounds like sodium bicarbonate which are helpful in counteracting acid in the stomach. Saliva is nature's antacid. It also contains enzymes which help break down food into simpler and more digestible forms. Saliva gets its slipperiness from a lubricant called mucin. Even that is important. Every time I do a physical on a horse, I run a finger into his mouth and then rub my finger and thumb together and smell it. It should smell clean and be slippery. Saliva that is tacky or has an off odor means you are looking at a horse that isn't right.

There are three-paired glands that produce saliva in horses. The major ones are just under the skin behind the jaw and between the jaw bones. The saliva is carried by tubes, called ducts. They open into the mouth. You can spot one set of them if you open your horse's mouth and move the tongue aside. Just a couple of inches back from the lower jaw incisors, right where the tongue usually nestles, you can see a pair of tiny flaps that cover two of the duct openings. The glands start secreting when a horse starts eating, and the flow slows down when the chewing stops. Nothing in the mouth means no chewing and very scant saliva. This is unlike you and me, who before, during, and after meals are continuously secreting saliva. Our mouths are always wet. Horses not so much, unless they are eating.

With this knowledge we are prepared to explore the how of horse feeding. Researchers, sitting on the ground out west, with their laptops and timers, have found that wild horses spend at least 85% of their standing time doing one thing. Their heads are down and they are eating. That horse on the prairie, eating almost continuously, is always producing and secreting saliva. Not true for Benny and many of our domestic horses. Ask your vet how many colics he or she sees in a year. Colic is extremely rare in wild horses.

When you leave for work like Sandra and throw a few slices of hay into a paddock or stall, there may be hours when the food is gone and the mouth is empty. An empty equine mouth means a relatively dry mouth because there is nothing to stimulate the saliva flow. The stomach has no food to work on and nothing much to buffer the acid. It adds up to a perfect ulcer scenario.

Years ago in my racetrack practice, I daily saw horses standing in their stalls with nothing to do, waiting for their next meal. Heavy grain and a few slices of hay two times a day was the diet. I'm not sure that it has changed, because horse traditions die hard. Diets low in roughage and high in grain don't produce enough saliva to neutralize stomach acids. Studies verify that 90% of race horses have ulcers.

Whenever possible feed minimum amounts of grain and make roughage continuously available. I tell owners that when feeding time comes around again, there should be enough hay in their stall or paddock so that a bird could build a nest. If you have a particularly easy keeper, you may have to feed less leafy hay, but don't, please don't, leave them for hours without something to chew on.

When I talk about continuous roughage, I get pushback from owners who are tired of throwing away hay that has been pooped on and walked over. Today's hay nets are an effective answer to that problem. They are the closest thing to turning a horse out on acres of grass. Some nets hold an entire bale. I like the nets with a tight weave so that each bit of hay has to be teased out. It keeps horses occupied and insures roughage in the stomach. You can jam the nets full and leave them right on the ground or on the stall floor. A side benefit is that horses are at their most relaxed when their heads are down and they are eating. As they chew, the saliva flows, the stomach has something to work on, and ulcers are minimized. The newer muzzles are also handy for limiting pasture for overweight horses.

To summarize, saliva is important for digestive health. Constant intake of roughage keeps it flowing. It is better than any purchased supplement for the prevention of ulcers, choke, and colic.

PS. Sandra changed her feeding routine. Benny is now fed from a hay net. By the time Sandra gets home, the net is pretty flat, but there is always a little left. He has not colicked in the last four years.

PPS. For a different look at saliva, see the chapter about horses who salivate too much, entitled, "The Slobbers."

59

Solitary

(isolating new horses)

U

Mary heard about the gray gelding and immediately checked him out on Face Book. Her favorite horse color—and handsome to boot! Just six years old, so probably not lame from overuse. Perfect! He had received no bids at the New Jersey auction and was headed for what is called "the feed lot." The old, not so nice, name for what was the killer pen. He would stay there for up to a week. If there were no offers to buy him for the set price, he would be put on the next truck to Canada or Mexico. That's a one way trip.

Mary read all the instructions on the auction site, contacted the agent at the feed lot, and bought him with plastic. She made calls to boarding barns near her and soon had a stall reserved. Ten minutes later she had transportation arranged and paid for. Within one hour Mary was a horse owner. Rescue horses are very, very easy to obtain. A week later the gelding was unloaded at the barn. Mary was there when the truck pulled in. The gelding came off calm, cool and collected. Everything she had hoped for. He didn't come with a name, but there was a tag on his right hip with the number 010, so Mary started calling him "Ten." Wow, the perfect Ten! Mary was excited.

It was a 12-stall barn, and two were open. The barn owner thought it would be wise to put him next to one of the empty stalls as a protection against any disease he might be carrying. Ten settled right in, and when Mary left an hour later, he was eating hay. She took that next week off and was at the barn Monday and Tuesday, getting to know him. She purred as she groomed him and went about the business of getting him fitted with tack. He was turned out for a few hours every day with an empty paddock between him and the other horses.

Wednesday morning Mary arrived at the barn at 9 AM and was greeted by the barn owner: "Ten didn't eat his grain this morning, and he seems kind of mopey." Mary borrowed a digital thermometer from the stable first aid kit and took his temperature. 104 degrees! My office was called to check him out. When I heard where he came from, I told Mary that I thought Ten's illness might be contagious, and that I would come out, but it would be the last call of the day. I arrived at the farm at 5:30 that evening and found Ten depressed, his temperature now 105 degrees. He had a snotty nose and was starting to swell under his jaw. I drew a blood sample and took a swab from way back in his nose. My recommendation was that he be totally isolated from the rest of the barn, hoping that he wouldn't infect the others. The barn owner put him in a round pen 30 feet from the barn and turnouts. I gave instructions on how and when to handle him.

The isolation and my recommendations came too late. On Friday morning a mare two stalls down from Ten started to cough. Ten's lab tests came in the next day and confirmed my suspicion of strangles. Typical of this messy upper respiratory disease is its slow march through a barn. Over the next two weeks three other horses in the barn got just as sick as Ten. A week later three others ran a fever with minor throat swellings and an occasional cough. Three others seemed unaffected, and looking into their history, we learned that two had been vaccinated for strangles a year ago, and the other had had strangles years before. The once busy barn became a hospital ward.

When one of the respiratory diseases hits, no one wants your horse (or you) at any equine activities. For a good two weeks after the last horse has recovered, barn visits and new horses should be banned. The barn owner that took Ten in told me a year later that her active barn was essentially cut off from the rest of the horse world for four long months. The show season for them did not happen that year. I will never forget a large dressage barn a few miles west of me that had a strangles outbreak several years ago. There was a split down the middle of the eight boarders as to how the epidemic and use of the indoor, etc. was to be handled. There were many arguments, barn meetings, and hard feelings, and a couple of boarders left, when they could.

Strangles and influenza are two highly contagious diseases of horses. The virus of influenza is easily spread through the air as an aerosol, and absolute quarantine with large distances from other horses is important. Strangles is a bacterial disease and is usually spread by nose to nose contact. However, as in this case, it can travel through a barn even with the precautions that were taken. Neither disease is fatal, but both make affected horses miserable and on the sick list for a long time.

I have never seen a time when horses have been moved as much as they are today. Equines with unknown histories are picked up at and by rescues. They are then trucked long distances with other horses from different locations. The confusion of an auction and mixing with strange horses is stressful, making them highly susceptible to infections. They may catch a bug, but may not show symptoms for a week. We should be super vigilant in guarding our horses' health when a new one is brought onto the farm. If you are bringing in outside horses, it's a good idea to talk to your veterinarian about what you might consider vaccinating against long before a new horse arrives.

I have a client with a lot of in and out horse traffic, and some are rescues like Ten. She learned how to handle the new-horse problem while working at a stable that had a strangles episode. She was determined that it would never happen at her barn. There, a new horse is put in a round pen located 50 feet away from other paddocks and the barn. No one is permitted within ten feet of the round pen except her. There is a three-sided shelter within the pen. In the morning she feeds by throwing hay over the top of the pen into the enclosure. The horse gets no grain in the morning. She fills the water pail with a hose running from an outside hydrant, which is a few feet from the pen. She doesn't touch the horse or even get within two feet of the enclosure all day. In the evening, after she has left her barn, she goes straight for the pen, wearing high rubber boots. She enters the pen and then gives the new horse his grain, from a bag kept in a secure metal container in the shelter. After he has finished his grain, she grooms and fusses over him. All grooming equipment and tack for that animal stays in the shelter. After giving him lots of attention, she heads for the house, takes a shower, and puts all her clothes into the washing machine. The boots get scrubbed and disinfected. This isolation lasts for two weeks. Her idea is that if symptoms were to develop it would likely be within that time. If the new horse does get sick, the outside stay is extended until he is symptom free for another two weeks. You will read various times for isolation, but I consider two weeks a reasonable time. It's a quarantine system that I call solitary confinement. It works.

It is natural to want to introduce your new horse to all the horses in the barn and integrate them quickly into the barn routine. Be smart. Put them into solitary for two weeks, and in the long haul you will save yourself all the worry and expense.

60

Stable Air

It was a mid-November day when her call came in. The owner of a stable that I had never been to wanted me to check out a horse with a persistent cough. I told Sandra to expect me at her barn the next morning. I got an early start that day. The half-hour drive to the farm was a delight. It had rained lightly during the night, and in the early morning hours a cold front had come through. The trees were sheathed in ice, and the branches, backlit by the sun, looked as though they were cut from fine crystal.

As I pulled up to the barn, I noticed that the window on the front of the barn had a heavy frost on the inside. From years of visiting hundreds of barns, I knew that this meant excess moisture inside.

I pulled open the big barn door and was immediately struck by the warm, sticky atmosphere in contrast to the crisp outside air. Sandra was sweeping the floor at the far end of the barn. She put the broom away and walked past the six horses' heads looking out over their Dutch doors. I was introduced to each animal and given a brief history of each one. Sandra told me that she had purchased the farm a few months ago and had recently moved the horses and her entire household up from Tennessee. She shared that she loved the beauty of winter but was having a hard time getting used to the cold. She was happy that I could come out that day, as another one of the horses had developed a cough just like the one she had called about.

As we chatted, I glanced around. Not only was the window in front of the barn frosted over, but all of the others were as well. Sandra seemed open to new ideas, and I knew that our conversation was going to be mostly about the tired old air in her barn, and what it was causing.

There is a season of equine respiratory problems. Every year, from October to April, there is a very predictable uptick in coughs and snotty noses. More serious diseases like the flu and strangles spread fast when horses are stabled. Cases of heaves often have their start in poorly ventilated barns.

The cause of all these issues is not the cold weather, but how we horse owners tend to react to it. We like to be warm and want our animals comfortable as well. So we tend to do what we do where we live. Shut the windows, seal all the cracks, and even insulate. We think we are being kind to our animals. The result is stable air like Sandra's, stale and filled with moisture.

Each average adult horse gives off a full gallon of water in his breath every day. Add to that the moisture from manure, urine, and sweat, and in a tight barn the air becomes super saturated with moisture. When barns are buttoned up, the heat given off by horses raises the air temperature. Warm air holds much more moisture than cold air. Dairymen have known this for years. They fit far more cows per space than we do horses. The temperature in a dairy barn even on a zero-degree Fahrenheit day would be well over 80 degrees if it weren't for big fans pulling out the stale air 24 hours a day. Viruses and bacteria thrive in the heat and humidity. It is almost impossible to clear up a respiratory problem in a barn where the air is rebreathed.

Sealing a stable to keep out the cold is well intended but is a big mistake. When you seal out the cold, you seal in the moisture. The evidence is seen on the frosted windows and walls where the moisture condenses on a cold day. Horses can withstand the coldest New England weather as long as they have plenty to eat, are kept on clean dry bedding, and there is good ventilation.

Our ancestors knew of the problem and built in a natural draft system to combat it. They designed their barns so that there was an air space under the eaves. The cold air entering there dropped down the walls, and mixed with the warm moist air. This tempered air rose and exited out the cupola on top of the barn. In almost all horse barns, this old natural draft system should work without depending on fans. Today in most cases ridge vents at the top of the roof take the place of the cupola. The beauty of a natural draft system is that it is self-regulating. The greater the difference in temperature between inside and outside, the faster the warm air will leave. The warm air with its capacity to hold water is vented out. In a natural air flow system, air inlets and outlets are equally important.

I was surprised by the amount of information online about the importance of barn ventilation. There are over 1000 articles listed! Of the ones I skimmed, the best is a 16-page article entitled, "Horse Stable Ventilation" from Penn State. It is quoted in many of the others' references and explains in detail, with lots of excellent drawings, how to build or retrofit a barn for ventilation and optimum health.

I examined Sandra's two coughing horses. Within two weeks of minimal medication, they were fine because with very little expense, the air in Sandra's barn was being changed four or five times every hour, and the flow distributed evenly throughout the stable. Sandra had learned the importance of fresh air and has not had a coughing horse since.

61

Stall Accidents

Every so often you will hear about horses running back into their burning barn. Why is that? It's because they are scared and confused and headed home. Whenever I am asked to look at the victim of a stall accident, I learn a little bit more about good stable construction. It always seems to be the small overlooked details that get horses in trouble.

One hazardous situation that I see almost every day is something that is missing on hinged stall doors that swing outward. The unsafe feature is having only one latch on the door. Usually that single latch is about waist high for our convenience. I remember a young athletic gelding that was apt to gulp his grain. Shortly after being fed one night he got a belly ache and went down in his stall. Unfortunately, he was lying so that the hind legs were within range of his stall door. As he lashed out in pain, the foot closest to the floor hit the door with enough force to spring the door out at the bottom. The plywood door was well built, and it snapped back, trapping his leg just above the hoof. Had there been a second, lower latch a few inches off the floor, the door wouldn't have moved. The nature of the horse is to struggle when restrained. If no one is around to release the leg (not an easy job), he will try to work himself free. In this case, it eventually meant putting this horse down. I am aware of two other horses that got into the same predicament that had to have long expensive therapies. Prevention is simple. A few dollars for a second latch placed down near the floor and less than 15 minutes to install it. It means bending down and undoing that second latch every time you have to open the stall door. If nothing else, it's another precaution against Houdini-type horses that seem to be able to open any latch. Is it worth the trouble? Because of the potential disaster here, I think so.

Stand in the middle of your horse's stall and look all around. Think about the natural curiosity of horses and the quick moves that scared or trapped horses make. Is there anything that your animals can get hung up on, over, or under? For example, there might be an old metal salt block holder screwed to the wall or a metal pail with a ripped edge. Are there protruding screws or nails? Any loose boards that need to be screwed back in? I have sutured up many eyelids caused by each of those things.

Every once in a while I see a stall that was built "on the cheap." That is, the stall was built with ¾ inch boards instead of solid two-inch boards. If plywood is used it should be at least ¾ inch. Anything less than sturdy lumber is easy to punch through with a hind foot. The punching through is not the problem. As you can imagine, it's pulling the leg back through the splintered wood that causes the damage. Using correct dimension lumber is an investment when building horse facilities. Equines get into enough trouble when you are doing everything right. No sense in asking for more.

Some stalls are designed for better horse-to-horse visibility and better air circulation by slatting the boards instead of making the walls solid. That's fine if you are careful about the distance between the boards. Ten years ago I had to free an Arabian filly that was exploring her stall and worked her lower jaw between two boards and then was unable to get it out. You can imagine the scene as she kept pulling back to free her jaw. First, I gave her a tranquilizer. We then had to saw through the two boards to free her. Finally, it was a trip to a surgical facility to get her fractured jaw repaired. If your barn has spaces between the boards, make sure that they are wide enough so that it's impossible for any part of the anatomy from jaws to feet to get caught. I personally like it when horses can see each other, and I do agree with the better air circulation. Just be careful about keeping the distance between the boards correct. Measure the distance to make sure a jaw or a foot can't get caught.

Similarly, the steel bars that protect windows should be spaced so that a horse's foot would be impossible to fit between any two bars. I saw this happen when a warm blood mare got cast upside down. Her stall had a barred window that was about four feet off the floor. When she tried to get up, she kicked one hind leg, and the power of the kick sent her foot between two of the steel bars. The bars closed on her pastern.

It was like being caught in a bear trap. I was called to tranquilize her so that the local fire department could free her with their "jaws of life." When we all arrived, she had been upside down for an hour. I never did have to tranquilize her because she lay perfectly still while the firemen spread the bars and released her. Outside of treating the scrapes on her pastern, there were never any aftereffects, which surprised all of us. I think it was because she had unusual sense for a horse. She realized that there was no way she could extricate herself, and so never struggled.

Do you have an unprotected light bulb in your horse stall? Once I was checking a horse's mouth to see if he needed dental work. He decided that this wasn't a good idea and went straight up on his hind legs. The top of his head hit a naked 100-watt light bulb. There was a loud zap and a long white lightning bolt that arced to the floor. No harm done, but it scared the wits out of the horse, his owner, and me. Anyone with unprotected bulbs should be aware that horses are far more susceptible to electrocution because they are more grounded than we are, especially if they are wearing steel on their feet. For the same reason any wires in a stall should be encased in conduits. Bored horses will happily chew on a wire. Outlets don't belong in stalls. Horses looking for something to do, can and will open the safety covers with their teeth and flirt with the electricity with their tongues.

I love rubber stall mats, but I hate to see ones that don't fit well and leave exposed edges for animals and people to trip over. Once bedding gets under a corner or an edge, more always seems to get under and build up. It takes some real grunt work with a good sharp knife, but once the mats are custom fit, the stall is a much safer place for all of us to be.

Stall safety is about paying attention to all the small details. Small, but important. A horse's stall doesn't have to be fancy, but is should be safe.

62

Steamed Hay

(help for heaves)

This year many of us will be dealing with hay that got wet. It may have looked OK when put in the barn, but now it's January, and when you break open a bale, a very fine, musty smelling dust rises up. That dust is not field dirt; it's a cloud of mold spores. As horses move the hay around with their noses, they inhale the spores. Horses exposed to mold spores are apt to develop a deep, persistent cough. This is an allergic bronchitis and is usually reversible. If there is a combination of continual exposure and poor ventilation in the barn, "heaves" may be the end result. Heaves or COPD (Chronic Obstructive Pulmonary Disease) can be helped, but not reversed. A similar process happens when a person is exposed to long term tobacco smoke. Heaves cripples horses in the same way that emphysema does people. It's interesting that cows seem to be able to eat that same moldy hay all day long and not have a problem. It's also worth noting that usually the mold spores don't seem to bother the horse's GI tract.

I usually tell clients in this situation that if the hay is fed wet, the spores don't get into the air, aren't inhaled, and so the problem is minimized. I have them do more than just wet the hay. I instruct them to put the hay in a clean muck bucket and cover it with water. The horses soon learn to get the hay that is under the few inches of water. Because it is soaking wet, the spores don't rise up off the hay and get inhaled. This works well until temperatures go below freezing. Of course, you could feed complete hay pellets, cubed alfalfa, or the packaged Lucerne products that aren't field dried. The downside is that these hay substitutes are all expensive

Great Britain has an ongoing problem producing quality hay.

Their climate of rainy and overcast days makes curing hay without it molding difficult. One of the ways that they have gotten around the problem is by feeding out steamed hay instead of dunked hay. There are at least two companies in England that produce commercial hay steamers. These are rugged containers somewhat bigger than a tack trunk. A bale of hay is put into the cabinet, and the lid is shut. A steamer attached to the side of the unit shoots steam up through the hay. After an hour or so the hay is "done." The hay is wet and hot, and the companies claim that not only do the mold spores not rise into the air, but they are actually killed by the steaming. The steamers seem to be effective, but cost around $2000.

One of my clients has a mare that coughs even when fed the best quality field hay. They found out about hay steamers on the internet but decided to build their own, which they did for under $75. They took a castoff refrigerator (you could also use an old chest freezer) and drilled a hole near its base to accommodate the tube from a wallpaper steamer. They put the steamer on a timer that turns on one hour before feeding time, twice a day. When the steamer comes on, the water in its reservoir boils, and steam shoots through the tube and into the old refrigerator. The refrigerator holds about a bale of hay on end. The steam works its way up through and thoroughly soaks the hay. At feed time the hay is warm, wet, and ready to be fed out. Just like water soaked hay, the steamed hay holds onto the spores which then don't float off into the air and into their horse's nostril. On a cold winter morning their mare tears into this nice, warm, and very safe hay without coughing. One more hay summer like we just had, and I suspect that hay steamers will become more commonplace.

63

Super Fly

(bots)

♘

It was a hot day in early June. I was in the paddock behind the barn at Mary's farm. She had asked me to check "Doc," a Quarter Horse with an allergy problem. She was holding a lead that was snapped onto Doc's halter. Mary has competed Doc for years. He's a seasoned horse and is always cooperative. That's why we were both surprised when he suddenly got fidgety, and we saw the whites of his eyes. He started stomping with his left fore and throwing his head. Finally, Mary and I heard a loud buzzing and realized what he was upset about. Doc was the target of a botfly. These insects are extremely aggressive. The females live only one week and have just one goal. Lay as many eggs as possible on the hair of any horse in the area. They are very determined and very fast.

The botfly darted in, laid a few eggs on a front leg, flew away a short distance, and then attacked from a different direction, her wings making that buzzing noise. These "super flies" may lay up to a hundred eggs on one horse. The fact is that she *will* lay those eggs unless you kill her. You have to slap her hard with an open hand against the horse the second she lands. Hesitate and, too late, she's off again. It's next to impossible to catch her in the air. Horses hate the noise of bot flies and their unpredictable actions. Equines at pasture will often take off running, totally out of control, when the botfly is at work.

The female botfly is unique to the insect world. She looks like a scrawny honey bee. Her body is bent almost double in the middle so that her egg-laying hind end is tucked under and faces her head. After she lays all her eggs, she dies. The male botfly's life is even shorter. His life is over just after mating with her. Neither the male nor female has mouth parts. They can't eat. Their only function as flies is to reproduce. The entire life cycle of a horse bot is one year, and at least 10 months of that time is spent not in the air as an insect, tormenting horses, but actually *inside* your horse.

Each egg that the fly lays is cemented to a single hair. They look like tiny yellow grains of rice. The eggs will stay glued to the horse's hair coat until you either physically remove them, or they hatch. From egg deposit to hatching is about five days. The hatch begins when the horse brings his mouth down to his leg or side where the eggs are. It is thought that the carbon dioxide from the horse's breath stimulates the hatching. The tiny released larvae get into the horse's mouth and burrow into the tongue or the gums. They stay there for a month. Then they burrow out, pass down to the stomach, and attach to its lining with their sharp mouth parts. In the stomach they grow to look like a grub that you might find in the woods under a log. They are fat, ugly, and about an inch long. Their stay in the stomach is like you on a ten-month Caribbean cruise. You have access to unlimited food and are a world away from the cold winter.

Somehow those bots, deep in the horse and far away from daylight or weather, know when the world gets warm. They release their hold and pass through the GI tract to go out with the manure. Once on the ground they burrow beneath the surface and stay there for a month. Just like a butterfly coming out of a cocoon, they metamorphose into the next stage, which is the flying insect—the botfly. Males and females find each other, and within hours the female with her fertilized eggs flies off to find a horse to lay them on, and the yearly cycle starts again.

I don't see as many botflies as I used to. I think it's because ivermectin and moxidectin (Quest) at the proper dose kills all the bots in the stomach, and most horses receive one of those wormers at least once a year. That doesn't mean that you won't ever see the botfly or her eggs, it's just that right now they aren't as common as they were 25 years ago. Perhaps they will develop a resistance to those medications over time. For sure they will always be around. If you buy a horse with an uncertain history, and its winter, it would be prudent to worm with one of the wormers mentioned. Incidentally, because the bots attached to the stomach don't lay eggs, there is no way to check for their presence in a fecal exam.

So, what are the implications for your horse? Actually, unless there are huge numbers in the stomach, horses tolerate them OK. The bot is one of those parasites that have it pretty well figured out. Attach to the host and get nutrition, but don't drain the horse too much, or you both lose. There are reports of bots penetrating the stomach and causing peritonitis, but it's rare. Given enough bots in the stomach, you can expect some general un-thriftiness. There are definitely problems caused by the super-fly female herself. Horses get spooked and sometimes crash into fences or do something equally silly to get away from them. If you are riding or driving a horse and hear that buzz, hang on! I have a theory about this. Horseflies (different species) also buzz, and they bite. They are large, triangle shaped, and have big eyes. The females bite to get a blood meal from any mammal, like us at the beach. The blood is necessary for the development of her eggs. Perhaps horses get frantic around botflies mistaking them for horseflies?

The best time to get rid of bots in the stomach is in the fall, one month after the first killing frost. By that time all of the bots have arrived and are implanted there. Personally I like getting rid of these parasites before they get to the mouth and stomach. If you see the tiny eggs attached to a horse's legs or flanks, get them off. They won't brush off because of the glue secreted with the eggs that binds them to the hair. Some people use a bot knife or a pumice stone, each made for that purpose. For me, a hoof knife works well. One of my early mentors always had a piece of glass from a broken bottle handy to scrape them off. Every egg that you remove will be one less bot inside your horse.

When summer starts, the bot flies are out, and sometimes it's your horse's behavior that will alert you. If you can't kill the fly as she pesters your horse, watch for those eggs on the legs or trunk. They are found in clusters, and usually on the front legs. Occasionally, you will see them on a shoulder or flank but never very far back. There is one species of bot that lays its eggs under the chin, and another that prefers the throat. Both of these are unusual in New England. Scrape off the eggs wherever you find them, and you have stopped the life cycle of the bot before it ever gets going.

64

Swamp Fever

—————————— ♄ ——————————

You may have never heard of Swamp Fever. If you are from Mississippi or Louisiana, you would know all about it. In parts of the U.S., Swamp Fever is the common name for the disease Equine Infectious Anemia or EIA for short. That still might not ring any bells. Even so, if you board your horse or compete at any level, you probably have a piece of paper that says that your horse has a negative Coggins test. That "Coggins" that gets you into boarding stables and horse shows, is your proof that your horse does not carry EIA. Both the disease and its blood test have an interesting history.

Back in 1843 a new ailment was described in France. Horses would get sick and die within a week. Some recovered and might get sick again months or years later and perhaps then die. Or, they could recover again but, once again, they might get sick. The disease was first recognized in the U.S. in 1888 and became a significant killer of horses here. We now know that EIA is caused by a virus and transmitted from one horse to another by way of the blood. It is spread most commonly by horse and deer flies. In fact, any biting insect can carry the virus from horse to horse. Hypodermic needles used on more than one horse in a stable can transmit the disease, and are considered the primary mode of transmission at racetracks. A foal can be born with the disease by way of exposure to his mother's blood in the uterus. Stallions can pass the virus on in their semen.

Once a horse has the virus it will *always* be in its body, but the virus numbers may not be high enough to make the animal sick. However, if that horse is stressed, and its immune system weakened, the virus will multiply rapidly. At that point the sick animal will be highly infectious to other horses that are exposed to its blood. Ponies, donkeys, and mules are all at equal risk. The disease is found throughout the world. In the U.S. it is more common in the deep South because biting insects are present year round. As you might suspect, it is more common in swampy areas where insects breed and thrive. In Cajun country horses with EIA are called "swampers." Two years ago in all of New England there were no positives, but there were ten in Louisiana.

The virus of EIA causes a rapid destruction of red blood cells. Affected horses run a high fever and become very weak. A massive swelling grows underneath the belly, and the legs become markedly swollen. Unfortunately, there is neither an effective vaccine nor a cure for the disease. The virus is similar to the HIV virus in people. Thankfully, we do have a blood test named after a Cornell Veterinarian, Dr Leroy Coggins, who was responsible for its research and development. This accurate test became available in 1970. Since only equines are susceptible, we should be able to eliminate EIA by destroying any horse that carries the virus.

The Coggins test on your horse that you show to officials or your barn owner is stamped as "Negative." If the test comes back positive, a stop-movement order would be issued for the horse. The state vet would soon be out to draw another sample. If that test confirms the first, you would be given two choices. You could either opt to have the horse euthanized or submit to a quarantine following very restrictive federal guidelines. A quarantined horse would be officially and permanently identified with a freeze brand and would not be able to be sold or moved off the property.

If the test has been around for close to 50 years, why is the disease still around at all? Great question. We have a pool of horses in the U.S. and worldwide that carries the virus and has *never* been tested. Each state has its own requirements, which you can find online. Enter your state and the phrase: "Equine Infectious Anemia regulations." Some states have a six-month negative Coggins requirement for entry, others one year. Most have regulations that prohibit the movement of horses within their boundary without a negative Coggins test. In Maine, testing is required every 36 months for horses that are going to boarding barns, races, or shows. There are many horses that fly under the radar and have never been tested. Pockets exist in Maine and around the country where

I suspect you might be met at the front gate with a shotgun if you tried to force testing.

It's astounding, but in doing research for this article, I learned that the incidence of horses carrying the EIA virus in Brazil is 30% of all domestic horses and 5% of wild ones! That is a significant reservoir of the disease. Fortunately horses cannot enter the U.S. without a negative Coggins test. There is some talk now about working to eliminate the disease in the U.S. by targeting areas that have a high percentage of reactors. Perhaps that will work, but I have my doubts because we have whole herds of wild horses and burros that might be tricky to pull blood samples on. I think that at least in states with winter, we have a pretty workable system that seems to keep the numbers of positive horses very low.

Back in the 70s and 80s, we had a number of horses in New England that tested positive. The few I had, surprised me. In every case the horses were 100% healthy on examination. But the positive Coggins showed that they were carrying the virus and so were a risk to other equines. During those years there was an outcry about the regulations, and meetings were held across Maine to protest the rules. I attended a couple and remember a hearing in Augusta with some impassioned speeches for and against the killing of seemingly healthy animals. Impassioned speeches are a fancy way of saying that there was a lot of finger pointing and shouting. In the end, the rules stuck, and to my knowledge all the horses that tested positive were put down because the alternative quarantine rules were so strict. In fact, the policy has worked, and I haven't seen a positive test in over 15 years. In the whole U.S., as late as the year 2000, there were 750 positives. By 2015 there were only 69. There is concern lately because of some recent positives in New York and Pennsylvania.

I mentioned that there is no vaccine. There is one that is made and used in China, but we don't really know how effective it is. Because of the ever declining number of positives, I'm not sure that any drug company in the western world would want to manufacture a vaccine as there would be little demand. Any vaccine for EIA would need to undergo both USDA and individual state approval. Not as easy as it sounds.

If present numbers hold and there was a vaccine, I would

probably not strongly recommend it to my clients, as the risk in New England is so low. In the meantime, it seems as if the current policy of testing horses that are on the move and euthanizing ones that have the virus is working. It's an expense for everyone but, as currently enforced, is a protection for our horse population.

My thanks to Dr Michele Walsh, Maine State Veterinarian, for her vetting of this article, and her excellent suggestions.

65

Symmetry

———————— ☙ ————————

I was called out to Sue's farm to check out her big Quarter Horse gelding, Carlos, for lameness. When I arrived, Sue said that she hoped this wasn't a wasted trip. She wasn't positive that Carlos was lame, but she knew he was not himself and had not been performing well. She offered to bring Carlos to me from his stall at the far end of the barn. I welcomed that chance so that I could watch him as he walked up the long aisle. Watching horses at a walk is important in lameness exams and often provides clues as to where and what the problem is.

I sat down on a bale of hay as Sue went to get a lead shank and Carlos. The old yellow barn tomcat jumped up and started rubbing against me. As I was patting and looking at him, something startled me. Sue's barn aisle floor is concrete, the barn itself is cavernous, and Carlos was shod. The sound bouncing off the walls was striking. "Clip, clop, clip, thunk. Clip, clop, clip, thunk," all the way up to where I was sitting. I laughed and said, "Sue, did you hear that?"

"Hear what?"

"The sound of Carlos walking!"

"No, I didn't. Guess I wasn't paying any attention."

"OK, turn him around, and let's walk him back to his stall. Listen for his footfall."

"Clip, clop, clip, thunk."

"Yes! I do hear it, he sounds way different when his right fore hits the ground, doesn't he?"

Carlos was light on the right fore, but not obviously lame. If he had been walking on rubber mats instead of the concrete, you wouldn't have noticed a thing. The footfalls were a place to start, and we began

197

watching how he landed on each foot. He was consistently landing toe first with the right fore. After checking the pulse strength above that foot and using hoof testers, I diagnosed soreness in the heel. The problem turned out to be a chronic abscess, which was easily taken care of.

The early hint as to what was bothering Carlos was that lack of symmetry as he walked. "Clip, clop, clip, thunk. " Left hind, left fore, right hind, and then the different sound of the right fore. We tend to think of symmetry as something we can see. Examples are a big knee, a swollen hind leg, a pelvis high on one side, or perhaps a half-closed eye. When we see something different like that, our eyes automatically go to the other side to compare. Symmetry is when they are the same, and that's usually good. Asymmetry is when they aren't, and that lack of "sameness" catches our eye. It is helpful in examining our animals to use *all* of our senses, not just what we see, but also what we hear, palpate (touch) and even smell. Outside of a few memorable occasions when I had my mouth open at the wrong time and got a squirt of one horse fluid or another, I think that taste is the only one sense I have never consciously used when examining horses.

When you see a big leg, it is helpful to see if even a light touch causes a painful reaction, which may mean an infection. Gently squeezing different areas may tell us if we have soreness in a bone, tendon or ligament. The symmetry here is to check the same areas on the opposite leg. Some horses don't even want their good leg squeezed.

If I am examining a horse with respiratory problems, I like to smell the air coming out of the nostril on one side and then the other. I cover one nostril with the palm of my hand and put my nose close to the other. When the horse exhales, I inhale. Then I do the same for the other side. Sinus infections that involve a bad tooth are super stinky and much more pronounced on that side.

Symmetry is also important when checking a painful eye. You can easily see that that eye is partially closed. Take the horse to a dark stall and look a little deeper. Use a flashlight to compare the size of the pupil in the painful eye, with the horse's other side. Serious conditions of the eye will cause a constriction (gets smaller) of the pupil on that side. Eyes with that lack of symmetry should be seen by your vet right away.

Checking symmetry is a handy tool because on the same horse

you have the other leg, the other eye, or whatever on the other side to compare the problem area to. I am thinking of a horse I see every year for his annual physical and vaccinations. As I listen to his heart, I always notice his eighth rib. It bows out away from the rib cage a solid inch. The first time I saw it, I thought that this must affect him in some way. It turns out that the eighth rib on the other side of his body *also* sticks out. There is no pain when the rib is manipulated on either side. As his owner says, "It goes with him." So, it's an oddity that is part of who he is and has never been a problem. He is symmetrical and sound.

The take-home is to recognize that ideally horses are symmetrical both in their body structure and in the way that they move, feel, sound, and even smell. Compare what you think is new and unusual to the other side, using all the senses that you can. By being observant and always checking symmetry, you will be able to catch problems more readily.

66

The Life and Times of Tapeworms

Ａ

Lynda McCann is the owner and editor of *The Horse's Maine and NH*. She recently emailed me about a warmblood gelding, Davey, that she has owned for two years. During that time, Davey had been a hard keeper despite the fact that he is a stocky-type horse. He also suffered a number of gas colics. This spring Davey started dropping live worms in his manure, and a small animal vet that happened to be in the barn identified them as equine tapeworms. Lynda wormed him with Zimectrin Gold and reported: "For a few days, we *really* saw the worms!" Now his coat is shinier, and he is gaining weight. Best of all, there have been no more episodes of colic.

We don't hear much about tapeworms and their effect on horses. Do some research, and you'll find those who say that tapes don't bother horses much. Others claim that 50% of all colics are caused by them. So, what *is* the truth? The fact is, yes, they usually don't bother horses that much, and the truth *also* is, as Lynda found, they can bother horses a great deal. To find out how both can be true, we need to look into just what a horse tapeworm is, and as we do, you will find out how to keep your horse totally safe from this parasite.

First of all, a name: *Anoplocephala perfoliata*. Long name, but this, our most common horse tapeworm, is actually only a few inches long. Other animal tapes, including the one that affects people, can be several feet long. The name tapeworm comes from the fact that they resemble a tailor's measuring tape, long and skinny front to back. Most other worms that inhabit horses are round, like earthworms. The roundworms include ascarids and large and small strongyles, the ones that we commonly worm for.

The equine tapeworm is probably the strangest creature that God put on earth. First, there is really no head. There is a front end, which contains four hooks so that the tapeworm can latch on to the horse's intestinal wall. There are no eyes or ears or other sense organs that we know of. They don't need any of them to survive and flourish. The most amazing thing is that there is no mouth or digestive tract. The tapeworm simply absorbs all the nutrition it needs through its outer covering. This is important to note as that is what is targeted when we deworm for tapes.

After the adult tapeworm attaches to the gut of the horse, it just dangles in the horse's intestinal contents and takes what it needs, 24/7. Behind the front section, there is a long chain of segments. The tapeworm has been described as a freight train with lots of boxcars hooked together in a line. Each of the segments has its own complete reproductive factory to make eggs. Perhaps we should call all tapeworms "she" because there is no male involvement. As the eggs in the last segments mature, the caboose (the last segment) drops off and that package, filled with eggs, goes out with the manure. When the eggs in the "new caboose" are ready, that segment is released.

There is an area of the horse's intestine where the small intestine empties into the cecum. The cecum is like our appendix, except that it is very large and is important in fiber breakdown. There is a valve that prevents backflow from the cecum to the small intestine. It is the spot where all the tapeworms hook on and literally hang out. It's not a big area, and so if a horse has tapeworms, the cluster of them will be found right there. If the group is small, let's say 20, they may not be a problem. One or two hundred may be more than irritating and can cause some serious colic issues, some of which can only be fixed by surgery.

So, to summarize, an adult equine tapeworm stays hooked in its permanent spot and is continually bathed in the horse's intestinal contents. The tape's food is absorbed through its "skin." No digestion is needed, the horse has already done that. The hind egg segments drop off when the eggs are mature. Now, some questions remain. What happens to the eggs after they go out with the manure, and how do horses get infected in the first place?

Unlike the human tapeworm, the equine tapes need a friend, another host. That "intermediate host" is a tiny creature, the Oribatid mite. It is about the size of the period at the end of this sentence. These beetle-like bugs live by the thousands in every square foot of soil and are just as important as earthworms in breaking down organic matter. As the mite works its way through the soil, it might come upon a real treat, an egg-loaded segment from the tapeworm. Tapeworm eggs hatch inside the mite and become tiny larvae. The mite is apparently not bothered by them. The mites also crawl up vegetation, and that is where the horse is apt to pick them up in a mouthful of grass. The horse digests the mites, and the tapeworm larvae are released into his gut. It takes several weeks for the larvae to turn into adult tapeworms. The adults hook on to the horse's intestine in that very specific place, grow into adult size, and the cycle starts again.

Your veterinarian probably is encouraging you to take fecal samples once or twice yearly and worm according to what is found. Those reports are on the roundworms that have always been a problem in horses. Round worms are continually releasing eggs into the horse's digestive tract. Tapeworms are different in that whole segments of the worm are being released, and the release is more sporadic. As a result, tapeworm eggs are rarely seen on fecal exams. The other issue is that when we do fecal exams for parasites, we use concentrated solutions to separate and float the eggs, and, wouldn't you know, tapeworm eggs don't float. So, the absence of tapeworm eggs found in the lab does not necessarily mean there are no tapes.

There are reports in the literature of a blood test that can be run to detect the protein of the tapeworm, but it is used mostly in research. Most vets take a practical route in dealing with potential tapeworm problems. In our practice we often recommend worming twice a year with one of the dewormers that is effective against tapeworms. We have found, for our part of the country, as long as good manure management is being practiced, twice a year is often sufficient worming to take care of all intestinal worms, round and tapeworms. There are four wormers available that are effective against tapes. One is the old standby Strongid. You need a double dose of the paste to get most of the tapes with this wormer. The other choices (Zimectrin Gold, Equimax, and Quest Plus) contain Praziquantal which is very effective against tapes and is very safe. Praziquantal works by affecting the outer covering of the tapeworm. Then, unable to absorb nutrients, the tapeworm dies and passes out with the manure. With hundreds of tapes, this die-off may take a few days. Incidentally, the most popular wormer of today, ivermectin, has no effect on tapeworms. However, used in wormers that combine it with Praziquantal, tapes, round worms, and bots are all taken care of.

Good manure management is part of parasite prevention. This means picking up poop regularly, and piling it to compost someplace where the horses can't get at it, and leaving at least six-feet all around the pile away from horse grazing. This prevents mites and the larvae of roundworms from re-infecting the horses on your farm.

Lynda's horse Davey had spent his life on 24/7 turnout until she took ownership. My guess is that it was a big pasture with no attempt at manure clean up. He had probably never been wormed with one of the products mentioned above. He was the perfect setup for a heavy infection of tapes, as evidenced by the tapes being passed spontaneously. There was just no more room, and so some had passed even before he was dewormed.

The take-home from all this is that, in the New England states, tapeworms in high numbers *can* cause un-thriftiness and colic in your horse. Chances are most horses that have never been dewormed for tapes are carrying them. I think it makes good sense to use the wormers mentioned on a rotational basis twice a year to insure that your horse is free. The wormers mentioned do kill roundworms as well, and I would rely on your vet to suggest the proper rotation. The ingredients and concentrations are unique to each product.

67

That Bottle of Pills

---- U ----

Two weeks ago I got a phone call from Lucy whose gelding was at a full gallop when he slipped, fell on rough ground, and slid for a few feet on his right side. After he got up, he favored his right hind leg for a minute and then seemed OK. Lucy asked if I needed to see him. I requested a photo. A few minutes later my phone screen showed a clear picture of the injured leg. There was a scrape ten inches long and three inches wide over the hip. All the hair and a few layers of skin were gone, but there was no blood oozing and no deep damage. It didn't need sutures or my attention. I called Lucy back and asked what she had done for him so far. "Well, I figured that he could use some Bute, so I gave him two grams and was sure that he needed antibiotics, so I gave him 12 SMZs. I have enough of those left to last a week. Is there something else that I should do?"

You probably have a few partial bottles of medicine of your own at home from past illnesses. If you are a horse owner, you're sure to have a few in the barn as well. I'm betting that among the supplement containers and the partial bottle of Bute, there is a half-used bottle of the antibiotic pills that we call "SMZ." If the expiration date on the bottle is current, it's a good thing to have on hand. It is a broad spectrum and well-tolerated drug that is effective for many infections. However, like other antibiotics, it is used far more often than it needs to be. I asked Lucy, "If you had scraped a leg like he did, would you put yourself on antibiotics?" She laughed, and said, "No, probably not."

I totally get it. You want to help when your horse has a problem, so it's natural to grab a bottle that might be of benefit because you want to do *something*. Is there any harm done? In addition to the cost, there is. Let's step back in history to find out why.

Back in the 1920s, Fleming, a British scientist, noted something unusual on the culture plates on which he was growing bacteria. Some mold had contaminated the plates, and wherever the mold appeared, there was a clear zone around it with no bacteria. He could have thrown away the plates because the mold had made them worthless. But, instead, he realized that something in the mold was killing the bacteria! Out of his continued research came penicillin, and soon after, the manufacture of other antibiotics.

Antibiotics were used heavily during World War II. It was soon noted that some weren't working as well as they had been. Bacteria multiply quickly. For example, single E.coli bacteria will start a new generation every 20 minutes. Mutations happen, and some of the "offspring" bacteria start life unaffected by the antibiotics they are exposed to. That resistance becomes part of the bacterial DNA and gets locked into subsequent generations. The widest antibiotic use, by far, has been in the meat industry where the drugs have been laced into the grain of young animals to promote markedly faster weight gain. The Center for Disease Control has stated that up to half the antibiotic use in animals is unnecessary and inappropriate and makes everyone less safe.

We are also somewhat at fault. When we are sick, we wonder whether antibiotics will help. If we don't recover quickly, we are tempted to use what is left of a bottle that has been sitting there since our last illness. When our animals are sick, we reach for the bottle even faster. However, many illnesses, ours and theirs, are caused by viruses, against which antibiotics are totally ineffective. There is a common misbelief that if a horse has a viral infection, a bacterial infection will follow, so you might as well put him on antibiotics. Antibiotics are not vaccines and do not work as preventive medicine. In other cases, like the skin scrape on Lucy's horse, antibiotics are not necessary. The body's immune system will take care of these minor issues.

I most often see horse owners reaching for antibiotics when their animals have respiratory problems. If a horse has a cough and/ or a nasal discharge but is not off feed and/ or running a fever, the infection is probably viral, and recovery is a matter of time and support, not antibiotics. Two examples are influenza and rhino. Some well-intentioned owners give antibiotics for a horse with the heaves, confusing it with pneumonia. Antibiotics are of no benefit for heaves.

Other than resistance, there are other problems. Some horses will colic when antibiotics are used because the drugs kill some of the normal bacteria necessary for digestion. There are even times when antibiotics are a hindrance to healing. An example of this is "gravel" (the common foot infection of horses). If the pus from an abscessing foot cannot be released from the bottom by your farrier or vet, you may have to wait for the infection to come to a head and break out at the coronary band. Antibiotics can delay that process. Veterinarians often do not use antibiotics for treating strangles for the same reasons.

Like most other health professionals, I would hate to practice without antibiotics, but I know that they are often unnecessary, and their over-use is having an effect on what they can accomplish. Today's biggest medical crisis is the presence of super bugs that defy *any* antibiotics.

When you have a sick or injured horse, first check with your vet as to whether antibiotics are necessary. If you are a good observer and can describe your animal's condition accurately, a phone call to your vet may be all that is needed. You can often keep that bottle on the shelf.

68

The Code
(behavior)

U

Until her retirement my wife Bonnie was a second grade teacher. She had classes of up to 33 kids. Somehow, single handedly she managed to keep reasonable order for six hours. On good days there was even some knowledge passed along. Earlier in her career she was involved in a special education room, assigned to just one pupil. Anna was in school just two hours a day, and for those two hours my wife was always by her side. One teacher, one pupil. Anna required every bit as much of Bonnie's attention as an entire classroom.

The school system labeled Anna as "special needs." She was not slow or stupid, and in fact had above average intelligence. The problem was that Anna's behavior was totally unpredictable. Bonnie never knew exactly what Anna was going to do next. Maybe punch someone. Maybe hug them. The reason for Anna's behavior was her home situation. No one ever took the time to instill in her a proper code of behavior.

You and I live by a behavior code. It is made up of thousands of unwritten rules that govern our daily behavior. If you go to a movie and find a line at the ticket window, you get in it. You willingly get behind someone else. You do so with the expectation that when you get to the window, those behind you won't push you out of the way. It's the give and take of daily life. At school Bonnie had to stand in line right next to Anna. Without my wife's restraint Anna might walk away, or just shove her way to the front.

There is also a people-animal code. We make and enforce the rules. You stand and laugh as your puppy plays with your kids on the floor. If the puppy bites, you intervene and correct the behavior. The puppy soon learns what is permissible. The rules aren't as many or as complex, but you gradually teach your animals the code, a way to behave around us.

Imagine the terribly dangerous situation when there is no code instilled in a 1000-pound horse. Put an untrained horse in a threatening situation, and it is possible that the animal will either retreat or attack. Retreat might mean a set of crossties ripped out of the wall. Attack can mean flying feet or snapping teeth.

It's been over 30 years, but I'll never forget an experience with a "no rules for me" two-year-old Standardbred colt in the third barn, first shed row, at what used to be the Lewiston Raceway. I was in the barn to pull some blood for a Coggins test on this young, wired-for-trouble horse. There were four experienced horsemen in the barn where this happened. We all knew by the way the colt was acting that he might react to the needle stick. However, none of us had any idea that he would explode. His trainer was holding him by a lead when I approached, patted him on the neck, and tried to slide the needle into his jugular vein. I never saw him strike, but I was sent flying through the air and landed sprawled over a tack trunk. The trainer's arm was broken when the same leg that hit me struck again. A two-hundred-pound horseman, standing near the colt's right hip, went flying six feet when the horse's hind legs connected with his chest. This all happened so fast that none of us that were hit saw a leg leave the ground. Total time elapsed was maybe four seconds. This colt didn't weigh 900 pounds, but he had speed, agility, and some pretty amazing moves.

Thankfully, this is a rare situation. Even with minimal training most horses have no intention of causing harm. I am just trying to underline the fact that they have the capacity to do so. With their size, strength, and speed, the potential for harm is always present. We would not want to diminish these qualities as they are the very things we prize in our horses. However, we must make take steps to insure that they are never used against us. Our horses must be taught the code. To use the horsemen's term, they have to be "broken." I have never really liked the term because it seems to imply a broken spirit. Just because I am willing to stand in line doesn't mean that my spirit has been broken.

I am thinking of a very high-performance show mare that was an incredible mover and always pinned in the show ring. What the judges or spectators didn't know was that it used to take the owner at least five minutes to get her bridled. Her head would go up, down, and sideways when the owner tried to get her to take the bit. This was more than annoying, as anyone who has been bonked with a horse's head will tell you. The mare also didn't like her feet picked up. If you finally got one off the floor, she would stamp it back down as soon she had had enough. More than one farrier left the barn in frustration, vowing never to return. Yearly vaccinations were more than difficult. The mare wasn't mean by nature, she just wanted her own way, and she got it. No one had ever taken the time to teach her that there are things you just have to accept. As a youngster she should have been taught to submit, but her owner was indulgent. She was just one of those horses that performed well but was no fun to be around and just plain dangerous.

You should be able to walk into any horse's stall with a halter but without a sugar cube in your other hand. Your horse should come out of the stall willingly, with you leading the parade. He or she should be able to stand on crossties without pawing as you work around them. If something in the barn falls with a loud bang, I expect a horse to look startled. I don't expect him to pull the barn down. Feet should be willingly given and tack accepted with no dancing around.

I have noticed that if any one horse in the barn has no code, the others usually don't have good manners either. Plainly said, the fault lies with the owner, not the horse. Horses are always looking for a leader, and like teenagers, really want to know the rules and that there will be consistent enforcement. If you think your horse doesn't measure up in the behavior department, and you aren't capable of teaching him or her manners, seek the advice of a good trainer. Your horse's behavior is a reflection of how much you care about him or her.

69

The Cooker

(about fevers)

───────────── ♘ ─────────────

One of the many, many amazing things about the body is how it maintains a very narrow temperature range so that all the body systems function optimally. In people, this range is about a degree above or below 98.6° F. Horses have a somewhat wider range, which is generally given as 99.5° to 101° F.

A horse that has been standing in a stall on a 0° F, New England day, might be expected to have a body temperature of down around 99.5. On a summer day, when the outside temperature reaches 100°, the same horse's temperature may run up to 101°. Think of it. A huge environmental difference of 100° but the body makes adjustments to keep the temperature within a very narrow range.

How does all this happen, and what happens when things seem to get off kilter?

There are nerve cells in a part of the brain that are temperature detectors. Some sense cold, others heat. Those cells act like the thermostat in your house to keep things within a normal range. Too cold and the furnace kicks on, too hot and it shuts down.

If you take a ride on a summer day, your horse's muscular activity produces heat. The warmed blood is carried to the brain, and the heat-sensitive cells fire. Messages are sent to the blood vessels under the skin to dilate and to the sweat glands to contract. The horse starts to breathe more rapidly to throw off heat. The body's activity has made the temperature go up a few degrees, but it won't get too hot because of all the cooling systems that are working. Within an hour after the ride, the temperature will be back within the normal range. On that cold day with the horse just hanging out, the cold-sensitive nerve cells in the brain sense the cooler blood. Hormones are released, blood vessels under the skin contract, the hair stands up, other heat preserving systems kick in, and finally involuntary shivering will start to keep the body warm. Normal body temperature is maintained.

Things seem to break down when a horse is sick. The body recognizes the bacteria or viruses as invaders, and defense mechanisms are turned on. The horse's white blood cells attack the organisms. As the white blood cells engulf them, their own lives are sacrificed. Toxins from the degenerating white cells are carried to the brain by the blood and the "thermostat" in the brain sets the body temperature at a higher range. Instead of 100° the horse's temperature may climb up to 106°. The body senses that this higher temperature should be maintained for a while, so the cooling system is not activated. This is actually a good thing. The invading viruses or bacteria have their own ideal temperature range, and the horse's high temperature starts to destroy them. The body's fever is acting like a "cooker" to kill the organisms.

Horses with fevers usually go off feed and act a little "out of it." It depends on the situation, but I usually hesitate to give a horse medicine to reduce the fever for a while, unless it gets towards the 105° or 106° range. The higher body temperature is helping to get rid of the bugs. You might have heard that a high unrelieved fever in people will cause brain damage. This doesn't seem to happen in horses. When you do give Bute or Banamine, the body's thermostat gets reset, and the horse may sweat profusely or sometimes pant like a dog. This is usually scary if you haven't seen it before. It is just the cooling system kicking in to make the fever break.

If you have a horse that isn't eating and seems dopey, by all means, take his temperature. Call your vet and report in with the temperature reading. Don't be surprised if the advice given is to hold off on the Banamine or Bute for a while. Let the body's cooker work.

70

The Decision

(colic surgery decision)

⚘

The call came in mid-morning. Gail was distraught. "It's Ben. He's bad. Real bad! Can you get here right away? I'm real worried about him. He's down and thrashing." I told Gail I would be there within the hour.

I thought about Ben as I drove to her farm. The big warmblood was Gail's first horse. He was in his late twenties now. Every once in a while Gail would ease onto his back, and they would slowly walk around the farm. It had been two years since he'd been saddled and really ridden. Gail had gone on to be an accomplished dressage rider, and for years Ben had been the farm's senior citizen. Ben was one of those horses who would never be traded or sold. He was just there to enjoy the grass and live his days out.

As I came up the long drive to the farm, I could see Gail on the front lawn with a lead shank on Ben. In the time it took me to park and get to the back of the truck, he was up and down twice. In an ideal situation I would do as I was trained. Make your diagnosis, *and then* treat your patient. When the patient weighs 1200 pounds and is throwing himself to the ground, that doesn't work. I quickly pulled up a "cocktail" of two strong tranquilizers, and the next time he leapt to his feet, I managed to find his left jugular vein and slipped the drugs in. Within a minute he stood with head hanging, and we had time to assess the situation and talk.

I asked the questions as I took his temperature, pulse and respiration, and listened for gut sounds. "How long has he been like this, Gail?"

"It's been about two hours. He ate all his breakfast, and we turned him out. He started to act like this soon after his meal. I gave him some Banamine, and it seemed to help for about a half an hour, and then the pain hit again. He's been so healthy. I just don't understand it. What do you suppose is going on?"

"I'm not sure. His temperature is normal, but even with the tranquilizer his heartrate is up, and I don't like the color of his membranes. I'm getting no gut sounds. I'll do a rectal. Maybe that will tell us something." I pulled on a long plastic OB sleeve and slathered it with lubricant. There was some manure in the rectum, but further forward it was just empty space, and I began to suspect some sort of blockage high up, beyond the reach of my fingers. I ran a stomach tube down his left nostril and into his stomach. Some stomach contents came back up through the tube, making my suspicion of a blockage even stronger.

"Gail, I'm worried about him. That was some pretty acute pain that he was going through when I drove up. Right now the tranquilizer is making him somewhat comfortable, but it isn't going to fix the problem." I told Gail that I had another stop just down the road and would check back in about an hour.

When I returned to the farm, Ben was starting to get uncomfortable again, and I knew that medicine alone wasn't going to solve this problem. Rechecking his vital signs showed me that he was worse.

"Gail, he's starting to crash. Normally I'd tell you that the only way to fix this problem is surgery, but given his age I'm not sure that we should consider that. He's old, and even if he got through the surgery, his recovery is apt to be mighty rough."

"You mean put him down? No way, not Ben, not now! I'll get the truck and trailer, and we'll take him to the hospital." All Gail could feel was her horse's pain. Her husband arrived and also tried to persuade Gail that it might be best to end Ben's life now, but she was not listening to him either. Within ten minutes Ben was in the trailer. As she drove out of the yard Gail hollered at me, "Call the hospital and tell them we are on our way." As she pulled away, I heard a big thump. Ben had gone down inside the trailer.

I called the hospital and explained the situation. They said that they would look him over when he arrived, and if they agreed with me, would try to dissuade her from surgery. I heard from them in the late afternoon. Ben had arrived wedged sideways in the trailer, and they had to use a "come along" to drag him out. Once he was out of the trailer, he stood up but was in a white lather from head to toe. Rectal exam with an ultrasound showed a probable entrapment, high up in the gut. Because of his age and his shocky condition, the veterinarians on duty were reluctant to proceed with surgery and suggested euthanasia, but Gail persisted. Ben was anesthetized after some IV fluids were given. The problem turned out to be a complicated entrapment of the small intestine in a small opening behind the liver. The gut was pinched in a tight place and its blood supply was cut off. To get exposure to this area requires an incision that is measured in feet and not inches. There were anesthesia problems, and they almost lost him twice. About two feet of intestine had to be removed. He was on the table for almost three hours. His recovery was difficult. He never really came to his feet. Finally after 24 hours of around the clock care, it was obvious that he wasn't going to survive, and Gail agreed to euthanasia.

Gail has told me since that she made the wrong decision that day, and regrets putting old Ben through it. What got her was that he got hit so hard, so fast. It was a knee jerk reaction to try to do everything possible for him. She was simply not ready to say the words that would end his life. She knew that he would have to be put down someday, but in her mind that was years away.

What I am going to suggest is a way of making the hard decision when it is not an emotional time. Margaret Gardiner uses a system to deal with this situation. There is a notebook in her barn with each horse's records. Every year each horse is assessed by the staff and the farm vet. As part of each record, one of three categories is used to describe what to do should a decision need to be made. The three are: heroic, medium, and relieve pain.

Here is an example of how this would work. Let's say you owned a horse like Ben. As a warmblood in his late 20s, you might well decide that, should he get colicky and need abdominal surgery, you might decline. The decision in this case would be to just relieve pain. In other words, if medicine given on the farm will take care of the problem, you would do that, but you have already committed not to send him to surgery.

The opposite scenario might be a four-year-old filly, showing a great deal of promise. The word here might be "heroic." That is, you would do anything you could to save her, and abdominal surgery with a good prognosis might be a "Yes, go ahead." A horse that you have set down as medium might mean something like, "OK, we'll go to a hospital and get fluid therapy, but we are stopping short of surgery." Finances may well enter into the decision. These days it is not unusual to have colic surgery and aftercare cost over $8000. The three categories that Margaret Gardiner came up with dictate her future actions for every animal on the farm. I like them because they are quite descriptive and are understood by staff that might have to make a decision in an owner's absence.

My advice is to sit down once a year, maybe on January 1st or perhaps on your animal's birthday and think about your horse or horses and what you would do if you were faced with a situation like Gail's. Put it down in writing for yourself and for a possible caretaker if you are away. Really important decisions are best made when you are clear headed and can think apart from the emotions that we all feel. Making these decisions for each horse is just good planning and part of being kind to your animals.

71

The Disappearing Foal

I usually write my articles to inform. If that is what you are looking for, you can stop reading right here, as you won't learn a thing from this one. It's a true story that happened some 30 years ago, and I am still laughing about it.

Don no longer has horses, and his barn in Minot where this happened is no longer there, but at the time he was a good client, a great hand with a horse, and no fool. His phone call came at around 6 AM one early spring morning.

"Doc, you remember my pregnant mare?"

"Sure do, Don, she was about due. Has she foaled out?"

"Well, not exactly, but…yeah, maybe."

"What does that mean, *yeah, maybe?*"

"Doc, her afterbirth hasn't passed yet. It's still hanging there."

"OK. Well, I should come out today, and we'll see what we can do about that.

"How's the foal. Do you have a colt or a filly?"

"Well, Doc, that's what has me a little befuddled here. There is no foal."

"Let me get this straight, you have a placenta hanging from the mare, but you don't have a foal on the ground?"

"Right."

I was suddenly wide awake and listening hard. "Is she straining?"

"Nope, and she's slack sided now…you remember how big she was? Well she ain't so big anymore."

"Is she eating?"

"Yup."

"... and no foal in the stall, have I got that right?"

"You got it right."

"I'm on my way."

On the drive to the Piper farm, I tried to reason this out. Happy mare, looking like she has foaled. No foal. The afterbirth hanging, but no baby. The reason the placenta is called the afterbirth is because that's when it's always passed. The whole thing didn't make sense, and by the time I got to the farm, I was anxious to see what had happened.

Don met me at the barn. I walked over to the mare's stall and leaned over the Dutch door. She seemed pretty happy, standing there eating her hay. It was just her in that stall. No foal. Sure enough, just like he had said, her placenta was hanging from her with some of it almost touching the floor. Don tied the mare's head to a ring in the wall and held her tail off to the side as I scrubbed up her back end.

"Well," I said, as I pulled on a long sterile sleeve and squeezed some lubricant on it, "whatever we find in there will be interesting for sure."

I ran my arm through the mare's vagina and into her uterus. I felt where the placenta was still attached, and it came away with very gentle traction. All 15 pounds of it splatted down onto the floor. I swept my arm around the now contracting uterus, and felt...nothing. I did it again, just to make sure. Empty. It had certainly recently held a foal, but there wasn't one in there now. I put some antibiotics in the uterus and then stood there totally bewildered. There should have been four living beings in that stall. Don, me, the mare, and her baby, but there were only three of us. All kinds of crazy things went through my head. Could someone have taken the baby? No, rustling a new born foal without its mom made no sense. We both felt foolish as we kept glancing into every corner of that foaling stall. I even kicked the bedding around a little as if there might be a foal under there somewhere.

We left the stall and walked around the inside of that big old 60 by 60 barn, poking into every nook and cranny. No foal, and even if it was out here, how did it get out of the stall? I asked him if the barn doors had been shut all night.

"All night long."

Way at the other end of the long barn, Don yelled, "Hey, the scuttle hole!" Don had one of those big old New England barns. You had to go up a ramp to get into the barn, and there was about eight feet of clearance under the heavy hemlock floor which was supported by big granite posts. Down underneath was where the manure was put during the winter. The men who built those old barns a century or more ago were pretty smart about saving steps. They never took the manure around the barn with a wheel barrow. It was dropped down through the floor of the barn through "scuttle holes." In this case the scuttle was about two feet square.

We peered down through the hole. The big pile of manure and bedding from the winter came almost up to the barn floor in a cone shape. We couldn't see much, so Don went out of the barn and down underneath, and there was a cute little filly, just hanging out with some Hereford cows. She was alive and still a little wet.

Don carried her up, around, and back into the barn and into the stall with her mom. The mare nickered, and with a little gentle pushing, we got the foal to her side, and she started to nurse.

As we watched her having that first meal, we got our heads together and pretty much figured out what had happened in the early morning hours. The Dutch door to the stall was made out of a sheet of ¼ inch plywood, secured just at the top with one latch. Apparently the foal had tried to get up and had fallen against the bottom of the door. The door sprang out, and she got up on the other side of the door. The plywood sprang back, leaving the door as shut as before. Now the filly was on the alley side of the door. We guessed that she had started wandering around in that big old barn, looking for mom who had suddenly disappeared. She got over to the open scuttle hole, fell in, and must have somersaulted down that tall manure pile to the ground below.

I'll never know why the mare never raised a fuss over baby's sudden departure, just exactly how the filly managed to spring the stall door, or why she wandered down the barn and fell into the scuttle hole. It was fortunate that the big pile of manure reached almost up to the barn floor and prevented an eight-foot drop onto the hard ground.

I haven't seen Don for many years, so I called to check with him before finishing this article to make sure I had all the facts about right. We both had another laugh over the whole episode, and each of us said that we had told the story many times. I'm sure I'll never have another farm call quite like it again.

72

The Dishrag and the Nail
(diagnosing ailments)

U

When you push the start button on our dishwasher there is a delay, then in a minute you hear the pump start, the upper and lower whirligigs spin, and the water splash around inside. This time there was the usual click when I pushed the button, but after that, nothing. No sounds of any type. I opened the door and pulled the racks out. Everything seemed OK. I pushed the racks back and tried again. All quiet. I figured this had to be an electronics problem, and knew it was over my head. I unloaded the dishwasher and called the appliance repair service.

The next morning Stan showed up with his tool box. I told him the story and how I had concluded that it must be the electronics. "Maybe," said Stan, then after a long pause, "but maybe not." He pulled the dishwasher door down, slid out the racks, and pushed on the bottom spray arm. It wouldn't turn. Stan turned to look at me and smiled. He unscrewed a plastic nut from the top of the sprayer and lifted the arm off its small upright pipe. A shredded dishrag was wrapped tightly around the base. It was keeping the arm from spinning. He explained that the dishwasher's computer sensed the problem, and as a protection, wouldn't allow the machine to start.

"How did you know?" I asked. "Seen it before," he replied, and picked up his unused tool box. "That'll be $65 for the house call." I paid Stan and felt foolish that I hadn't looked a little deeper into the problem.

Clients, thinking they know nothing about colic or lameness or whatever, will call our office in what might turn into a dishrag trip. Here's an example that I've experienced more than once. Joan calls us and says, "I have a lame horse. It's so bad he won't put his foot down."

220

I come out, I pick up the foot, and there, sticking out of the sole, is a roofing nail. I pull out the nail, noting the direction that it went in and take appropriate further action. I am not saying that this scenario doesn't need veterinary attention, but I am saying that a little investigation on the part of Joan would have been wise. Sometimes, as you may have experienced, your vet can't get to you right away. In this case Joan's horse will avoid stepping down on his foot for hours or maybe the next day. He'd like to, but each time he does the nail point causes pain. Years ago I learned that when I get a phone call about a horse not weight-bearing on one foot, I should always ask two questions:

1. Have you picked up the foot?
2. Did you check for a nail?

Those would be good questions to ask *yourself* if your horse suddenly goes lame. It's smart to ask yourself questions every time you have any horse emergency. In the case of a horse showing signs of belly pain, some pertinent questions would be:

1. How long since the horse has made manure?
2. Running a fever?
3. Heart rate / minute?
4. Color of the gums? Odor from mouth?
5. Gut sounds on both sides behind the rib cage?

If you don't know how to check for these things, talk to your vet who will show you the next time he or she is at your place. There are a series of unique questions for every emergency that comes up.

Some ten years ago a neighboring veterinarian showed me his new cellphone. He told me that besides being a phone, he could take pictures with it. I was amazed at the technology and even more amazed that he would pay good money for a silly feature like that. Now, of course, I have one and use it daily for taking pictures of all kinds of horse situations for my records or for sending to another vet for an opinion. I often ask clients who call with a cut horse to take pictures and text them to me so that I can decide if the horse needs sutures. Texting your vet with photos of your problem is helpful to vets in dealing with anything that visual. I have received pictures of knocked-out teeth, bite marks, porcupine quills, crooked legs, injured eyes, and all kinds of skin problems.

Don't take the position that because you don't have a degree in veterinary medicine that you are helpless. Don't be like I was in dealing with my dishwasher. Don't assume that the problem is way above your skill level. Do all the personal investigating that you can, and *then* call your vet with the information you have gathered. In the process of calmly assessing the horse, you may find that a vet farm call might not be necessary. It won't be a dishrag that is causing the problem, but it may turn out to be something equally simple that you can deal with.

73

The Donkey Difference

———————— ♘ ————————

In the last few years, our area of northern New England has seen quite an increase in donkey numbers. Many are rescues from here and there, and some came as gifts: "Since you are buying those two horses, I've decided to throw in that little donkey over there." Every once in a while a donkey is actually purchased. I have two donkeys myself. One I bought outright because I was looking for one and liked his face. The other was a rescue that I bought just to get him off an incredibly dirty trailer.

What is there about donkeys that make people grin and want to have one? It's a question that comes up for me on those cold, dark winter mornings, and I have to get up, bundle up, feed up, and muck out. As soon as I'm outside and headed for the barn, Shamus starts to bray. Typically that deep throaty noise lasts for 10 to 15 seconds. Fortunately everyone in our neighborhood gets up early anyway. The haunting sound puts me in the same mood as a faraway train whistle. It makes me grin, and I'm back to liking asinine ownership.

If you are considering a donkey on your place, be aware that they just don't sound and look different from horses. In fact, they really *are* a distinct species. Donkeys have 62 chromosomes. Horses have 64. Just close enough so that a donkey stud (jackass or jack) can breed a mare and produce a foal. That offspring will be a mule with some characteristics of each parent, but will have 63 chromosomes. It can also go the other way, and a horse stud can breed a female donkey (jennet or jenny) and will produce what is called a hinny. Hinnys are rare, and as far as I know, I've never seen one. With very rare exceptions both mules and hinnys are sterile.

All donkeys alive today, big or small, trace way back to the African wild ass. Archeologists tell us that the first were domesticated in Egypt about 5000 years ago. I wonder if they helped build the pyramids. In the world today, most domestic donkeys are working for the world's poor engaged in subsistence agriculture.

If you have ever been on the outskirts of Las Vegas, you might have seen herds of wild donkeys. These free-range animals are called burros. They are all descendants of domesticated donkeys that escaped or were let loose. There have never been native donkeys in our hemisphere. All of their ancestors came over on a boat at some point.

Besides the obvious huge ears, big hee-haw, and skimpy tail with its tufted end, there are other differences that a potential owner should be aware of. The most important is that since they are all descended from the wild desert ass, their metabolism is very efficient. They *cannot* handle rich feed. If you have acres of green grass, you will have to fence them *out*. Second cut hay should never be served, and they really don't need grain. I, like many donkey owners, give a handful or two of timothy hay stretcher pellets instead. Feeding them like horses will result in ugly fat deposits under the mane that get large enough to cause the crest to flop over. Fat also forms along the flanks and over the tail head. These fat collections are there forever, and even extreme diets will not shrink them. Donkeys can suffer laminitis and possible crippling for life if they have access to just a few hours of rich spring grass. The hard and fast rules are that the hay should be first-cut hay, and paddocks with limited grass. Lush green pastures are deadly. It's OK to let them graze once the spring and summer grass turns brown.

Because of their desert origin, donkeys don't have an undercoat that tends to hold in heat. To make up for it, their winter coat is very dense. No undercoat means that they feel every drop of rain, and don't like it. I recommend a simple outside shelter if you are not always able to get home to get your donkey out of the rain. Their desert ancestry has also made them camel like in their ability to go far longer than a horse without water. The heat resistance and the limited water tolerance made donkeys the pack animal of choice during the gold rush days in the southwest. Donkeys are much stronger, pound for pound, than horses.

You may find your veterinarian less than excited about castrating your donkey. The jacks have large testicles with a rich blood supply.

Sometimes extras steps have to be taken to prevent excessive bleeding. Donkey anesthesia can also be a little tricky. It is interesting that when you have a donkey upside down for a castration, you will see a nipple on each side of the sheath. The nipples are not present in male horses. On the other hand, donkeys don't have chestnuts on their hocks like horses do.

The donkey foot seems tiny and is set on at a steep angle, but those little feet are tough, and shoeing is usually not necessary. Regular trimming is really all they need. As little as the feet are, the ears of course, are just the opposite. Perhaps it's "better to hear you with." Some believe that the large surface area of the ears is a help in dissipating heat, important in the desert.

Both donkeys and mules have an acute sense of impending danger, and if they feel that a situation is unsafe, you will have a hard time forcing them to move. For example, they are not at all interested in walking on ice and if you insist, expect a fight. This is where their reputation for stubbornness comes from. Their training has to be different from horses.' Donkeys resist being pushed into submission and react better when they understand the process. Once they learn something, they have it forever. And ever. They remember every experience, good or bad.

Donkeys have a high tolerance for lungworms and are not clinically affected by them. Horses are. This means that while donkeys are unaffected, they do shed lungworm eggs, which horses will pick up. When I see a horse coughing who is stabled with donkeys, I always consider that lungworms could be the problem. Fecal exams from both donkeys and horses will show the lungworm eggs. When we see these eggs in either species, I recommend worming both with the appropriate dewormer. The coughing horse is wormed to treat that cough, and the donkey is wormed to stop the source of the infection.

Generally speaking, donkeys are hardy and often live to be 40. Problems like colic, so devastating to horses, are rare in donkeys. I am grateful for that as we often stomach-tube horses with belly aches. Donkeys have very narrow nasal passages and extreme care with the proper size tube is important.

Another interesting difference is the vocal folds in the back of the throat. In donkeys they have a scalloped appearance, which some anatomists say is the reason for the peculiar sound of the bray.

Donkeys are used as guard animals for sheep because they have no love for anything canine. If a dog gets in with them, the automatic response is to attack. If you are looking for a guard donkey, get a full size donkey who will not be intimidated by more than one dog or coyote, as a mini donkey might be.

Donkey uniqueness is part of their charm. Even if you never "do anything" with them, they are easy to keep and long lived, and just plain fun to have around.

74

The Guardian

(sleep deprivation)

―――――― ♆ ――――――

Every night before turning in, I do barn check. By the time I get there, my donkeys have almost always "put themselves to bed" by coming into their shared stall from the paddock. Invariably Shiloh stands at the stall door facing out at the world. His buddy Shamus is stretched out, fast asleep. Shiloh is the barn watchdog. Whenever there is more than one equine in a herd, there will often be one self-appointed guardian that watches over the others. In the natural horse world, this is usually one of the mares of the herd. When this job is taken so seriously that the watcher never gets a chance at sleep, things start to come apart for him.

Research has shown how important sleep is for both us and for horses. Horses have three levels of sleep. They need about two hours of a very relaxed drowsiness and three hours of "slow wave sleep." For these first two levels, the animal is still on his feet and easily aroused. The last phase is called REM (rapid eye movement) sleep. In REM sleep the horse is either flat out or on its sternum with head turned to the side. They don't wake up right away when stimulated. Horses need 30 to 60 minutes of this deepest sleep. If you watch carefully, you can see the eye movement, even through the closed lids. In this deep stage, the brain waves change and the restoring, healing work of the body takes place. (Humans need two to three hours of REM sleep.) If horses get less than their requirement for a few days in a row, interesting things start to happen. Basically, the sleep deprived horse tends to fall asleep on his feet. These horses will sway forward and back and actually buckle at the knees and go down, often catching themselves after the front of the fetlocks or the knees hit the ground. There are some videos of this, which you can access by googling "sleep deprivation horses videos."

Veterinarians often recognize horses that are sleep deprived by noticing scarring on the front of the foreleg fetlocks. Some horses need that sleep so badly that they will sway and go down in crossties when feeling secure while being groomed. We have all experienced what this must feel like as we try to stay awake when driving after a night of little or no sleep.

I am embarrassed to say that years ago I diagnosed horses that fell down from a standing position as being narcoleptic. Narcolepsy is a specific neurologic problem in people in which one goes from wide awake into a coma-like state at inappropriate times. I have a friend who used to fall asleep right into a plate of his food, until he was put on the right medication. It turns out that narcolepsy is extremely rare in horses. In looking back, each horse that I and other veterinarians thought had narcolepsy, was most likely sleep deprived. Dr Joe Bertone from Western University in California is credited with being the first to recognize the syndrome and how to deal with it. Why would horses *not* relax, lie down, and go into deep sleep? After all, as far as we know they don't carry the load of worries or party late like us. There are a couple of reasons that have been identified. One is the social situation. The "guardian horse" feels he must stay awake to protect the herd. Perhaps the animal is in a noisy or scary stabling situation. This is the case at week-long horse shows where the lights are always on, and the activity level is high 24 hours a day. There are also some animals that don't want to lie down because they have arthritic joints, making getting up and down painful. These horses may get their first good sleep in weeks when put on anti-inflammatory medication.

There are some issues that should alert you to the possibility of your horse missing out on deep sleep. A very natural and daily activity for horses is going down and having a good roll. If you have never seen your horse roll, it may be because he or she has some soreness that makes this activity painful. If a horse doesn't go down to roll, he or she probably won't go down to sleep. Evaluate for soundness any horse that you never see rolling. Obviously, sleep deprived horses will not perform to their potential.

Whenever the social situation changes, as it does at horse shows, be aware that your horse may become sleep deprived during that time away. Sometimes it helps to change who the horse is paddocked or stabled next to. Putting a pony in with a sleep-deprived horse may allow him to relax and catch up on his healing sleep. I think that some horses won't lie down because there just isn't enough room in their stall. I generally recommend a 12 by 12 foot stall for a 1000-pound horse.

If you suspect a horse with this condition in your barn, talk to your veterinarian. For sure he or she has seen this before and will have suggestions based on your situation.

75

The Horse's Stomach

⚘

When my phone rings at 6AM, I'm pretty sure it's not a social call. "Dr J!" she shouted, "I think we're in trouble! You know my gelding Zeus? Well, he somehow got out of his stall last night and into the grain room, and it looks like he ate about half of that bag of sweet feed, and right now he's not looking so good." It's the kind of call every equine veterinarian dreads. The morning schedule, including my own breakfast, was trashed, and as I drove to her farm, my hope was that Zeus had gobbled all that grain within the last hour so that there might be a chance of saving him.

Why are horses so subject to problems like this? After all, last Thanksgiving I ate way too much and was a bit uncomfortable for a couple of hours, but I didn't have to call my doctor! One reason that horses can't take this gorging is because they have unique stomachs.

Although they are herbivores, horses don't have huge ruminant stomachs to break down fiber the way cows, sheep or goats do. In the horse the relatively small stomach churns the food, secretes acid and enzymes, and moves the food on down to the small and finally to the large intestine where the real fiber digestion happens. Although the stomach doesn't hold food for long, it is the site for some real problems.

Most people have heard that horses can't vomit. This is true for two reasons. The horse has a very strong sphincter muscle at the entrance to the stomach. It acts as a one-way valve and won't permit food to go back up. Vomiting is also prevented by an abrupt turn of the esophagus at the stomach entrance. This turn gets kinked when the stomach is full. Throwing up is no fun, but we all know how much better we feel when it's over. For horses this inability to vomit is not only extremely painful, it can be fatal.

Stomach issues usually arise when horses are fed inappropriately. Horses are grazers and do best when eating small quantities all the time. Because the stomach size is limited, huge meals or just heavy grain-feeding twice a day can bring trouble.

Zeus, the Houdini horse, hadn't eaten for hours, and while he was waiting for someone to get to the barn in the morning, he fiddled with the latch to his stall door until it opened, and he found his way to the grain room. He chowed down so fast his overloaded stomach couldn't empty. His inability to vomit meant a very real possibility of it rupturing. This would have meant certain death if the stomach contents had spilled into the abdominal cavity. In this case we were able to prevent that from happening, but it was needless agony for the horse and a large, unanticipated vet bill for the owner.

Another chapter in this book recommends three barriers to keep horses from getting into this situation. These are the stall door, the grain room door, and the grain container. All three should be secure. Every year our practice gets at least a dozen calls from clients whose horses have gotten into the grain and pigged out.

Here are some quick rules for keeping *all* stomach problems to a minimum. In most cases roughage should be available 24/7. This is actually the best way to prevent stomach ulcers as well. Grain should be considered a supplement and never the main part of the diet. Any feed changes, such as grain type or access to green grass in the spring, should be made gradually.

The word colic means belly pain, and the stomach is just one place it can happen. Colic that originates here is misery for horses, and it is mostly preventable by good feeding practices.

76

The Landing

My sister-in-law, in experiencing advancing age, remarked that she was glad that no one was around to watch her get out of bed in the morning and take the first few steps to the bathroom. She said, "It's not a pretty picture." After a horse has been standing in his stall all night, it's not always a pretty picture either. But those first few steps are full of information for someone who is observing closely. I have had several mentors in my lameness education. The good ones have each said that watching a horse walk can often give you as much information as watching them work at the faster gaits. Doubly true when they first come out after being stalled overnight or for just a few hours.

Here is a recent example. I was asked to look at a gelding that the owner said had a front end lameness that he seemed to warm out of. I told her that I'd like to examine him before he worked, preferably first thing in the morning. I asked her not to take him out of the stall until I got there. When the day came, I stood far back from his stall door and kept my eyes on his feet when he was brought out. As each foot hit the barn floor, he literally tiptoed. That is to say, the toe of each front foot hit the ground first, and then the heel dropped down. This is totally abnormal. Horses should land just about flat. Actually, recent super-slow videos reveal that normal horses at work do hit their heels first, just a split second before the rest of the foot lands. However, in a normal horse, what we see with the naked eye is a horse landing flat.

When this gelding was turned as he came out the stall, he was obviously favoring the leg on the inside of the circle. I asked the owner to turn him in the other direction, and when she did, he was off on *that* inside leg. At this stage my thought process was: *OK. This gelding is*

232

lame in both forefeet. He's landing hard on his toes probably because the back part of his foot hurts. I had the owner take the horse into the indoor and free lunge him, and sure enough, within a few minutes, he started to warm out of his lameness and land more normally. His gait was still somewhat stilted, but definitely better. Five minutes later he was able to turn fairly comfortably. I suspected that he might have early navicular disease, and subsequent nerve blocks and X-rays revealed that to be the case. First clue? It was the way he landed toe first coming out of his stall.

Unfortunately, when the grass is richest in the spring, we always have some horses that get laminitis. This extremely painful disease affects the toe of the foot. As a result these horses tend to land *heel* first, and then the toe flops down. Once you see one with this "heel-toe" gait, you never forget it. If you are standing well in front of them, you actually see the bottom of the sole for a split second. Again, the horse with navicular or other heel lameness tends to land toe first. The horse with laminitis lands heel first. Each is landing in the way that causes the least discomfort. Imagine a thumb tack in your shoe at the toe or at the heel. You would naturally walk to avoid the pain of stepping on the tack. Horses mildly affected with laminitis or navicular disease will tend to improve after several steps and often really do "warm out" of the lameness. Again, it is that first look, when the horse is "cold" that is so revealing.

A few times a year I will see a horse that strikes the outside of the front foot when he lands and then eases down onto the inside. If you walk this way for a few steps, you will feel how this strains the lower joints in your own leg. I see this most often on horses that have a tendency to toe out. Farriers often trim feet to achieve symmetry and balance of the foot, which is usually not what these horses need. The tendency to toe out comes from higher up in the leg. In my opinion, feet should be trimmed so that they land flat, regardless of how balanced the foot looks when you are holding it between your knees. These horses often need to have the outside wall lowered so that they land flatter. This will make them toe out more, but this is what the upper leg is dictating anyway, and in a mature horse you have to go with it to some extent. I wish every farrier would take the time to really watch all horses walk and trim accordingly. Farriers are a critical piece in keeping horses sound.

The landing of the foot is also something to be aware of in the hind end. Watching a horse walk away from you can prove helpful in deciding if a horse has a stifle or a hock problem. Horses with stifle joint issues tend to swing the leg wide. Inertia then carries the foot through that outside arc and a little bit toward the midline. The result is that they tend to land a little bit on the inside of the foot. If this has been an issue for some time, there will be wear of the inside wall if they are barefoot, or a shine to the inside branch of the shoe if they are shod. If the horse has a hock problem, the tendency is for the leg to swing in, and then land a little bit on the outside of the foot with subsequent wear on that side of the foot or branch of the shoe. Again, the landing is best observed when the horse has not been exercised.

There are other things to look for as a horse lands, but these basics are a good start. If practiced regularly, your observations will increase your awareness of your animal's bio mechanics and their well-being. My suggestion is for you to get in the habit of watching how those feet land on every horse you see for the next month as they come out of the stall in the morning. You will have gained an important skill.

77

The Mountain behind the Barn

(manure)

———— ◡ ————

Horse manure. You've shoveled, forked, lifted, pushed and pulled your share of it. You might not want to read about it, but the condition of that manure can be a clue to your horse's health.

Have a horse long enough, and you might start grumbling about the quantity of all that poop. A good-size horse will produce somewhere around 50 pounds a day. That adds up to nine tons a year! Unfortunately, this is just a fact of life that goes with animals on a mostly roughage diet. We grumble about the amount, but if a horse hasn't made any for a while, it's time to be concerned.

Impaction, or as the old horsemen used to say, "stoppage," is the most common cause of lack of manure in a horse that is eating. An impaction is a tightly wedged mass of food material in the large intestine. Impacted horses will show some signs of colic. The pain is less severe than a gas colic or twisted intestine, but can last days instead of hours.

I don't feel like I have completely examined a horse until I have walked into the stall and kicked some manure apart. The amount, form, color, consistency and smell can all provide clues as to what is going on inside the horse.

Horse manure is formed in balls because of the anatomy of the last several feet of the horse's intestine. This section is not just a smooth flexible pipe. It looks more like a long garter snake that has swallowed a string of tennis balls. Water is absorbed from the fecal material on its way through, and toward the end it is easily molded, taking on that ball shape. When the manure loses its form and become more like cow patties, there may be a problem. Some horses get loose when they are nervous, but if a watery diarrhea persists, it's time for a vet visit.

There are other things to watch for. Long, obvious pieces of undigested feed in the manure may be an indication of a dental problem causing improper chewing of roughage. The next time your vet is out, I'd have him or her examine the teeth.

Some horses graze very close and will pick up gravel or sand as they graze. This grit in the horse's intestine tends to collect in the colon and can cause sand colic. You can check for this by taking a good handful of manure and putting it in a gallon Ziploc bag. Mix well with water and hang the container with one corner down. Within 15 minutes the heavy sand will settle down to the tip. Sand can be cleared out by feeding psyllium (the ingredient in Metamucil) on a regular basis.

Internal bleeding anywhere along the intestine also shows up in the manure. If the bleeding occurs in the stomach or small intestine, the blood will be partially digested and will darken the manure. If the bleeding in the large intestine, the manure will have streaks of red in it.

Internal intestinal parasites use the host's manure as a vehicle to get their eggs out. For this reason, it's important to keep your horses away from the manure pile. Letting horses graze around the manure pile multiplies worm problems. Manure provides an easy way to check on your horses worm load. When your vet visit is scheduled, save some from the morning cleanout to be analyzed. Put a sample (a tablespoon) in a quart labeled Ziplock bag for them to take back to the lab.

Some people are quite adept at noticing a difference in the smell of manure. I had a technician years ago who could tell by that difference that a horse was about to get sick. She would know a good 24-hours before there were any other signs.

All this boils down to knowing what normal manure is for *your* horse. You handle it every day anyway. Get into the habit of tearing a ball or two apart with your foot, shovel, or fork before it goes into the wheelbarrow. It soon becomes a habit and is just another part of good horsemanship.

78

The Problem with Competition

———————— ∪ ————————

A few days ago our bookkeeper came into the office with a dilemma. Her five-year-old grandson wanted a special football jersey for Christmas. It had to say Tom Brady on the back, which meant the number 12 on front. She priced the jersey at Olympia Sports. That size eight jersey was $70. Cecile knows the value of $70 and considered the price outlandish. Her grandson, of course, has no idea of value and by next season will have outgrown the jersey. But Cecile loves that boy and bought a Brady shirt later that day, but online where it saved her $45. Common sense prevailed.

It made me think of what is goes on in the competitive horse world, and how the desire to win (look at me!) can be somewhat out of proportion to common sense. When things get extreme, it's the horse that suffers.

The example that gets the most press is what has been done in some circles with the Tennessee Walking Horse. Walkers are a wonderful breed. They are easy to work with and have a wonderful natural gait that translates to a very smooth ride. Some of our clients with bad backs have Walkers for that reason. There is a split within the breed when it comes to competition at horse shows. One set of owners and trainers emphasizes the natural gait and prohibits devices or practices that exaggerate it.

The darker side of the Walker world favors a very animated style in the show ring. Its trainers comply by using enormously stacked up feet and heavy shoes. Because of the expense of applying this type of shoe, it is rare to find these horses turned out. In addition, in a practice called "soring," painful irritants are rubbed into or painted around the pasterns.

When a foot hits the ground, the horse immediately snatches the leg back up because of the pain. Soring produces an artificially high and extended gait known as the "big lick." It draws a rambunctious and enthusiastic crowd. Consider the price that the horse pays for that exhibition. There are federal laws outlawing it, but there are not enough regulators to stop these practices. In New England the emphasis at shows is on flat-shod gaited walkers, without all of the excesses seen in the South.

Some of the southern Walking-horse tactics are being used in part of the American Saddlebred and show Morgan world. As in Walkers the favored look or style is an exaggerated gait. Stacked shoes, although usually not quite as radical as the Walkers, keep the horses stepping high. Tails are "nicked," meaning that the muscles at the base of the tail are cut, and then the tail is placed in a "bustle" or brace for days to train the tail to stand up. When the brace is removed and the horse is performing, the tail will stand up and flow out. A little ginger applied to the finger and into the rectum of the horse just prior to competition assures that the tail will be high. "Training" methods such as throwing strings of firecrackers and discharging fire extinguishers as the horses go by, play on the horses' natural fear and give the eyes that wide-open look and the animated style. Chains are fastened like bracelets around the pasterns to irritate the lower legs for more action. As with the Walkers, the community of owners and trainers is split, and there are shows that prohibit these practices. We have both types of Saddlebred and Morgan competitions in New England.

The opposite extreme can be found in some (not all) Western Pleasure classes. I had a non-horse person ask me if all the Quarter Horses with their heads way, way down were all tranquilized, or maybe sick. The term "peanut roller" has been used to describe the exaggerated super-slow gait with the head almost to the ground. It looks like the horses are on their last legs. To get this effect, practices like tying a horse's head up high from the ceiling all night have been used to tire the neck muscles. If you have ever sat in an audience with a seat way to the side and then for hours had a crick in your neck, you can appreciate how the horses feel. There has been a swing away from the peanut-roller way of going, but in a few shows, and under some judges, it is still rewarded. It fosters an attitude of: "You tell me what you're looking for, and I will do what I need to do to win."

The dressage community has been struggling with "rollkur," the forcing of a horse's head behind the vertical as a shortcut to get a collected look. When you view the horse from the side, the neck is bent so much by rein pressure that the chin is close to touching the chest. This is ironic in a sport that prides itself in having horses respond to minimal aids. Any accomplished dressage rider will tell you that all true collection must ultimately come from behind. Rollkur, practiced consistently, is a copout to get the effect of a collected horse without all the hard work that it takes to truly accomplish it. If done consistently, the result of rollkur can be an inflamed poll, with a guarded prognosis for future soundness. Fortunately, the dressage industry has recognized the problem, the FEI has banned it, and it is becoming less of an issue.

More than anything, I hate to see draft horses with bobbed tails. These horses have had most of the tail surgically removed for the sake of style. A shortened tail makes the hind end look more massive. Once done, for the rest of the animal's life, he is unable to flick away annoying flies. The excuse given for bobbing a tail is that it prevents reins from getting locked under the very strong draft-horse tail. There are ways around this without amputation. Draft animals trained for pulling competitions at fairs are sometimes subjected to an electric prod to encourage them to throw themselves into the collar to jerk the sled loaded with massive concrete blocks. On the other hand, there are now farm draft-horse competitions where the animals and their handlers are judged on such skills as how straight a furrow can be plowed. This is a far better test of the skill of both man and horse.

I have used a few examples where things have gotten out of hand in different disciplines. Each can easily be found in still pictures and videos on the internet. If you are in one of the equine sports above, I recommend being fully informed. If yours is a different competition, there is probably some abuse in *your* sport too. Please understand. I am not against competition. It makes us focus on what we are doing, and, within limits, it's why we see outstanding performances. Competition amongst people in business and in their sports moves things ahead. But stock manipulation and baseball spitballs are really cheating just to get ahead, with no regard for who gets hurt. I believe that horses, used in mindful competition, enjoy it as much as their handlers. But, when an animal is abused for the sake of a blue ribbon or cash, it shouldn't be a surprise that so many have ulcers. Abused horses usually suffer in silence, but the strain is there.

Lest you think that I am a goody-two-shoe on the outside looking in, over 40 years ago I made most of my living at the racetrack. I am ashamed to say that I regularly injected the joints of very young horses and gave many IV treatments containing vitamins and hormones at trainers' requests so that their horse could get a check at the next race. I never felt good about it and eventually left track practice. Once in the pleasure horse business, I got a reputation for doing a good job at nicking the tails of Saddlebreds and even bobbed a draft horse or two. I never felt good about doing those things either. My excuse at the time was that if I didn't do it, someone else would. That is never, ever a good reason for doing anything. If you are an active participant in some kind of activity that sometimes keeps you up at night, in the end it's not worth it. I have left that behind and sleep well now. There are barns around that I am not invited to anymore, but that's OK by me.

If I have hit home, what's next? If you are feeling a little queasy about some of the training methods you have been taught, stop. Don't be part of it. Find an equine competition where the horse is not being abused just so a ribbon can be tacked on a wall. If you feel that things in your equine world are getting shady, know that others feel the same way. Be the leader. Be brave, and don't participate. If you are in an audience where you know that animals have been abused, talk to the management, and next time stay home. There was a slogan that came out of the mess of Vietnam, "What if they gave a war and nobody came."

My thanks to ethical competitors Tanya Rennie of Vienna Farm and Sherrye Trafton of Sable Oak for reviewing this piece and offering solid suggestions.

79

The Slobbers
(clover-caused salivation)

U

It was midafternoon on an early spring day. I was scheduled for spring shots at Charlotte's barn. I gave her a call when I was 30 minutes out, so that she would have time to get the horses in. As my technician Erin backed our truck up to the barn door, we saw Charlotte bringing up the last of her four horses from the lower pasture. We hadn't seen Charlotte for a full year, so we spent a few minutes catching up and then began the annual exams and vaccinations. First on the list was Zip, a six-year-old Quarter Horse gelding. I began my usual physical. As the last part of my exam, I always look in a horse's mouth to see what the oral membranes look like and to check the teeth. A glance at the first few molars told me that he needed floating to reduce the sharp edges. As I was checking him over, Erin was busy getting his vaccines ready.

After Zip was vaccinated, Erin and I approached him with a mouth speculum so that I could see way, way back in his mouth and begin filing down his sharp points. We fitted the speculum plates over his upper and lower incisors and snugged up the leather strap around his poll. Erin and I worked as a team and pulled steadily down on the arms of the speculum. It went through a series of clicks on the ratchets as his jaw opened wide. In equine dentistry feeling the edges of the teeth is just as important as looking, and I have learned to trust the speculum to protect my fingers. I ran my hand back to the last molars. As I suspected there were sharp edges all the way back. What caught me by surprise was the volume of saliva that started pouring out of his mouth and running down my arm. As I pulled my hand out the saliva started to pool at my feet. Charlotte, Erin, and I stood there dumbfounded as over three cups of saliva gathered in front of Zip, with more coming in a steady stream. I glanced up at the roof of his mouth thinking that perhaps a stick was jammed across the roof of his mouth between the molars on each side. That will sometimes cause a horse to hyper-salivate. There was no stick, and my bright LED light revealed no other abnormalities, but that saliva just kept coming! I was still scratching my head over this when Charlotte exclaimed, "Hey, look, Pablo's doing the same thing!" Charlotte's stalls are built so that each horse can see all the others. Erin and I glanced next door, and sure enough, Pablo was drooling just like Zip. We released the speculum, removed it from Zip's mouth, and walked down the barn floor checking each stall. Every one of those four horses had his head slightly lowered, and saliva was pouring out of their mouths as if a faucet inside their heads had been left running. No horse was in distress, but in front of each horse a slippery puddle of saliva was gathering.

The fact that every horse was affected woke me up as to what was going on. I said, "I think we need to take a walk around your pasture." The day pasture is a two-acre field, and down in the lower corner was a large patch of white clover, about 100 feet by 100 feet. Instead of the usual bright green color of the leaves, the clover looked a little dull. On closer inspection we could see small dark dots on the leaves indicative of a fungus. Its official name is *Rhizoctonia leguminicola*. The common name is black patch, and it produces a toxin called slaframine. The toxin irritates the tongue and gums and causes copious salivation. The text book name of the problem is slaframine poisoning. Most everyone calls it "the slobbers." It had been a very wet and cool spring, and Charlotte had not opened that lower pasture until that very morning because it had been so boggy. When let out of the barn, her horses must have immediately headed for that tasty clover that they hadn't seen since last fall. By the time we arrived, the effects of the toxin were just being felt. Not every horse likes clover, so it was a little surprising that all four horses were affected. Incidentally, we put off floating the horses for another day when we wouldn't get our shoes slimy.

We expect calls about slobbers in cool wet weather when the fungus is active. This was the first time that I had been on the scene to watch it develop, and I was as surprised as Charlotte. It is truly amazing how much saliva a horse can produce. The books will tell you that a normal adult horse will put out ten gallons of saliva a day. Horses with slobbers produce even more. Since it is spilling out, it doesn't get recycled, so it has the potential of causing dehydration. Slobbers isn't strictly a pasture problem. If hay is baled with the fungus on the leaves, the same thing can happen when it is eaten. I am told that the longer it is stored, the less effect it has. I understand that buttercup can also irritate the mouth and cause salivation, but it has been my experience that horses avoid it, and I personally have never seen it cause a problem. The fungus can grow on alfalfa, but I haven't seen that either, probably because we don't grow much of it in northern New England.

I remember one case, right in my town, when a mare with a funny appetite chowed down on a rhubarb plant growing in the paddock. I'm not sure if it was the leaves (known to be poisonous) or the stalks that that caused the problem, but she came down with slobbers that just wouldn't quit. The owner was pretty panicky, but after she learned that the mare wasn't going to die, she got curious and put a pail under the mare's head, and collected almost a five gallon bucket before she got bored and turned the mare out to drain. To this day I wonder if it was a fungus toxin, or just the puckery taste of the rhubarb that caused her slobbers.

The good news is that usually within four to eight hours, the salivation slows down and finally stops. There is no medical treatment other than keeping plenty of water available to replace all that has been lost. Electrolyte supplementation is wise as minerals are lost in saliva that drools out. One article suggests taking the affected animals outside and flushing their mouths out with a hose. I've never tried that, but if you had a well-broke horse that would permit it, it would be something to try, and makes sense to me. Another source recommends giving a horse atropine, but I don't agree. This powerful drug will dry up the saliva, but too much of it will shut down the gut, potentially causing the far worse problem of colic. I'd much rather see them salivate and flush out the toxin.

I called Charlotte after we got home that evening, and she said that the problem was just about over. Charlotte mowed that pasture close and fenced it off for a while, and there has been no recurrence to date. The bottom line in Slobbers is that there is no need to panic, but a call to your vet, who may have further thoughts, would probably be in order.

Slobbers is always from the mouth. A horse that is choked will have saliva, but not as much, and usually mixed with feed, coming out of the nostrils. Choke is described in another chapter, and as noted there, it is much more serious.

80

The Sound of Hoofbeats

(rare vs common)

───────────── ♘ ─────────────

It's a saying all veterinarians know, "When you hear the sound of hoofbeats, don't look for zebras." In other words, unless you happen to be on the plains of Africa, if you hear hoofbeats, they are most likely coming from horses and not zebras. The meaning is, *consider the ordinary before the exotic.*

Here is an example of horses vs. zebras. A good part of my day is spent looking at lame horses. If an owner walks a horse out of its stall, and the animal is hippity-hoppity lame in one front leg, I am not thinking that this horse has laminitis or navicular disease. It could be one of those, but those would be zebras. Most likely, since it's just one foot and he is acutely lame, the chances are "horses" that he has a foot abscess. I never assume that it can't be a zebra, and so I start at the shoulder and quickly run my hand down the entire leg, missing no joints or muscle bundles on the way. That will take less than a minute, and it's an important minute, but I'm still betting "horses" and will concentrate on the foot, looking carefully for an abscess. As I move to the foot, my exam slows down and I check the pulse in both digital arteries, use my hoof testers to see exactly where he is sore to pressure, and use my hoof knife to try to find that abscess. It's just a question of asking what is most likely and then concentrating on that.

What does all this mean to you as a horse owner? Here is something you may have experienced. You come out to the barn to feed up and notice that your favorite mare doesn't greet you as usual. She stands in the back of the stall with her head down, looking depressed. You see that she hasn't touched the hay you put out last night. So, you are hearing the sound of hoofbeats. How are you going to investigate?

In this case the hoofbeats are saying: perhaps colic, maybe a fever. It's time to check both her temperature and her gut sounds. Then maybe check her membranes and listen to her heart.

Same mare, same depression and you might start looking for the zebras. "Well maybe she is depressed because I yelled at her last night when she was chewing the stall door. Or maybe she is upset at the pony next door. I'll just wait a couple of days and see if she gets over it. Not a good idea. Go with the most *likely* thing and check it out.

Around 800 years ago, there was a Franciscan Friar named William of Ockham (also spelled Occam) who stated that the simplest, most sensible answer is most often the correct one. Another way of saying this is: if you have two theories to explain your observation, go with the least complicated one, the one that makes the most sense. In medicine we look for the fewest possible causes that will account for all the symptoms. This has become known as Occam's razor. The razor part refers to trimming away the unnecessary and focusing on the most likely. Are we ever absolutely, positively sure what is bothering a horse? Not often, but if we think of all the possible causes and then pick the most likely, the treatment for that cause is most apt to help.

I took my truck to the garage the other day to see Ted. When I arrived he was talking to a customer of his who said: "I'm not a mechanic, but…" I wish I had a dime for everyone who has ever said to me, "Well, I'm not a veterinarian, but…" Just because you aren't a vet doesn't mean that you shouldn't ponder what is going on with your animals. Check out all the symptoms you are seeing and come up with your own possible explanation that makes sense. If you are totally ignorant on how to take a temperature, listen for gut sounds, or determine what an abnormal foot pulse feels like, ask your veterinarian to show you these things! Vets love informed clients. My conversation with a client who has educated herself on horses' health is far different from my conversation with a horse owner who has not.

I'm sure you know the saying, "A little knowledge is a dangerous thing." I saw a client's horse the other day that had a markedly swollen front leg. The owner had been online, looked up swollen legs, and came across the term Elephantiasis, and wondered if that might be the problem. Actually that is a problem in people in tropical countries which is caused by a parasitic worm. It happens to be responsive to ivermectin, which is one of our horse wormers, but my client's idea of giving this horse a dose of wormer would have been a total waste of money and of no benefit. Hearing the sound of hoofbeats, the owner went to his information source and found…right, a whole herd of zebras thundering by.

What is the take-home? First, when your horse has something wrong, don't panic. Think about what your vet would want to know. For example, if your horse is off feed, take the temperature, check his pulse, and listen for gut sounds. Gather as much information as you can, in a calm collected way, and then call your vet. Assuming the worst or jumping to crazy conclusions (zebras) is not good for your own mental health and does your horse no good at all.

81

The Squirts

(diarrhea)

‐‐‐‐‐‐‐‐‐‐‐‐‐‐‐‐‐‐‐‐ ♆ ‐‐‐‐‐‐‐‐‐‐‐‐‐‐‐‐‐‐‐‐

It happened again today. It was one of those "while you're here" conversations we all have with our health providers. In this case it was Andrea asking about her aged warmblood gelding, Whiz.

"The other thing, if you have time. It's not a big deal, but it's annoying to me, and I'll bet it's annoying to him too." I was writing Andrea's bill, and nodded my head to show that I was listening. "When Whiz makes manure its usually pretty well formed, but then there is this juice that comes out right after. Sometimes his manure is loose too, but mostly it's just the brown liquid right after he poops. I call it 'the squirts.' It gets all over his hind legs, and well, it just bugs me. I'm forever cleaning him up back there. Anything we can do about that?"

I think I am asked this question, in just about the same way, no less than once a month. What is funny about it is that everyone always calls this particular problem "the squirts." I never heard about it in vet school (as I remember). You can't find it in any equine textbook. It is never mentioned at veterinary meetings, but ask your vet about it, and for sure, they will be knowledgeable. From their experience you will get a long list of possible causes and cures. Although it's not in the books, you *will* find it talked about online at one of the many horse-owner chat sites. If you Google just the two words you can join the conversations. Surround the two words in quotes and you will get a bunch of raunchy entries that have nothing at all to do with horses.

My wife was an elementary school teacher. One day in her classroom she picked up on a distinctive odor. Bonnie walked up and down the rows of seven-year-olds at their desks. The smell got stronger right next to Carl. She bent down and said quietly to him, "Carl, do you feel OK? Would you like to go down and see the nurse and get cleaned up?" Carl said, "No, Mrs. Jefferson, I'm OK. I just got the squirts." I guess we all just know the term from a young age.

In the stomach of healthy horses, food mixes with water and saliva. As it passes into the small intestine, it's a thick liquid. In the large intestine most of the water gets reabsorbed. In the colon the body recycles more, and the ingesta are compacted and take on the form of the familiar fecal balls. Anything that interferes with the reabsorption of water means that the manure will be less solid. This can mean pure diarrhea, but in horses like Whiz we will see the usual fecal balls and those liquid squirts. The "anything" can be something simple that irritates the gut, like too many acorns or apples. An overgrowth of some bacteria, protozoa, yeasts, or viruses can do the same. I own a donkey that gets the squirts when he is nervous.

In my experience horses with the squirts are usually mature, often in their 20s. It doesn't seem to make a difference if it's a stallion, mare, or gelding. I think I have heard the complaint from owners of every breed. I have seen it in the best managed stables and in some very marginal ones.

If your horse has this problem, mention it the next time your vet is in the barn. Hopefully he or she will do a thorough physical exam. If it is more than occasional, a fecal test and or blood work may be indicated. Don't be surprised if everything checks out OK. In most cases I end up talking about possible causes to see if any ring a bell with the owner. We often arrive at a diagnosis through the backdoor of "stopping this or trying that" until we find an answer. Not the textbook way to arrive at a diagnosis, but the situation often dictates this approach.

Sand picked up from close grazing can cause it. Its gritty nature can irritate the lining of the intestine. An irritated intestinal wall doesn't reabsorb water well. Psyllium given regularly will pick up sand from the gut and take it out. It is available as a powder or in pellets.

There was an older mare just two towns away from me that had the squirts. Sometimes the liquid would come out in an explosive way and hit the stall wall with a splash. We tried different things over a course of weeks, but any relief was only temporary. Her farrier was getting a bit annoyed because her squirting episodes were unpredictable. It wasn't a pleasant environment to be working in. He is known as a man of few words, and one day dropped the hind foot he was working on said, "I think you should take her off this coarse hay and put her on hay pellets. I bet she'd bind up proper." The owner ran this idea by me, and I told her it didn't make sense to me, but we had tried everything else. Sure enough, within two days of being on hay pellets, the squirts stopped. Was the coarse hay irritating the intestinal wall? I'm not sure, but in retrospect I remembered that she was missing a few teeth. Her manure stayed normal until she died at a good old age. I don't expect that to work on every case, but it is something to try.

I will never forget crusty old Charley and his mare, Star. I would describe her problem as squirts on steroids. One day formed manure, the next day she might have explosive diarrhea. Through it all she stayed happy. At the time I owned an equine hospital. Charlie just showed up one day with Star and dropped her off.

"Fix her. Call me when she's better." I took it on as a challenge. Blood and fecal samples were sent off. I tried supplements, antibiotics, and all kinds of drugs designed to slow down the gut. I tried homeopathy and acupuncture. My staff gave her every possible combination of feeds. We did everything but call in a witch doctor. Nothing worked. Charlie would call every day or two and get the no progress report. Finally after three weeks, with no warning, just like he had arrived, Charlie showed up to take Star home. He loaded her in his trailer and paid his bill, which I discounted because of my total lack of success.

As he latched the door on the trailer Charlie said, "Tell you what I've decided. I'm turning her out on that lush ten-acre field way out back that has the pond. I'm not going to even look at her for a week." I told Charlie that all that spring grass might make the diarrhea way worse. She might die! Charlie replied, "Kill her or cure her, one way or the other that mess from her hind end is going to be over." A week later my phone rang and I recognized the number. I dreaded picking up as I figured that old Star was gone. "She's all better. No diarrhea and no squirts." To this day I get razzed by Charlie about him switching to Dr Grass to cure Star. Would it work on another horse? I don't know.

I usually recommend as a first treatment to put a squirting horse on probiotics, or more lately also prebiotics. The problem can be caused by a bacterial imbalance, and sometimes a daily dose of "good" bacteria will overwhelm the bacteria that might be causing the situation. My second recommendation is often psyllium. Next would be Bio Sponge powder or paste. Sometimes the supplements for hind gut ulcers are helpful. Pepto Bismol or Kaopectate can tighten up an acute case. Protozoa such as Trichomonas or Giardia may be responsive to the antibiotic Metronidazole.

So the annoying situation of the squirts has many possible causes and just as many possible solutions. With the help of your vet try to figure out the why, and then try what makes the most sense. Without a definite diagnosis, you just have to experiment. "One at a time and give it time" is a good slogan. Don't be tempted to try everything at once as you won't learn what is working. You have time to work it through. It's like bad manners. The squirts are annoying but never fatal.

82

The Stall Door

———————————— ♘ ————————————

There are two things that I like to see hanging on the door of every horse's stall. One is an information paper, under plastic, that gives information about that particular horse. The other thing is the horse's halter, with lead attached.

An incident that happened several years ago in a stable (now closed) illustrates just how critical the paper can be. A client called about a mare that belonged to one of her boarders. The mare got into a scrap with a pasture mate and suffered a laceration on her right hind leg. When I arrived, I saw that the wound needed suturing and asked if the owner had been notified. The barn owner said that she had tried but couldn't reach her. I knew that the wound repair couldn't be put off, so we decided to go ahead. The mare had a bit of an attitude, so we took her outside on the grass and gave her a dose of IV tranquilizer. My thought was that if she was still kicky under the tranquilizer, I could then give her a short acting anesthetic, ease her down to the ground and safely suture the leg. I checked her heart, lungs, and temperature. She was young and quite healthy.

I gave her the IV tranquilizer and went back to the truck to gather instruments for repairing the leg. As I returned with my arms full of stuff, I glanced at the mare and noticed that she was acting funny. She had started to breath erratically. Then she began to buckle on the front end. She staggered a bit and sank slowly down. Remember, I had only given a common tranquilizer which has a large safety margin. Her respirations became more and more labored, and despite some heroic efforts to bring her around, she died about 20 minutes later. It was devastating!

The owner was finally reached and was understandably terribly upset. She drove out to the barn, and after she calmed down told me that before she moved to this stable, the mare had been tranquilized at another barn, had suffered a huge reaction, and almost died. When she moved the mare, the owner had never passed on this vital information. I suppose she thought that she could always be contacted if there were a problem. Had she had an information sheet on the door that said, "This mare has had a severe reaction to such and such a tranquilizer," I, of course, would never have given her that same drug. The owner had left no such notice with the stable. The result was a terribly needless loss.

So, what should be on that sheet? I like to see the horse's name, age, and general description. For example, it might read: "Suzie, four-year-old chestnut Quarter Horse mare with blaze face and hind stockings." I have seen a few stall information sheets which included front-on photographs of the animal's head and side views of the whole horse. The owner's name should also be there, along with all phone numbers where they and at least one other responsible person can be reached. The information sheet should also include the name of the horse's veterinarian with their contact information. Finally, I would put on any special instructions such as: "Sensitive to some medications. Check with owner or barn manager before giving any drugs."

The second thing I like to see hanging on every stall door is the horse's halter, with lead shank attached. This is important because in an emergency no one has to search for it. I have heard the argument that if you keep your horse's halter on 24/7, it might save a few seconds if there were a fire. I don't buy it. *Every* horse should immediately accept his or her halter from *any* person, no exceptions. If your horse won't stand willingly while you or anyone else puts the halter on, it is time for some basic training. It really shouldn't take any more time to slip a halter on than to attach a lead to the halter. My opinion is that when you leave the stall, you should leave with halter in hand. I have attended a number of horses who suffered severe injuries when their halters got caught on something in the stall. When that happens, the natural reaction is for the horse to jerk back, hard. With no give the horse feels trapped, may panic, and can get hurt in their frantic efforts to pull away. It is always wise to keep in mind that the horse is a prey animal, hardwired to cut and run.

Both the horse information and the halter can be vital in barn catastrophes. We all worry about barn fires, but in the past few years a number of barns in Maine have gone down under snow loads. What if no one from the barn was there, but someone driving by happened to see smoke coming out of the barn or a roof collapsing? What if one or more of the horses were trapped or injured? In all the confusion and probable horse panic, the halter on the door would be right at hand. In trying to sort things out, the facts on the stall door about each animal and who to contact would be crucial.

I was working on this article when I began to feel like a hypocrite. So, I went out to my barn, took the halters from the tack room, and hung them where they should be. I own two small donkeys, both of whom live in one stall. I made up an information sheet, enlarged the type to bold, enlarged it so it could be read six feet away, and slipped it into a clear plastic holder. The paper identifies both animals and gives a few peculiarities for each.

To summarize, if there is a horse in a stall, an information sheet and a halter with lead should be hanging on his or her door. These two precautions will give you a sense of security and could save your horse's life.

83

The Trouble with Breeds

———————— ♘ ————————

Over 25 years ago I got a call from Richard, a Quarter Horse breeder, who had just moved to a farm a few miles from my place. He had come to Maine from down south and was looking for a vet. We made an appointment, and a week later I backed my truck up to his barn. I slid open the big white barn door and walked in. I didn't see Richard, so I started walking through the barn to get a feel for his animals. By the time I reached the fourth stall, I was starting to think I was in Disneyland. Every single one of his eight horses was buckskin. Every one! I have always liked the color, maybe because I don't see that many, so they always make me look twice. I had never seen a barn full of them.

Richard came into the barn from the house a few minutes later. We introduced ourselves, and I commented on his horses. "Yup, I breed for that. I won't have a horse that isn't buckskin. I will tolerate a dun, but they come out any different than that, and they're gone." As I listened to him talk about each horse, I realized that he was practicing very close inbreeding so that he could keep getting the color. It was father bred to daughter, sister to brother sort of thing. I have always believed in hybrid vigor, and this was going against that and everything I had ever been taught or read. My trips to his barn were infrequent, and after two years he moved away. He felt that there wasn't a market here for his animals. The fact is that the constant inbreeding was causing all kinds of conformation issues, and we Maineiacs just weren't buying his nicely colored but deeply flawed horses. Selecting for just one thing was causing big problems. Richard was "color blind," unable to see beyond the appearance that he wanted. Select for just one thing and sooner or later those recessive genes will come home to roost.

Most of us are drawn to one breed of horse. Maybe it's the one we grew up with and know. Sometimes we like a particular one because that's the one whose best at what we like to do. I googled the term "horse activities," and found 97, running from trail riding to hunting wild boar on horseback (with a spear!) Then I tried "breeds of horses," and found *hundreds* worldwide. I got tired trying to count them, so I just counted the breeds whose name starts with A, and found 38! There are actually six breeds that start with the word American! All breeds were started by an individual or group of horse people who wanted a horse that would look or perform a certain way. A Belgian weighing close to a ton can plow a field or pull a hay wagon loaded with 50 adults up a hill. Don't try those things with an American Saddlebred. But *that* peacock of the horse world can bring a stadium of people to their feet cheering as he prances around the show ring. Each breed has an activity that it does best. The consumer (horse owner) demands the traits, and the breeders respond. The term that best describes what is going on here is "Fashion vs Function."

Let's look at vehicles for an analogy. You drive the one you have because it fits you and what you need it for. No point in having all wheel drive in Florida unless you like to race in the sand. However, your own drive home on stormy winter nights may require that extra traction. As a consequence we have all kinds of vehicles, fitting every need. If a new need like 50 mpg arises, the need is met, and hybrids start coming down the line. The difference between horses and vehicles is that vehicles are stamped out on an assembly line. The 100th vehicle leaving the line that day is just like the first. Not so with horses. The more you use the same genes, the bigger the problem down the road.

As an example of what happens with the "manufacture" of horses, let's look at the Appaloosa breed. The Nez Pierce Indians found and bred a horse that could handily carry a warrior *and* be flashy. Lots of white men liked the look of the colored Appys, too, and that "blanket" over the hind end became selected for. Whenever one trait is selected for and others are forgotten, other things start to happen, and it usually isn't good. The result has been a weakness of the Appaloosa eye. Many in the breed suffer from periodic opthalmia which can result in early blindness. There is also a tendency toward night blindness and, way at the other end, an often skimpy tail. It would be GM deciding to make the most incredibly advanced all-wheel drive ever seen, but letting everything else like brakes and safety get shoddy.

There are many more examples of what happens when a narrow set of traits is concentrated on and selected for. The Morgan horse was born in the hills of Vermont to answer the need for a hardy horse able to take the family in a buggy to church and the next day get hooked to a plow to till the garden. Maybe that night the teenage boy in the family would throw a saddle on to go visit the pretty girl down the road. Justin Morgan, the foundation sire, was such a horse, and stamped the breed. The old style Morgans are still hardy, and as every vet can tell you, they are almost *too* hardy. Many have metabolic syndrome and have to be kept away from grain or green grass. Some Morgan owners decided to go in another direction and make their horses look and act like Saddlebreds, and the easy keeper trait of the breed has gotten lost in that pursuit.

There are many more Quarter Horses than any other breed in the U.S. Some people like to show them in halter, and for a time it was the extraordinarily muscled horse that took the blue ribbons. In selecting for that one characteristic, other things were left behind. The Quarter Horse stud "Impressive" had this quality like none before and threw lots of babies who at birth looked as though they had been lifting weights in the womb. The problem was that other items like feet and legs were ignored, and his descendants had a hard time doing any degree of athletics because there was no foundation to support it. They were also subject to HYPP, a debilitating muscle problem, later proven to be thrown by Impressive.

"Minis" of all breeds are popular and have enabled owners to have a horse on the property without the need for acres and acres. The prime trait selected for has been small size, and again, things that pop up on the way are often ignored. As a result minis are sometimes born with dwarf characteristics like misshapen joints and heads. They often have dental problems because they get issued the normal number of teeth without enough room to house them all. These recessive traits can surface even if both parents are normal.

Consider the racing Thoroughbred. The fastest Kentucky Derby was run by Secretariat 42 years ago! Every year records are broken in every sport. Granted, Secretariat was exceptional in every way, but there have been improvements in training and tracks since then. The racing Thoroughbred has been selected for early speed as a three year old. That's where the money is. You can't have both early maturity and a long life. Many in the breed are old and creaky in their mid and late teen years. In a northern New England winter, it is hard to keep their ribs covered. Thin walled and shelly feet are a common issue, and many have to be shod with glue-ons because they can't take a nail.

An extreme example of the inbreeding issue leading to recurrent problems is the Friesian breed. They are flashy movers and several Hollywood films have added to their popularity. Demand has meant constant inbreeding which has led to immune problems. They are not the easiest horse to settle when bred and have many more problems associated with foaling than other breeds. Veterinarians dealing with them on a regular basis all have stories about their issues.

Arabians, long noted for their endurance and excellent conformation have suffered dictates from the halter-horse group of owners. The unique dished face has been selected for to the point that it is a parody, and there will be a price to be paid in these horses not getting enough air if they are asked to do more than stand around and look pretty. I was sad to see an example of this on the cover of a recent leading Arabian magazine.

If I have not mentioned your breed, it is only because this article would get a little tedious. Whenever and wherever animals (all types) are bred and a trait or two is selected for, there will be issues. So, what's to be done? First, I think it is wise to deeply research any breed you are interested in. The official breed website will rarely mention its genetic problems, even though *every* breed has them. The breeders themselves are likewise quiet about issues, even though they live with them every day. Dig deep enough and you will find references to them. You may have to do an end-run and do a search for a particular problem in the veterinary literature. Usually every such article has a paragraph on predilections, which means the breeds that are apt to have the problem. Talk to your vet about his or her experiences with the breed. Before you take possession of a horse, check the pedigree for inbreeding. There is a mathematical way of quantifying this, called the coefficient of inbreeding, which can tell you what the risks are. If its performance you want, don't be afraid of the horse of mixed breeding. Like mutts in the dog world, they are often healthier and live longer than horses locked into generations of careless breeding.

84

The Value of an Annual Exam

♘

It was early spring and I was vaccinating at Virginia's boarding stable. I find spring vaccination the ideal time to do annual physicals. It is time consuming, and there is a charge, but the information gained can be huge. I like to have owners there. It's the perfect time to discuss what vaccines the animal needs and the significance of the findings on the physical exam. Cocoa was one of Virginia's own horses. I had not met him before and asked her about him. I was surprised when she told me that the hunter was 26 years old. He could have passed for 12.

The first thing I do when examining a horse is to stand back a good five or six feet and get a general impression. I look at the animal's conformation which gives a hint as to possible future leg problems. I ask myself if the animal's condition is about right for the horse's age and activity level. I watch the rib cage move in and out. Cocoa was bright and alert, in good flesh, with a nice easy breathing pattern and was standing square on all four. His conformation was excellent. I walked in closer and used my pen light to check his eyes. Both corneas were clear. I used an ophthalmoscope to examine the deeper eye structures. There were no floaters or cataracts, which are often found at this age. Both eyes were perfect right down to the retina. I remember thinking, *Remarkable horse.*

The next step on my exam is to check the heart and lungs. Uh oh. Cocoa had what sounded like a heart murmur. Murmurs can be heard when blood escapes back through a valve that isn't fully closing after the heart contracts. I asked his owner if he was exercise intolerant, meaning, does he tire easily. She said no, he's been a great performer, and despite his age he just gets out there and does his job. The extra sound was quite distinct on both sides of the chest wall, but since he was in such great shape and didn't tire, I thought maybe I was mistaken. Sometimes what sounds like a valve problem might be what we call a flow murmur, the sounds of blood splashing within the heart. A similar sound can be heard if the heart is rubbing on a lung or the chest wall. I asked if I might listen to him sometime this spring before, during, and after exercise, preferably before he began this year's competitions. She said, "Sure," and after watching him trot in hand I vaccinated him. I wrote my findings: "Possible systolic heart murmur heard on both sides. No exercise intolerance reported."

Just a few days later Cocoa escaped from his pasture and, leading a herd of his equine buddies, came galloping in through the open barn door. Sparks were flying as his steel shoes slipped on the paved barn floor. He ran straight down the alley and right into the big indoor arena. He made an impressive turn at the far end and came galloping back. Virginia quickly shut the gate to the indoor so he couldn't run back out. He came snorting up to the gate and then started to tremble and wobble behind. Then he went down and lay flat out. Virginia remembered my comment about his heart a few days before and thought this might be the end. She called my cellphone and asked if I could come right over and check him out. By the time I arrived, Cocoa was back on his feet and had been led back to his stall. He looked totally normal, but when I listened to his heart I could hear that murmur again, now compounded by an irregularity that wasn't there before.

I was thinking that my first impression of his heart must have been correct, that the extra heart sound I heard days before really was blood escaping back through an incompetent valve. The excitement of getting out and the mad dash with a heart that wasn't working right was too much. Not enough oxygenated blood was getting to the hind end. As a result his legs gave way, and he fell over. After he was down a while and the body wasn't calling for as much blood, up he came and was "normal" again. I discussed the option of bringing him to a clinic and having a treadmill test done with an EKG. Virginia asked what I thought we should do, and I replied that no matter what any further tests might show, I personally would not allow my own daughter to ride him. Virginia wisely said, "I think maybe it's time to retire Cocoa." I think this was a smart decision as, no matter what the test revealed, you would always wonder whether he might collapse at a jump and go down on his rider. Had I not done the initial exam, everyone in the stable would have just thought that him going down was just one of those things. I think him going down was a blessing to possible future riders.

A thorough physical exam can reveal all kinds of things. Another extreme example happened over 20 years ago. A young couple in Yarmouth had just bought their first horse from a dealer who had taken the horse on a trade a few days before. I was asked by the couple to come and vaccinate him. In this case my exam never got further than the horse's eyes. Cataracts on both sides had left him essentially blind. He was one of those horses who was totally trusting and would follow you anywhere, so the owners had absolutely no clue that he could only see dim shadows. I'm not sure what would have happened when they started to ride him. I called the dealer, who was as surprised as anyone, and the horse was exchanged for another the next day.

Every year I find a few horses with breathing problems that the owners were not aware of. My first clue is by watching them breathe by watching the rib cage. The motions of breathing should be effortless. When there is too much of a push to get the air out, I know I have a horse with a respiratory problem which might not show until the horse is put into work. Listening to the lungs, and perhaps checking throat and lungs with an endoscope, would be the next step. Caught early, many respiratory issues can be helped by good management and sometimes medication.

Part of a good physical is to watch horses in motion, to see if they are off at all, and to watch each foot as it hits the ground, looking for early signs of feet out of trim or upper leg problems. Again, some early imbalances are easily corrected early on once a competent farrier is notified.

These are just a few of the situations that your vet's physical exam can reveal. Look on the yearly physical as a time to learn more about your horse and identify potential problems.

85

The Walk

(walking colic)

──────── ♘ ────────

One night last winter, I got a phone call from an anxious client. His 20-year-old Arabian mare was in distress. Ordinarily this is a very cranky animal, but tonight she was depressed. She kept pawing with one front leg, and every so often would look around at her left flank.

What concerned this man the most was the fact that the mare kept trying to lie down. He and his wife had been keeping her on her feet by walking her. In fact, when he called the horse had already been walked for two hours. I had some trouble talking to him, because every few seconds he would interrupt our phone conversation to yell out to his wife, "Keep her walking. Don't let her go down!"

After I had seen the mare, and the situation was under control, I asked him why he had been so insistent on walking her. He replied that he had always heard that colicky horses should be walked. I've often heard this myself, but after many years of attending colics, I no longer agree.

When you see a horse in pain, it is natural to want to help. The something that everyone *can* do is to snap a lead shank on the horse and start walking. Often when I pull in a barnyard on a colic call, I spot the two walkers. Some people will walk their horses about 100 feet, turn and walk back. Others seem to favor a large diameter circle walk. Sometimes, before I get called, "the walk" has been going on for a long time, and there is a deep groove in the dirt where the horse has been walked. By the time I arrive, the owners seem to need help as much as the horse.

I am speaking with empathy. At vet school we students had to walk colicky horses. Because the walk is slow and without specific

263

destination, after an hour your feet start to trip over each other. It's like walking aimlessly through a huge museum or department store. It doesn't take long before your eyes start to glaze over, and your feet and back start to ache. In most cases, I think it's unnecessary.

Think for a minute. If you had a belly ache, would you go out on a two-hour walk? If you are like me, you'd probably head for bed. You would twist and moan until you found a comfortable position, and then stay right there. That's exactly what a colicky horse wants to do. He will go down, may flip, and get into some real peculiar positions. As he hits the ground and rolls, he may pass some gas. If he gets no relief, he will probably jump up, walk several steps, and then go down again.

Most colics are no more serious than our occasional stomach aches. The pain is often from some portion of the gut distended by gas. It hurts. The lying down and rolling is an attempt to somehow relieve the pressure. It may help. I don't buy into the theory that a rolling horse may twist his intestines. Lots of horses roll plenty when turned out in the morning, with no harm done.

A very small percentage of colic cases are in real trouble. One example is a complete twisting of the intestine. You may have to keep this horse walking to keep him from seriously banging his head on the ground until help arrives. You certainly don't have to walk every horse that has belly pain. Call your vet and describe what the horse is doing. We will often suggest Banamine and have you watch the horse for an hour. If he wants to go down and doesn't have a roomy stall, turn him out where he has room to lie down without injuring himself. If the Banamine isn't effective within the hour, call back. If your vet thinks that the colic is serious enough to warrant hospitalization and possible surgery, it's always a case of the quicker the better. Hours of walking won't help.

86

There Comes a Time
(euthanasia decision)

———————— ♄ ————————

Red turned 28 in the spring. For the past ten years the Bensons called him "Old Red." If we can judge such things, Red had a good life. All the children learned to ride on him. When family stuff would get intense, Red could expect a visit to his stall from one of the kids to talk things over. Over the past year Red had started to fail. His teeth were at the gum line, and the twice-a-day mashes were keeping him going. One eye was blind because of a cataract, and there was one starting in the other. At night he would occasionally bump into the walls of his stall.

It was November, and the family realized that his time had come. I was asked to lay him away before the ground turned hard. He was to be buried out back, by the stone wall, near the old pine, close to two family pets. We all knew that this was the thing to do. He might have made it through one more winter, but it would have been hard.

As sophisticated as veterinary medicine has become, there will always be conditions we can't deal with. The fading horse like Old Red, the draft horse with a fractured hip, the pony so badly foundered it can't get up. The list is long. The only option in such cases is humane destruction of the animal. The correct term is euthanasia. This is a word from two Greek roots which translate as "easy death." It doesn't mean easy decision or easy solution. It can mean immediate relief from incurable suffering or a lingering death.

It's a sensitive subject. However, many people have questions about it. How exactly is it done? What does the horse feel? This article may be as emotionally hard to read as it is to write. I am doing so to help clear up some misconceptions and perhaps relieve anxieties you may have about it.

The American Association of Equine Practitioners has a document on euthanasia of horses. The acceptable methods must be quick and painless. There are many ways of killing animals, but only a few meet these two criteria.

Most veterinarians use an intravenous solution and may give the horse a sedative first, depending on the situation. The actual euthanasia drug is a highly concentrated pentobarbital solution made for this purpose. It is injected into the jugular vein, which is very accessible as it runs from behind the jaw down and into the chest. The jugular empties directly into the heart. A few seconds after injection, the solution is pumped from the heart to the brain. The part of the brain that makes us aware of our surrounding is quickly affected and usually, within a minute, the horse loses consciousness. There is no anxiety or pain. We know this because the drug, a barbiturate, has been used for years on people.

The horse goes down, but is unaware of doing so. Some horses sink slowly in a slow motion way, and others go down with a crash. Again, there is no awareness that they are going down. Within a few minutes the brain centers that control the heart and lungs shut down. During this period, there may be some muscle twitching and slow leg movements, but the parts of the brain that perceive anxiety or pain are gone. During the whole procedure the horse has felt nothing except the prick of the needle. Veterinarians will generally stay until they have insured that the horse's heart has stopped beating.

For decades the traditional method for the euthanasia of horses was physical damage to the brain by way of a bullet. This is quick and painless, but is objectionable to many horse owners. There are rare instances when it becomes the only way. The last time I had to euthanize a horse with a gun was over ten years ago. The horse had a broken leg and was so full of fear and pain that he could not be restrained or approached with a needle.

There are some dos and don'ts concerning burial. I ask owners not to dig the hole before the horse is put down. Horses are afraid of deep holes. Lead horses near a hole, and they will naturally shy. I feel that euthanasia should be as easy on the horse as possible. The best plan is to dig the hole next to the animal *after* he or she has been put down. Another reason is the very real issue of human safety. Remember, the horse has lost consciousness before he drops. There is no way of predicting or controlling which way he will fall. Sometimes you have to move fast to get out of the way. That in itself is enough to think about. You don't need the added worry of falling into a hole while avoiding him landing on you. This has happened to me, and I'm not anxious to repeat the experience.

Lately there has been interest in composting dead animals. When properly done, the horse's body is totally decomposed within six months. There is a science to this, and to be effective it must be done correctly. There are composting facilities in the state that offer this service. There are also facilities in Maine and other New England states that will cremate horses.

When called to euthanize a horse, I often hear the comment, "This must be the hardest part of your job." Actually, it's not. I won't put horses down just for the convenience of the owner. It is always because, in my judgment, the horse really needs to be released, and I feel that this is the last, kind thing that can be done for an animal in trouble.

Don't worry about your ability to make a decision when it's time. I can assure you that when the time does come, the decision makes itself. The actual laying away is often the only solution to a problem that has become unbearable. It is nothing to dread ahead of time. Part of being a caring animal owner is the willingness to accept responsibility for an end-of-life decision. When in doubt, a good question to ask is, "Am I keeping this animal alive for his or her sake, or my own."

87

They Are What They Eat

$$\Omega$$

It was getting toward noon, and three cups of coffee that morning had me on the lookout for relief. The problem was that I heading south on the Maine Turnpike and the next exit was ten minutes away. There is a small rest stop just below Gray that I was happy to pull into. On my way out of the building, I walked by the Starbucks coffee counter and many snack racks. Trying to be efficient, I decided to grab some lunch there. The only "real food" was a personal size prepackaged "Chicago style" pizza. The clerk offered to heat one up in their small five-minute oven. I told her to go ahead and was soon sitting down with a drink and a pizza that had way, way more dough than cheese. Looking at it, I thought, "Do they really eat these things in Chicago?" My first bite told me that this had been a bad idea, but it was lunch time, so I wolfed it down anyway. I walked back to my truck feeling like I had swallowed a small, but heavy bowling ball. The afternoon was busy, and when I got back to my farm about 6:30 PM there was a trailer in the drive with the last horse of the day waiting to be seen. My wife quickly assessed the situation, and as I drove up the driveway to the barn, she headed out to The New Gloucester Village Market to get us a quick supper. She came back a half hour later with the one thing I did not want to see—a great big cheese pizza. I climbed into bed that night feeling like the Pillsbury dough boy.

We can get away with days like that occasionally, but doing that day after day will cause health problems. We tend to feed horses the same diet every day. If we don't feed them the right stuff, they will pay the price. Here are a few examples of how improperly feeding our equines can put them at risk.

There are two extreme body types in horses, one typified by the Shetland pony, and the other by the racing Thoroughbred. Shetlands are built like boilers, short and chunky with all body bones well covered. They do just fine in the most severe weather conditions without blankets. Thoroughbreds are built like radiators, lots of rib evident, and because they lose heat easily, don't do so well when the weather turns cold. As Thoroughbreds age, it's harder and harder for them to keep weight on, but those ponies just keep getting rounder. These two types have to be fed very differently. Thoroughbreds need lots of good quality roughage, and often need grain as well. Ponies do just fine on less leafy roughage and, for extras, maybe a handful or two of hay stretcher.

Ponies have been described as having a "thrifty gene." Their metabolism is incredibly efficient. Many Morgan horses are the same. The condition is exaggerated even more if they also have the condition called Equine Metabolic Syndrome (EMS). In terms of management, these "easy keepers" are best kept in dry paddocks far away from green grass. Some well-designed grazing muzzles will slow them down to the point where they might be able to graze, depending on how lush your grass is. Equines exhibiting signs of EMS should not be fed high carbohydrate grains or even treats like apples or carrots. Treats to an EMS animal is like putting a type 2 diabetes person on a diet that includes daily candy. Fortunately, all of the major grain companies are aware of the problem and can steer you to their low starch and carb feeds. If EMS animals are overfed, they develop harmful fat deposits in all the wrong places and are likely to experience the terribly painful foot condition of laminitis. Another metabolic disease is Cushing's. Horses with Cushing's also do best on low-carb feeding plans with the addition of daily medication.

Improper feed can also cause respiratory problems. Hay quality varies tremendously. You can feed hay that has some poor qualities such as less leaf and more stem, but no horse should ever be fed musty hay. When you open a bale and see a cloud of dust come up, you aren't looking at dirt, you are seeing thousands of airborne mold spores. Horses inhale those spores while they are eating and react to them with an acute allergic bronchitis. Keep feeding that musty hay and they will become "heavy," which is similar to COPD or emphysema in people. Mold spores have the same effect on horses' lungs as smoking does to ours. Horses with the condition can have their symptoms eased with medication, but there is no cure. All it takes is a few bales of bad hay, and you can cause a horse to become a lifetime respiratory cripple.

The draft breeds, and many Quarter Horses, are likely to develop a feed related muscle situation called Equine Polysaccharide Storage Myopathy, or EPSM. The Quarter Horse Association calls it PPSM. This is caused by a gene mutation that results in sugar in the diet (glucose) being stored as glycogen, which the horses can't use. Debilitating muscle stiffness and pain can follow. Just like the chunky ponies, these heavily muscled animals must be kept away from carbs. Their proper feeding involves substituting carbs with fat. Veterinarians in New England often recommend adding Vitamin E and selenium to their diet to help the stiff muscles. As you might know, out west there are areas where there is too much selenium, and supplementing it could be potentially harmful.

I titled this article, "They are what they eat" because if horses are fed too much or too little of the wrong things, they will become something other than what you want, and in fact do become a reflection of what they eat. In my opinion it is important to know the type of horse that you have in your barn and what feeding restrictions or supplements are recommended for each breed and individual. If you have questions about this, spend some time with your vet the next time he is in the barn. Have him assess your horse and possibly run lab tests to come to a diagnosis and diet plan. Most of these animals can be managed to live long useful lives.

88

Those Strange Sarcoids

───────────── ♘ ─────────────

Sarcoid is the most common cancer of horses. I suppose I should say on horses, because sarcoids are skin tumors. They can grow to be very large, but they don't spread to internal organs. Although common, I don't think I've ever been called out specifically just to look at one. That's because at first they usually don't look very impressive. As a result, owners tend to wait until their vet is on the farm looking at something else. Then it's usually, "As long as you're here, would you check out this skin bump?"

Sarcoids don't follow any of the usual rules for cancer, and as much as they have been studied, we really don't know exactly why they act as they do. They aren't like other cancers. First, they tend to occur in younger and not older horses as you would expect. Secondly, they appear in a wide variety of shapes. Most of the ones I see are what we call nodular, just a hairless bump on the skin. Initially they can be mistaken for a tick bite. Sometimes, instead of a smooth surface they are wart-like with fringy fingers. Others are totally flat and look like a piece of old bumpy leather pasted on the skin. Rapid growing ones may look just like a cauliflower, and can get every bit as big. Because of their size, these stick way out from the skin and bleed when they get bumped. Some grow on stalks. I have seen a few that are a crazy mixture of all these types. An internet check will bring up photos of types of sarcoids. Google "horse sarcoid images."

Sarcoids are often found where there has been a wound or trauma. For example, a horse that has had many IV's may develop a sarcoid on the skin over the jugular vein. Despite the skin damage that saddles can cause, I've never seen one on a horse's back.

When pathologists study sarcoids, they often find the DNA of the bovine (cattle) papilloma virus deep inside. It is thought that flies carry the virus from cows to horses. When I see a sarcoid and question the horse's owner, I am often told that the horse has had contact with cattle at some point.

The state of a horse's immune system when exposed must also be important, because horses that get sarcoids tend to get more. Their herd mates might never have one.

Veterinarians will back away if you start a conversation about doing a biopsy of anything that looks like a sarcoid. When cut into, they tend to start growing more aggressively. Even if it's a small one and you make wide incisions in order to get every cell, there is a pretty good chance of the sarcoid coming back bigger. So, as a treatment, surgical removal is usually not a good idea.

In general, sarcoids are not a great health risk, but if they are growing on areas of the body that are apt to get knocked about, it's best to get rid of them. There are many treatment options, which tells me that nothing works all the time. Some sarcoids disappear without any treatment at all. There are also medications which can be injected into sarcoids that will cause them to shrink and hopefully finally go away. The two most popular are Cisplatin and BCG. Typically, you have to inject them many times over a period of weeks. Sometimes the injections cause local inflammation and make the area painful.

I have had good luck using liquid nitrogen sprayed on the nodular types to kill the cells. Mostly this has worked with little recurrence. There are also some veterinary herbal preparations. The most popular is Xxtera. The active ingredient of this ointment is blood root, a flowering plant whose extract has been used for skin growths since colonial times. A small amount applied daily will cause smaller sarcoids to shrivel up, but it may leave an unsightly scar.

A few topical medicines made for people have been used on equine sarcoids. Examples are Aldara, 5-Fluorouracil, and Acyclovir. More are always being tried. Some work by affecting the immune system, others are antiviral. Intense local reactions may occur. These human preparations are usually quite expensive. Lasers have been used with some success. The literature reports that radiation therapy may be the most effective treatment, which means several costly trips to a university or major surgical center.

There are all kinds of sarcoid home remedies that have been tried by horse owners. One of the most interesting is the daily application of Crest toothpaste. You've got to wonder how anyone came up with the idea. Some feel that the fluoride in the toothpaste is what shrinks the sarcoid. An online report claims that fluoride mouthwash sprayed on a troublesome sarcoid in the groin made it disappear. That one shows colored photos which show the tumor shrinking. Would it have gone by itself? Perhaps. Certainly it would be worth a try and couldn't hurt.

Equine veterinarians have become pretty adept at identifying sarcoids by their appearance. It's never an emergency, but the next time your vet is out, ask if that newest bump might be a sarcoid. Generally, sarcoids tend to be slow growing and not a cause for alarm.

89

Thoughts on Strangles

⎋

As I write this article, the racetrack at Saratoga, NY, has shut down their facility for two weeks because of an outbreak of the upper respiratory disease we call strangles. What we know about strangles today is pretty much what has been known for decades. Strangles is caused by the bacteria, *Streptococcus equi*, that has adapted itself specifically to the horse. People and other animals are not affected by it.

Think about having the absolute worst head cold and sore throat you've ever had, with a fever reaching 106 degrees F. Now imagine that your lymph nodes are five times normal size, and you can get some idea of how miserable horses are with this disease. It's hard for them to swallow, and even hard for them to breathe. Horses with acute full-blown strangles are in a lot of pain. The lymph nodes between the lower jaws and around the throat latch get so big that they may rupture, oozing a thick yellow discharge. Although penicillin is effective against the bacteria, most veterinarians (me included), tend not to use the antibiotic once a horse has the disease because the abscesses are so thick-walled that the drug usually doesn't have an effect. One belief is that the antibiotic treatment can drive the infection to other parts of the body. Strangles is mostly an upper respiratory disease. When it goes to other parts of the body, it is called bastard strangles which can be even more of a problem.

I've seen a number of strangles outbreaks in Maine and would like to share my personal observations about the disease in this state. The literature reports that the biggest outbreaks of the disease are among weanlings and yearlings. Taking the nation as a whole, that is true. That is the most susceptible age group, and outbreaks are common on farms that raise a crop of youngsters for sale each year. After six months the weanlings no longer carry the maternal antibodies from their moms and so are apt to contract this highly contagious disease. This is especially true on farms where the barns are crowded, and the ventilation is poor. There are areas of the country where the farms anticipate that each new crop of youngsters will get the bug.

Since we do not have a lot of farms in Maine raising big numbers of foals, almost all of our outbreaks tend to happen in barns when a horse is brought in from a sale or auction barn. For this reason it is important to isolate any new horse from those sources, and especially those who are stressed by a long (several hours to several days) truck ride. The literature varies on the time that a new horse should be kept apart, but I like to see at least two weeks in a separate barn or shed with no contact with other horses. If the horse goes off feed, I recommend taking the temperature twice a day and watching for the telltale swellings. The bacteria are easily carried from horse to horse on hands and clothing. My suggestion is to feed and take care of the isolated horse after everyone else. Obviously there can be no shared buckets or equipment. Even with all these precautions, there is still some risk taking in a horse from a sale barn. There are asymptomatic horses that carry the bacteria in the guttural pouches deep inside the head and can be sources of infection for long periods of time.

Strangles is rarely fatal, and most horses recover completely. When it does hit, it often means that an active barn will be shut down for two to three months. This means no horses in, and no horses out. My experience with the disease is that it doesn't sweep through and infect all the horses within a short time period. A slow march through the barn is more typical. There will be one sick horse, and then a few days or even a week later, another, and so on. Typically, out of ten horses two or three will get very sick, four or five others just run a fever or have a cough, and two or three will not be affected at all. If you do have it on your place, don't visit other barns without a complete change of clothes and a shower. You probably wouldn't be welcome even taking those precautions. When I know I'm going to an active strangles barn, I make it the day's last stop, and all the clothing from that day goes into the wash, and my footwear gets totally disinfected.

Strangles in a boarding barn often results in a highly charged emotional atmosphere for owner and boarders. It pays to have as many barn meetings as necessary with all the horse owners and the barn veterinarian to discuss developments as they occur. Everyone should be allowed to express his or her concerns. Some of the issues that always arise are: whose fault this was, who should be moved and where, who can use common facilities such as the wash rack or the indoor, what is the disinfection protocol, and whether it is or isn't too late to vaccinate a horse that hasn't been exposed.

There are two types of vaccinations: one is a killed type that is injected intramuscularly, and the other is a modified live vaccine that is squirted up the nose. Every veterinarian has his or her own preference. The vaccines don't always completely protect against the disease, but the vaccinated horses usually have an easier time. Personally I tend to vaccinate those horses at most risk. For me that means the relatively young horses and those that are going to be traveling, particularly if they will be stabled at a facility overnight. When a horse has had the disease, his immunity lasts for years, so I, and many other vets, do not recommend revaccinating these horses. On occasion doing so may result in an allergic reaction called Purpura, which is really scary and can be fatal. You need to rely on your veterinarian's advice as to which horses to vaccinate, and with which type of vaccine. It would be a mistake not to rely on your veterinarian when dealing with an outbreak, as each is different and needs to be handled with his or her expertise.

90

Three Barriers

(preventing gorging)

———————— ♘ ————————

Every year I can count on a half dozen calls from clients whose horses have found the grain supply when no one was in the barn. You may come home from a dinner out and find your horse in the grain room, having his *own* dinner out. You surprise your horse, which until your arrival had his head deep in a bag of sweet feed. You yell, and it's funny how he knows he's done something wrong and scrambles back to his stall.

Even worse is the "morning" discovery. You find that one of the horses has gotten out of its stall. Because he enjoys company, he has let a couple of his friends out as well so they could all have an extra meal together.

Sometimes they make such a mess it's impossible to tell how much grain is missing. That raises two big questions: how much *did* he eat, and is he going to get sick. If a horse eats somewhere between two and twenty times what he should be getting, you can be sure that he will, at the very least, have a good belly ache. Most grain is carbohydrate rich and too much can cause laminitis, which may lead to founder, a seriously crippling problem of the feet.

If you discover that one of your horses has gotten that extra meal, try to remember how much grain was there before the incident. Then, if you can, try to determine *when* the horse got into the grain. Those are two questions that your vet will ask you when you call. Sometimes mineral oil by stomach tube and injectables given in time will prevent complete absorption of the grain excess and its effects.

You can prevent this from happening at all by using what I call the three-barrier system to prevent unwanted equine visitors to the grain room.

The first barrier is the horse's own stall door. Make sure that the door is properly closed before you leave. Most barn door hardware has an extra hole to slip a snap through to foil the horse that delights in opening doors. Some "Houdini" horses will spend hours trying to get the door open. Take that extra few seconds to insure that they can't.

The second barrier is the door to the grain room. All of the same precautions apply.

If someone has been sloppy about securing doors or if your horse is really determined and *does* gain access to the grain room, I would make sure that there is a third barrier. Put your unopened bags of grain into an old chest-type freezer or some large chest that also has a snap or an arrangement that a horse can't figure out. If your open grain is in a five-gallon bucket, make sure that the lid can be screwed on so that if tipped over and rolled, it won't open. Never, ever leave open *or* unopened bags in a grain or tack room without that third barrier of protection.

Do your horses a favor. As you are leaving the barn each time, ask yourself, "Are my three barriers up?" and run through them mentally. Then leave with peace of mind.

I have treated many horses for grain overload. I have never done so at a farm that religiously practices the three-barrier method. It's just a part of being a responsible horse owner.

91

Three Roads
(different treatments)

U

Every time I am out west, I am surprised by the roads. They go ruler straight for miles! They're nothing like our roads in northern New England. We have all these hills, lakes, streams, huge granite boulders, and other things in the way of road builders. Any road around here, running straight for a mile, is rare. So, when I plan a drive to the next farm, I usually have three choices as to how to get there. Two are pretty much even as far as travel time, and then there is the very roundabout way, which is often more scenic and may have the advantage of going by a good donut shop.

Healthcare choices today are a little bit like New England roads. As owners of animals, we have options to choose from in arranging for their health care. The vet who makes a call to your farm is probably mostly mainline. He or she graduated after eight years of college and practices medicine by the book. They keep up with current trends, but tend to walk a narrow road to keep within the currently accepted "standard of practice." Even so, more and more veterinarians are exploring other options such as acupuncture, chiropractic, and laser therapy. Of course, veterinarians aren't the only ones working on horses in the healing arts. Horse owners often consult with and use the services of communicators, massage therapists, Reiki practitioners, aroma therapists, and many others. The horse owner's thinking seems to be, "Whatever works."

While driving on unfamiliar roads in our part of the world, it's easy to get into trouble. It is becoming common practice to use a GPS device rather than consulting a map. I use my GPS on occasion, and more than once have found myself in the middle of a very sketchy road with no way to turn around. It is also possible to go down some wrong roads in making health choices.

I am not saying that any or all alternative therapies are wrong, but I am saying that you need to use some thought in their selection. Here's an example. Last fall I was asked to see a horse that had severe hind-leg lameness for two weeks. Because I have a reputation for having a relatively open mind about other therapies, the owner confided that when the horse came up lame, she first hired a communicator to check in with the horse. As a result of that conversation, she had a massage therapist out. The therapist found several knotted muscle groups in the hind end. Two treatments later the horse had not improved, and our practice was called. I was able to go out the next day. My lameness exam revealed an increased digital pulse going to the foot of that lame leg. With my hoof testers and thermograph, I was able to locate a hot and very sore spot. My hoof knife found and released an abscess. By the next morning the horse was sound. Yes, there were muscle knots in the hind end, but they were the result of the horse's abnormal stance trying to relieve some of the pain he had been going through for two weeks. The owner was out $150 before I ever got there.

I am not saying that veterinarians have all the answers. I am also not making a stand that alternative or complementary therapy is not valid or effective. I myself go to an outstanding chiropractor and an excellent massage therapist once a month. Life would be a little harder without their services. I also recognize that it sometimes takes more than one discipline to alleviate health problems in horses. I have come to appreciate the competence of many non-veterinary therapists who work on horses and often send them referrals.

What I am saying is that as a horse owner, you owe it to your animal to take some well-traveled and safe roads before exploring others avenues when your horse is acutely lame or sick. In general, because of their years of training and experience, veterinarians can usually pinpoint issues fairly quickly. Then, with the help of specific blood tests, nerve blocks, digital ultrasound and X-rays and other great tools, they can usually be confident as to what and where the problem is. My suggestion is that if you have a lame or sick horse, a call to an equine vet is probably the first one that should be made.

92

Tradition

We have one of those big coffee-table art books at home. Its colored pages show vases, statues, and pictures through the ages. If you are at all interested in horses, you immediately see that they have been a favorite subject of artists for thousands of years. This isn't too surprising, since the horse has played such an important part in man's history. What *is* striking to me is how the horses looked, were tacked up, and handled through the centuries.

My favorite is a photograph of, what many consider, the finest equestrian statue ever cast. It is "Colleoni" by the sculptor Verrocchio and was standing in Venice, Italy, before Columbus discovered America. It depicts an imposing military commander on his incredible horse ready to leap into battle. The rider makes the Marlboro man look like a sissy out for a Sunday ride. Someday I'd like to see it for real, but googling the sculptor and the statue will give you some appreciation of how timeless solid conformation is.

Through this study of horses in art, we learn that superior horsemanship didn't start just a few years ago. We know by records, that horses have been appreciated and used by our ancestors as far back as cave drawings can take us. Breeds have come and gone, depending on fashion and use, but the really good blood from thousands of years of selection is seen in our animals of today.

We are at the receiving end of this long tradition of the partnership of mankind and horse. You are the present holder of a body of information that has come the distance. Your horse knowledge has, for the most part, been passed down orally. You didn't learn how to muck out a stall from a book. No manual told you how to gently place a bit in a horse's mouth or how to pick up a foot. Someone showed you and me, and someone showed the one who taught us. Every once in a while there is a brand new idea. If it's good, it survives. For example, within the past 20 years round-pen training has gone from an oddity to a well-established training technique that will probably last. If something new is just flashy, it dies, just like all styles do. Think of all the new horse shoes that hit the market each year, most of which don't last.

Our horse knowledge has been passed down orally in every language known to man. Some of those languages have died out, but good horsemanship stands the test of time. There are many good books, lots of articles, and a wealth of information on the web. These sources are helpful to both experienced and new horse owners. However, if all the written material were burned tomorrow, it wouldn't matter much. The knowledge would pass down just as it always has. However, there are also some disadvantages to oral tradition. Misinformation is also passed down. Some old wives tales will never die because they seem to make sense.

I used to work on Maine's Standardbred racetracks. One of the things that always bothered me was that many trainers in this sport liked their horses with long toes and low heels. I'm talking about significantly long toes and very dropped heels. When I would ask why they would have their horses trimmed and shod this way, I got one of two responses. "A long toe makes the horse's stride longer," or "That's the way we've always done it (tradition)."

The longer stride could be argued, but the opposing argument is that a horse can't push off properly with low heels. I used to argue that shoeing this way causes misalignment of the pastern bones, and eventual lameness in the upper joints. I would ask the trainers how their legs would feel if they tried to run in long-toed clown shoes with the heels right on the ground. "Don't know, but this is how my dad always had his horses shod." I finally learned that arguing with tradition is an uphill fight, and most of the time you can't win.

So, appreciate those who have gone before, both your ancestors and their horses, and be willing to part with tradition when good common sense tells you to.

93

Trapped

(horses imprisoned)

⚘

We see it in our practice quite often. A horse gets a leg trapped and struggles for release. He may get out on his own or, if lucky, may be found soon and released. If he pulls and jerks long enough, the damage that is done may be irreparable, and the horse will have to be put down. Let's examine what happens in these cases and how to prevent this tragedy happening to one of your animals.

First, we have to remind ourselves that the horse is a prey animal. For thousands of years, like other herbivores, they have been the hunted. Locked deep in their hardwiring is a fear of being trapped. Being trapped is actually quite rare in the wild. Conceivably, a leg might slip down between two heavy stones, or the whole horse might get caught in quicksand or the muck of a deep marsh. They will struggle for release, and if they can't get out will die there.

Entrapment is much more common for the domestic horse because of our own construction efforts to "keep them safe." You probably know of at least one horse that has gotten all wound up and hopelessly caught in fencing.

I'll never forget two that reared up in their stalls and in striking out, punched a foot between iron bars. In one case it was the bars on a door, and in the other the bars on a stall door window. Both of these horses ended up literally hanging by one leg because the foot is wider than the pastern. Both made enough racket to alert the stable owners. The horse caught in the window bars was released by the town of Gray fire department. The bars were so strong, they couldn't pry them apart and had to spread the bars with their jaws of life. This is the hydraulic apparatus used to pry auto wrecks apart to release those inside. The horse caught in the bars of the door had to be put under anesthesia for 30 minutes so that the door could be removed, and the bars spread with two long iron pry bars. These two horses were OK because they were found in time. Some aren't so lucky.

Just this winter I was called to come help release a horse that was caught in one of those big cattle-pipe hay feeders. The feeder was round, probably ten feet in diameter. The successive storms we had this winter kept piling snow deeper and deeper around it. Horse traffic around the feeder turned the snow into ice. A young stud slipped and got his leg caught between the feeder and the ice. When the family's kids found the horse, no one was sure how long he had been lying there. By the time I arrived, the horse had been freed by the owner's husband who used a Sawzall to cut the pipe of the feeder. I checked the horse's legs, and all I could see was just some skin scrapes on the leg. He actually walked and trotted sound. However, within a week he went lame, and we finally had to put him down because all of the tissue around the area that was trapped had started to slough away. He probably struggled quite a bit when he was first trapped and did a huge amount of damage to the soft tissues of the leg.

The most common way that I see horses get trapped is by getting a leg caught under a stall door. Whether you have a sliding or a swinging stall door, you should always have a latch a few inches up from the floor. Horses that go down from colic and kick out a hind leg that is near the door can pop that leg under the door for a split second, and then the door springs back, trapping them. Get them out quick enough, and they are usually OK. If they are caught for any length of time, the damage that is done to the leg when they struggle may not be fixable. It does take an extra few seconds to secure a bottom latch as well as regular one, but it might save a life some day.

I'm remembering another horse that in winter slid off of an icy ramp that ran from the barn down to the ground. One of the legs got caught under the ramp and fractured when the animal struggled to get up.

Try to make your place as safe as you can. Bars should be placed so that a horse kicking out can't separate them enough to get his foot caught. I've also seen a couple of jaw fractures from young horses that put their head sideways and stick the jaw through the bars. When they turn their head straight up and down, they get caught and usually panic. It probably doesn't need saying, but barbed wire and horses don't ever mix. It's bad enough for a horse to be wrestling with a wire fence wound around him, and pretty horrible when it's barbed.

Because they are a preyed-on animal, when trapped they can do lots of damage in their struggle to get free. Minimize those situations by checking around your place and thinking: "If I were a horse. . . "

94

Tug

(one thing affects everything)

U

If you have ever enjoyed one of our national parks, you can legitimately thank John Muir, at least in part, for its existence. Muir was born in Scotland in 1838. When he came to America, he discovered our magnificent wild areas and became their champion. He has been called the founder of the environmental movement and started the Sierra Club. His influence as a speaker and writer in saving our wild areas from development is profound.

Muir's quotes are all worth reading and thinking about. My favorite is: *"When one tugs on a single thing in nature, he finds it attached to the rest of the world."*

Have you ever noticed what happens when a row of pine trees next to a road gets cut down to widen the road's shoulder? Within a few years the pines behind the missing ones start to lean and will eventually fall over. Each pine depends on the interlocking root system of its neighbors. When enough are lost, the remaining trees cannot stand. The tug is cutting down several dozen trees that were literally attached to others, and the rest of the woods are affected.

The quote holds true for all living things. A good part of my day is usually spent doing chiropractic work on horses. I am often asked how a horse's pelvis, withers, or any other part could have gotten out of alignment. To answer the question, I will often use that quote of Muir's. "Tug on a single thing. . ."

Let's say that your left stirrup is a couple of inches lower than the right. Can you see how this would cause your horse to rotate his trunk to the right to try to stay straight? Over time, if the situation is not corrected, the muscles attached to the spine on the right side, tugging

286

on the spinal vertebrae, will pull them out of alignment. This action also affects the vertebrae above and below that area. Eventually the forces and counter forces influence every part of the body, and if you are lucky only the gait will be affected.

If you wait too long to get your horse trimmed or reshod, the usual result is long toes and low heels. This puts a strain on the ligaments around the lower joints because the bones are out of position. At the same time, the tendons that attach to the lower legs are affected. This results is muscle imbalance, and soon the horse becomes sore all over. Long toes are the tug, and the eventual result is a horse too lame to ride.

The other day I noticed that a client's horse was carrying way too much weight and getting a cresty neck. There were three tugs pulling on this horse. The first was that she is a Morgan. Morgans are well known as easy keepers. The second tug was a diet high in carbohydrates. If you haven't already guessed, the third was the fact that the animal hadn't been exercised in weeks. Correcting her diet and getting those feet moving may keep her from contracting laminitis, a disease of the feet. There doesn't seem to be an obvious connection between diet, exercise, and laminitis, but thousands of affected horses tell us it's true. "Tug on a single thing. . ."

My point is to think about the eventual effect of everything likely to tug on your animal. The consequences of lazy or ignorant horsemanship can be expensive and sometimes disastrous.

95

Two for One

(surprise pregnancies)

Mother and daughter run the farm together. They have had horses for years and know what they are doing. This April I was asked to do chiropractic work on two of their horses. I did that, and then they said, "Hey, while you are here. . ." It turns out that they had bought a mare for a good price just after Christmas. The complaint was that she wasn't doing as well as they had hoped under their care. She was a bit potbellied, and they wondered if she might have worms. They had already mucked out her stall before I arrived, so there was no manure to take back and analyze. I asked permission to get some manure from her rectum. I slipped on a sleeve and slathered lube on it. There was some fecal material right in the rectum. She was a nice mare to work on, and something told me to just go a little further in and see how things were internally. I was surprised to find a close to term fetus, alive as could be. The owners were more surprised than I, because the mare had been in heat a few times since the start of the year. It turned out that the previous owner had been having employee issues on her farm, and that at least one of her studs had gotten in with this mare in June.

Any equine veterinarian will tell you that these surprises do happen. My first experience with this was a racing Standardbred mare. She had been in a claiming race in the fall, and her new owner had given her every chance to prove herself. As the spring season went on, her times got slower and slower. He didn't cull her from his racing string because there was just something about this mare that he liked. One morning in the spring, he called me over to his barn and said that he found out why she had been racing so poorly. I asked him why, and he said, "Just stop over at the barn before you leave the track." I did, and he motioned me over to the mare's stall. As we looked over the split door, I saw her nursing her new colt! She had actually raced the night before! She hadn't finished well, but amazingly, she was still trying. There was no history of her being bred, and again, since she had been showing heats all spring, neither he nor I suspected that she might be pregnant. Pregnancies can be pretty well concealed in stocky mares, and while it's not common, some mares will cycle through their pregnancies.

Another surprise foaling I remember was over 20 years ago, and cross my heart, this is a true story. The owner, whose place I had never been on, called to say that she had a new foal to check out. She added that she had always owned the mare and knew for certain that she had never been bred. I asked her if there might be a neighbor with a stallion who was adept at jumping fences, and she said there were no stallions in the neighborhood. Three days later I stopped at her farm and saw a very obvious stallion in the stall next to the mare. I said, "Could this be the father?" She replied that the two were sometimes turned out together, but he certainly couldn't be the father. I asked why, and she replied, "Don't be silly, Doctor, that's her brother!"

There are lessons to be learned from these three stories. Anytime you take possession of a mare, be suspicious that she might be bred. Ask the owners how long *they* have had the mare. If they have had her less than 11 months, it could be that she was bred before they got her. When you buy a horse, you often don't get the story that that goes with them. This seems to be common in "rescues." Some mares come from wild or poorly managed herds where everyone runs together, and, of course, those mares are more apt to be pregnant than not.

Just when you think that you have things figured out by counting elapsed months on your fingers, be careful. The books will tell you that mares cycle from early spring until fall. This is not always true. I knew of one mare that would only settle in early November. That meant that she would foal in October, and she did it every year, no matter what we did to make her "normal."

If you are having a pre-purchase exam done before buying a horse—always a good idea—ask to have a pregnancy check done unless you don't care if you are buying into a "two for one deal." Even if the news is surprising, it would be nice to know about when the package will arrive.

96

Ugly Pogo

(EPM)

U

For many years (decades) there was a daily newspaper cartoon about Pogo, an opossum, (sometimes just called possum) that lived in the Okefenokee Swamp. He hung out a lot with an alligator named Albert and an owl whose name I forget. Pogo the opossum was cute and clever. One of his famous quotes was "We have met the enemy, and he is us." I don't know about clever, but in real life opossums aren't cute. They don't look anything like Pogo. The fact is, they are probably one of the ugliest animals you'll ever meet.

The first one I saw was a roadkill, just two miles from my house about six years ago. A few months later, I met one in our barn. I walked in to do night check, and there he was, as big as a cat, and a bit scary. Any other wild animal would have scurried away. Opossums tend to stand their ground. This one opened his mouth and hissed at me. Their open mouths are quite impressive, holding 50 teeth, more than any other animal in North America. I'm sure that he was visiting my barn to help clean up the food that our barn cats had left.

Opossums have quite an appetite. They are true omnivores, eating anything and everything: insects, small rodents, anyone's leftovers, and all varieties of roadkill. They often become roadkill themselves while eating out. They have very coarse, scraggly hair. Someone said, "Every day is a bad hair day for an opossum." The hair doesn't insulate well and helps to explain their appetite. They have to eat plenty to keep warm.

The opossum tail is long and hairless. They are excellent climbers and nest in hollow trees and burrows in the woods. The myth that they hang from their tails is not true. What *is* true is that they really do "play possum" when badly threatened. Their nervous system goes into "play-dead mode," flops them over, and to the rest of the world they look gone, to the point that their eyes glaze over. I understand that you can't even pick up a heartbeat—and I'm not going to try. Predators lose interest.

They are North America's only marsupial. The very tiny young are born after just 12 days of pregnancy, and their first journey is to Mom's pouch where they spend a couple of months nursing and then work their way up to her back where they are carried for another month or two.

Why do we care about this strange creature? They carry a one-cell parasite called *sarcocystis neurona*. They pick this up from eating dead birds, skunks, raccoons, and even cats. The parasite is found in the muscles of these animals. It ends up in the opossum's intestines. Apparently this doesn't bother the opossum, but when the parasite matures, an immature form passes out with the fecal material. This is then picked up by small animals and birds, and the cycle continues.

If a grazing *horse* picks up the parasite it goes to the brain and or spinal cord and not the muscles. It is the cause of the disease EPM (Equine Protozoal Encephalomyelitis). This is a debilitating neurologic disease that can cause a variety of symptoms depending on where it ends up in the nervous tissue.

EPM is relatively rare in Maine. Opossums used to be rare as well. Will the influx of opossums mean a higher incidence of EPM? For sure. Here is what you can do to help discourage them. Keep your horse feed in tightly covered bins. Put out cat and dog food in amounts that will be cleaned up and not left around, especially at night when Pogo comes around looking for snacks.

97

Up Through the Nose

(choke)

U

My phone rang at 10:30 PM that winter night. In a vet's house when the phone rings after 9, you can bet it's not a social call. I had been Julie's vet over 15 years, but I didn't recognize her voice right off. She was panicked.

"Dr J! You know I've had horses forever, but I've got something here I've never seen before. I think you need to get right out here. It's Pete, my old gelding. He was OK at feeding time tonight. He gobbled down his grain real fast like always and seemed fine. But I just got back from barn night check, and I think he's dying."

Through the years I have found that if I deliberately talk slowly when I have an excited caller, the panic at the other end seems to lessen, at least somewhat. I tried it.

"Julie, what is Pete doing? Is he down?"

Slightly slower: "No, no he's not down, but he's sure not right."

"Julie, tell me what you are seeing."

The pitch of her voice started to rise again. "You are going to think I'm crazy, but I think his brains are coming out of his nose!"

At this point it was hard for me to keep to my slow pace as Julie's excitement was starting to affect me. I forced myself to speak calmly, "Did I hear you right? His brains? Through his nose?"

The words spilled out: "Oh Doc, it's awful, it's all whitish green and foamy. He gurgles in his throat, his neck is all tight, and he keeps going in circles in his stall."

That was the tipoff for me, and I realized what was probably happening.

"Julie, I think I know what's going on and can probably help.

This is what I need you to do. Get all the hay out of his stall and take the water pail out. I'll be there within the hour. Chances are we can fix this."

I pulled into Julie's barnyard about 45 minutes later. Pete's stall was the first on the right, and Julie was in there with him, rubbing his neck. He was one uncomfortable horse. His eyes were wide open, and he kept flexing his very tight neck. Sure enough, greenish white foam was bubbling out of both nostrils.

"Julie, it looks like he's choked."

"Oh, is that what's going on? I've never had that happen. That means he's got some food stuck partway down his throat, right?"

"Exactly. What you see coming out of his nose is a mixture of saliva and some feed. I remember that you said he gobbled his grain. Did you happen to have any beet pulp mixed in with it?"

"Yes, how did you know that? I like the beet pulp because it's low in sugar."

"That's right, all the sugar has been extracted out of the beets, and what is left is a good feed, but the process makes it very dry. That's why I recommend soaking it for several hours. Two parts water to one part beet pulp is about right. If it's not served wet, it can get stuck on the way to the stomach."

"I haven't soaked it because I'm feeding a pelleted beet pulp that you aren't supposed to have to soak."

"I've heard that too, but in the last couple of years we have had it cause some chokes. There is also a newer form of beet pulp which is shredded and sometimes mixed with soy. It is probably less dangerous, but in any form I recommend the soaking."

As we talked I drew up some IV tranquilizer for Pete so we could try to move the mass in his neck. After his head dropped, I passed a stomach tube through his nose and down his throat. I hit the obstruction about halfway down his neck. With some warm water pumped in and gentle pushing, the mass passed down into the stomach.

Pete was an old timer. They seem more prone to choke, perhaps because they don't drink as much as they should. In our practice we see many more cases in the winter, probably because of the partial dehydration, but also because summer grass has so much more moisture than dry hay.

Pete had three things going against him: it was winter, he tends to bolt his grain, and he was eating beet pulp. Unfortunately we can't do much about winter other than warm the water which does encourage drinking. Adding oral electrolytes also gets horses drinking more. If you feed beet pulp or other dry food, make it a rule to soak. If you have a grain gobbler, a dozen golf ball size rocks in the grain dish will slow him down some. This does make for noisy feed times. A common practice on the race track is to feed hay first to take the appetite off a bit so that horses don't dive into their grain with quite as much gusto.

When food gets stuck in the esophagus on the way to the stomach, it causes a buildup of saliva on top of the mass. Once a bolus of food is caught, the saliva and any food that a horse eats after he is choked will back up in the throat and finally start running out the nose. It can't come out of the mouth because of the horse's long soft palate. It tends to foam because as the horse breaths his wind cutting through the saliva produces bubbles, and yes, sometimes it really does look like brains coming out of the nose.

Most chokes clear without intervention. Saliva may soften the food bolus, and the muscles of the esophagus can then push it along. If the mass doesn't move, the situation has the potential of becoming more serious. Saliva continues to be produced, and the horse keeps swallowing. As quarts of the slippery fluid back up to the top to the throat, the whole mess starts to come up and out through the nose, especially when the head is lowered. The potential danger is that some of the backed up fluids may spill over into the trachea and down into the lungs, potentially causing inhalation pneumonia.

It's important to keep a choked horse from eating or drinking. More food and water just makes the condition worse. As a first aid measure, I will sometimes tell owners to give a couple of raw egg whites to a choked horse in the hopes that their slipperiness will lubricate the stuck food and help it to pass. A relatively new drug, Buscopan, relaxes smooth muscle and has proved helpful in treating choke. Even so, some horses that have been choked for several hours may be difficult to relieve. Banamine is often given to relieve the inflammation, and antibiotics are commonly given in case some of the backed up feed gets into the windpipe. Surgery may be considered as a last resort.

Choke is uncomfortable. If you have ever made the mistake

of swallowing too big a bite of food and having it catch momentarily on the way down, you can appreciate a horse's distress, particularly if the condition goes on for hours. Call your vet early on if your horse is choked. The advice may be to wait a bit, as most chokes do clear spontaneously, but if the situation persists your vet will want to take action.

98

Upside Down!

(on being cast)

♘

You may have had horses all your life, and it's possible that you've never experienced an upside down horse. It might also be that you own a horse that gets cast on a regular basis. "Cast" in the equine world refers to a horse that is down and can't get back up because of the position he or she is in. The horse is usually up against a wall, sometimes truly upside down, with all four legs sticking straight up into the air. Others will be found on one side with all four legs tucked in and their hooves against the wall. They get in these crazy positions and aren't able to gather everything together to get up. It takes a certain amount of momentum for a horse to rise, and this gets difficult when he is on his back or jammed next to a wall or another obstacle. Horses can and do get cast next to fences, round-pen panels, feeders, or any immovable objects. Our first clue that a horse is cast in the barn is usually the loud banging of feet against a stall wall.

Years ago I knew a mare named Daisy who would get cast at pasture with no wall or object in sight. She preferred to lie down in gullies. I think she liked the depressions in the earth that must have been like a giant cradle for her. After a nap in the sun she would try to get up and end up with her legs waving in the air, like an upside down beetle. This happened so regularly that if her owner didn't see her grazing as she looked out from her kitchen window, she'd head out to the rescue. Through trial and error, she knew just how to slide ropes over Daisy's legs. When the mare made an attempt, her owner pulled on the ropes and flopped Daisy onto her side. From there Daisy would jump to her feet and start eating grass. As the mare got older and a little arthritic, getting up became more of a problem, and she had to be fenced off from her favorite pasture depressions.

Colicky horses are apt to lie down and roll to find a comfortable position, and may get cast in the process, but in my experience, most cast horses don't start with a belly ache.

Finding your horse cast can be unnerving. Every so often I get a midnight call asking me to come out and tranquilize their cast horse. This is really not necessary. Cast horses will lie still for a while and then go through some all-out efforts to get up. As they struggle, they scrape and bang their feet against the stall wall. It sounds like someone trying to knock the barn down with a sledge hammer. So, while it's scary, it is not a medical emergency.

If you keep your cool, you can straighten things out yourself with the help of a couple of friends. If the horse is on its side with legs all jammed up against a wall, the safe way of getting him untangled is to spin his head end away from the wall. Approach the horse from the horse's back. *Never* get next to the wall near those active legs. Position your team along the length of the mane, and have everyone grab two good handfuls. Then all pull together in a coordinated effort straight back. This will rotate or spin the front end away from the wall. Now the down animal has enough room to get up by himself. This spinning is most easily done in a stall with a smooth floor. It's hard to do on dirt.

If your horse is against the wall and truly upside down, the technique is different. The goal here is to get the animal back on its side, with the legs in the middle of the stall instead of against the wall. Carefully slide a rope over the front and hind legs that are next to the wall. Ideally the loop should be just under the hoof, around each pastern. It is best not to tie a knot. Just make one turn around the pastern so that the ropes will drop off once the horse is right side up. Using ropes gives you good leverage and keeps you out of harm's way. This is a three-person project. One for each foot, front and rear, and one to cushion the head as it comes over. The two on the feet pull steadily towards the middle of the stall to flop the horse onto its side, away from the wall. When the legs come over, the body and then the head have to follow. All hands should be ready to move out of the way quickly as the horse comes over. This procedure should be done quietly, with the person at the head reassuring the horse the entire time. Once the horse is on its side, everyone should leave the stall and give the horse a chance to rest for a few minutes. Usually he will soon get up by himself.

Some horse owners report that banking the bedding in the stall very heavily (three or four-feet out, and at least two-feet high) against the walls will keep their animal from getting cast. You can also attach anti-cast strips to the stall walls. This can be anything from a simple 2 x 4 to the commercially available hard rubber strips designed for this purpose. Screw the strips or the wood into the wall at about the same height as a chair rail in a house. This gives the horse something to dig into with his feet and helps to get him away from the wall.

A prevention that has worked for some is an anti-cast roller. It looks something like a vaulting rig, and it goes around the horse's wither area and cinches up like a saddle. There are big iron rings on the top which make it impossible for a horse to go all the way up on its back. The problem I see with them is that you never know when a horse is going to get cast, so as a true preventive, it would have to be worn all the time. Unless you have a horse that repeatedly casts himself, there would be no point in making this investment.

It's probably not a bad idea to have two- 12 foot ¾ inch diameter (or more) soft cotton ropes in the barn ready to use for a cast horse. Having one for each leg works best. Lunge lines and lead shanks can be used, but they can be hard on your hands and on the horse's legs when you are trying to flip him over.

Getting cast shouldn't be a cause for panic. It's just another interesting thing about horses and the situations they can get into. Having a plan and keeping a cool head, and you (with some help) will be able to correct the situation.

99

Veterinary Medicine as a Career

———————— U ————————

S everal times a year every veterinarian I know is approached by a client who says, "My daughter/son is incredible with animals and wants to be a vet. What do you think?" Looking back on my long career, I have no regrets, and most of the time I'm still excited about starting my day. However, the road to becoming a vet is long and expensive and if you, or a relative, are thinking about it, there are some things you need to know.

When I ask teenagers why they think they want to be a veterinarian, the answer is usually, "I love animals!" This is a good start, but just as important is an ability to get along with people. Every animal that needs a veterinarian's attention comes with an owner at the end of that leash or lead shank. Do you remember how you felt when you last had a sick or lame horse? Owners in this situation are upset, and as their vet, you must have concern for them and an understanding about how they feel. In other words, it takes more than a love of animals and a lot of college to become accepted as a veterinarian. You must sincerely like people and want to help *them* as much as their animals.

The education is not quick or easy, and the competition to get in school is stiff. Veterinary schools today require at least three years of education in a good college before applying. Actually, most students are finishing up their bachelor's degree before they apply to vet school. Those years of undergraduate work include about ten science courses. The chemistry courses alone take five or six semesters. Usually two math courses, a year of physics, and two English courses are also necessary. Vet schools like well-rounded individuals, so it's a plus to take a foreign language and other general education courses. Letters of recommendation and an acceptable grade on the national Graduate Record Exam is usually required as well.

Veterinary college itself is a full four-year program. Whether your primary interest is dogs, cattle, horses, or zoo animals, everyone in vet school has to sit through all the same courses. There is some room for specialization while in school, but it is mostly on your own time, and as you are in class 30 to 40 hours a week, there isn't much free time. Each year every course must be passed before you can move on. There is no such thing as failing a course. In medicine, knowledge builds from one course to the next.

There are 30 regional vet schools in the U.S. Each must continually meet all the requirements of an accreditation committee. Some schools have strengths in specific areas because of their location. For example, if you are interested in pigs as a career, a Midwestern school might be your first choice. In general, however, schools will give first preference to students from their area.

Adding the undergraduate and graduate (vet school) years comes to a commitment of eight years of college. It's not all a grind, a lot of it is exciting and fun, but it does cost lots of money. In 2014 the average debt for graduating seniors was $135,000. Some graduating seniors will be repaying their loans until their retirement! A recent graduate is quoted as saying, "I didn't realize the implications of my debt until I was living with it." The current economy has hit the horse world hard, and new graduates interested in equine work are making less starting pay than those graduating five years ago. Rural states are realizing the shortage of large animal veterinarians, and some are starting to offer some loan forgiveness if there is a commitment to doing large animal work in underserved areas.

This article was not meant to discourage, but rather to lay out the facts. If you are interested in veterinary medicine, sit down and have a serious talk with your own vet. Most veterinarians are happy in their work and are interested in helping others join the profession.

100

What I Want You to Know
(pointers from a vet)

———————— ♘ ————————

My equine practice is 95% ambulatory. That word in vet medicine means, "We come to you." This article is drawn from my experience as a farm call vet. I am sure that your own vet will agree with what I have to say. Equine vets with haul-in hospitals may not concur. Here are some things that my ambulatory colleagues and I would like you to know.

First, *I want you to know the basics on what to do if your horse is not acting right.* If you don't know how, or are lacking the simple tools to take a Temperature, Pulse, and Respiration from your horse, I urge you to ask your vet for some education the next time he or she is at your place. If you call about a sick horse and provide us with just those three observations (the TPR), plus gut sounds, we will know whether he needs to be seen, and how quickly. Total cost of the digital thermometer and a stethoscope at the drug store is right around $25. Cheaper than an emergency farm call. By far.

I share emergency calls with five veterinarians. In our association, each of us is obligated to take emergencies for the other practices one weekday night and one weekend in six. Under this arrangement it is not unusual for me to go on an emergency call to a farm I have never been to, meet an anxious horse owner for the first time, and examine a sick horse that I have never seen before. To add to the drama, this often happens in the middle of the night.

A week ago I was on night emergency duty and got a call from an owner who uses one of the vets I was covering for. The call came in at 10:00 PM. "My horse Pepe has been doing the craziest thing all day. He is holding his left hind leg off the ground and is shaking it. Then he puts it back down and touches his toe to the ground and then jerks it right back up and starts shaking it again. Can you come out to see him?"

"Do you mean tonight? Like *now?*"

"Oh, please! I know I can't sleep tonight if he isn't helped. I think he has a broken leg."

Here is a fact. Horses (or people, I suppose) with broken legs never, ever shake them. I knew that he had an abscess, and some horses do find some relief from that pain by shaking their leg, just like you might shake a hand that has just been injured. I tried to explain this and told the client that Pepe could wait until morning. I suggested she call either her own vet or a farrier then. I explained that, given the hour, the charge for the emergency visit would be high. All my talk wasn't persuasive, and after a few more minutes on the phone, I decided it would take less energy for me just to drive out to her place. She told me that GPS didn't work well in finding her farm. I found out that her directions didn't either. I finally arrived well after 11 PM. The barn wasn't wired for electricity, so I had the owner hold a flashlight. After some digging I was able to release Pepe's abscess with my hoof knife. Two tablespoons of pus squirted out, and within a few minutes he was standing on the leg. No more shaking. I got back home around 1 AM. Guess who couldn't get to sleep then. *I want you to know that if you notice something during the day, that is the time to call for help. Please don't wait until 10 PM. It's so much easier on your horse and on the vet.*

I am more than annoyed when someone bad-mouths another vet in front of me. It's helpful to hear what Dr X came out and did for your horse, but I have no patience for, "I just don't think that he has any idea what he's doing." When Dr X was out to see your horse, it was a different day under different circumstances, and what the horse was exhibiting that day may have been very different as well. *I want you to know that farm vets talk to each other all the time. We see each other at CE meetings, call each other about puzzling cases, and in most cases we are friends. Please refrain from the criticisms. It doesn't make any points with us.*

Over several months I have been attending a horse that had Lyme disease. Subsequent lab reports show liver damage. I have been in touch with a clinician at a referral hospital and an internal medicine specialist about the case and have followed all their suggestions. If you saw the horse today, you might say that he looks fine. However, he just isn't the horse that he was. Despite great owner compliance, and all the high level advice that we have implemented, I am stumped as to why there hasn't been significant change. There are times when some problems in some horses just leave me baffled. *I want you to know that sometimes we just don't know.* I often refer cases, and sometimes *they* don't know. These situations are frustrating for both owners and vets.

It used to be that large animal practitioners were lone wolves out there from sunup to sundown, getting tired at days end, and perhaps making mistakes in judgement. Many of us have found that we can get more done, and far more effectively, when we have a good technician with us. I always hire techs that have been in the horse business for years and are skilled at handling animals. Many times I have been saved from a kick or bite by an observant assistant who is aware of how a horse is about to react. *I want you to know that if a vet's assistant says to you, "Let me take the lead," it is because she senses that there may be trouble brewing.* Give it up willingly. Everyone will be safer as a result.

A few months ago I was driving down a road that I haven't been on for five years and saw a farm that I used to call on. I recognized a couple of horses in the paddock, so I knew it was the same owner. I wondered why they switched vets. Was it something I said or did? Whatever the reason, my hope is that they are happy with their new vet. Your choice of a veterinarian involves many factors, and it's not just his or her head knowledge. Who you pick and stay with is based on who you can depend on and trust. This often comes down to a personality issue. *I want you to know that I recognize that some personalities just don't click, and once realized, it might be time for a parting of the ways.*

Finally, here is my take on social media. Years ago I was accused, through Facebook, of ignoring someone's urgent need for a veterinarian. We log in every call that comes to us, and that supposed call never got to me. I had a number of clients ask me later, "What was that all about?" To this day I don't know. Unless you know the facts, and actually, even if you do know the facts, refrain from spreading that juicy news about someone's barn, vet, farrier, or dentist. Consider the source. Information passed from one person to another is quickly distorted. *I want you to know that no matter how sophisticated social media gets, rumors and gossip will always be just that.*

I have aired some things I'd like you to know. Care for equal time? As a horse owner, what would you like *your* vet to know? The question makes me a little apprehensive, but still, I'd really like to see your comments. You can contact me by email: *dajdvm@maine.rr.com*

101

What Makes Them Special

There are many things that attract us to horses. We love their spirit. We celebrate the speed of racehorses and the strength of the draft breeds. We are amazed by the extreme athleticism of sport horses. We love our horses' willingness to enter into partnership in our activities. Best of all, most seem to be pretty happy hanging out with us. Besides all these qualities, there are also some anatomical characteristics of horses that are either unique or finely tuned as compared to others in the animal kingdom. This article will focus on some unusual characteristics of the horse's head.

Our eyes are on the front of our head. As a result, unless we turn our neck or body, we are always looking forward. This is true of all animals that are hunters. Lions, dogs, and cats all have this type of eye arrangement. It gives us great depth perception and focus

Horses' eyes are set on the *side* of the head, which is true for all the prey or flight animals. This would include the giraffe, antelope, and rabbit. Having the eyes to the side is the perfect arrangement for the hunted as it gives them almost wrap around vision. They can see a full 350 degrees out of 360 without turning their head. The only limit to their vision is the few feet directly in front of them and the few directly behind. This is pretty important when something is looking to have you for lunch. It is also something for us to remember when we are back by their hip. A horse might seem to be looking straight ahead, but can very accurately throw a foot your way. Horses have color vision, but it is not as refined as ours. For this reason jumps should be painted in bright colors, and for your safety the rails should not be painted in earth tones unless you'd like to wear some (earth that is). Finally, the night vision of horses is far superior to ours. Go out into their pasture some very dark night when you can't see a thing. You might well bump into a horse, but they will never bump into you.

Horses also have an exceptionally long soft palate. When your horse has a speculum in its mouth to have its teeth worked on, ask to take a look. You'll be able to see all the teeth, but not as far back as the pharynx where the swallowing happens. Their elongated palate actually rests on top of the tongue, blocking the back view. When food like dry beet pulp gets stuck part way down the esophagus on the way to the stomach, the horse is "choked." Horses are continually producing huge amounts of saliva. The saliva in a choked horse gets swallowed, but doesn't make it to the stomach. It hits the obstruction, and as more saliva is produced it backs up, against gravity, all the way back up to the back of the mouth. That long soft palate prevents it from coming out of the mouth, so it continues up and starts to spill out of the nose as froth when it mixes with the air. It's sort of like Coke coming out of your nose if you have a mouthful and start to laugh. To relieve the choke, your veterinarian may have to pass a stomach tube through the nose into the esophagus to alleviate the problem. It can't be done through the mouth as that long palate would be in the way.

Another unusual feature of the horse's head is the paired "air sacs" called the guttural pouches. About the only other large animals known to have these pouches are rhinos and tapirs. The pouches are just to the side of the large space, called the pharynx, at the back of the mouth. In a 1000-pound horse, their capacity is between two and four cups each. It is thought that their purpose is to equalize different pressures within the head. Running through each pouch is one of the large carotid arteries which supply blood to the brain. Some researchers feel that the air in the pouches cools the blood in those arteries. In this way the air in the pouch acts like a radiator.

Guttural pouches can be trouble. After a horse has the messy upper respiratory disease that we call strangles and has recovered, the strep bacterium that causes it can hide out in the pouches. Some horses will carry the bacteria there for months. This makes them a source of infection for other horses.

The pouches are also an ideal place for molds to grow. One of the places the mold settles on is that large exposed carotid artery. The mold has the potential of eating into and eroding the wall of the artery and causing it to rupture. This is like puncturing a fire hose that is pumping water. The bleeding can be so severe that horses have been known to bleed to death out through the nose. Most nosebleeds have other causes and are not as serious, but it is good to check with your veterinarian who may want to do an endoscopic exam if you have a horse that is dripping blood for an extended period of time.

One interesting survival mechanism peculiar to horses is the huge capacity of the equine spleen to store red blood cells. Whenever the horse is alarmed, the spleen contracts, and millions of red blood cells are released into the blood stream. This reserve system is one of the reasons that horses can lose a great deal of blood before bleeding to death. It is also why veterinarians prefer to take a blood sample from a horse that is not excited. When a horse is anxious, the spleen contracts, and if a blood sample is pulled during that time, the blood will show a much higher red-blood cell count than it would if the horse was relaxed. If your horse is sick and you think a blood test may be in order, have your vet pull the blood *before* he or she does a physical exam which may cause anxiety and spleen contracture.

Mares do not go through anything like menopause. Right up until death, they keep growing new eggs and having regular cycles which run from mid spring until early fall. Even though your mare may not show outward signs of being in heat, the cycles are still going on. People will frequently ask why their mares seem to be coming into heat so frequently. The fact is that you can expect them to be in heat from four to eight days, and out for about 14, which means that every two weeks you can expect another heat. Although they do cycle all their lives, it's unusual for an aged bred mare to carry to term. They often do not maintain the proper hormone balance to get them through an entire pregnancy. If you want to breed an older mare, ask your veterinarian for help with assessing and supplementing hormones to help her go to term. Just be aware that you are fighting Mother Nature.

You have probably heard that horses can't vomit. This is one of the reasons that horses are so apt to colic. If a horse's stomach doesn't agree with what was just eaten, it's not easy to get rid of it. A very strong muscle surrounds the entrance to the stomach and acts as a one-way valve to prevent vomiting. We also have a muscle there, but the heaving of our stomach can overcome it. That strong sphincter muscle in horses means that they are destined to bear stomach pain. Occasionally, so much pressure can build up that a horse's stomach will rupture. This is one of the reasons your vet may pass a stomach tube and release the fluids and gas in the stomach as part of a colic treatment.

When we see our winter-coated horses, we can understand how they can look comfortable in a New England blizzard. But how do they stand on that frozen ground with no foot protection? The quick answer is that horses have an amazing blood supply to the foot. Blood to the foot is carried by two large arteries that run behind each fetlock down into the hoof. Have your vet or farrier show you how to take the pulse there. This is a great skill to learn and is handy when you are assessing a lame horse.

Deep within the foot is a network of veins, unusual in that they do not have valves to prevent blood from flowing back down to the foot. Instead, when a horse is in motion and the foot hits the ground, all its tissues are squeezed and virtually all the blood is pushed back up the leg. This works because the hoof capsule is relatively rigid. Once weight is on the foot, the blood has nowhere to go except back into the circulation. When the used blood has been squeezed out, a space is created for the blood pumping down from the arteries to fill the foot again. The fill is immediate, and the new warm blood has totally replaced the old. This constant turnover keeps the internal structures of the foot toasty warm, even in subzero conditions. One take-home from this is to be sure that your horse has room to move around in the winter. I often see horses just standing in one spot, because it hurts their legs to break through the crust on snow. Break it up for them, and put the hay in different spots in their paddock so they have to walk and keep that blood flow going more effectively.

Horses have the unusual ability to "lock" their hind legs so that they can stand for long periods of time using minimal energy and no muscle exertion. There are three ligaments that connect the patella (knee cap) to the tibia (the bone between stifle and hock). One of the ligaments can slide over a knob on the femur (the big leg bone) and literally lock that leg in a standing position. This is handy because with one leg locked, the horse can rest the other. This neat feature of horses can be a problem when the hind leg locks or catches as the horse is moving.

This doesn't cause any pain, but it bothers the horse to have a hind leg go straight out behind and not be able to flex. We see this most often in horses that aren't getting enough exercise. The intermittent locking can affect horses of any breed but is by far more prevalent in ponies. Programmed exercise including hill and trot pole work to strengthen the quads often corrects the condition. If not, there a new simple surgery that can be done on the standing horse that will usually fix the problem.

These are just some of the interesting differences that make horses what they are. Knowing a little bit about these hidden workings of horses helps us in understanding and managing them better.

102

Wheeze, Rattle, Rumble, Roar

(horse noises)

U

I just rented the movie Secretariat. Hollywood horses are perfect. The stallions look shiny and "studdy." They challenge the world with piercing whinnies. The mares are soft, motherly, and nicker a lot. In westerns the pack of horses that make up the posse gallop loudly, especially when they cross the wooden bridge. Those film horses never seem to make some of the other noises that real horses do. Real live horses make all kinds of unusual sounds, most of which are curious, but not a problem. Others can be a clue to something that isn't right.

Most of the noises come from the head. Any obstruction of the airway may cause a horse to make some different sounds when trying to breathe. Generally they are louder when the animal is being worked, because the air is being exchanged at a much faster rate. The head noises are exaggerated by the fact that horses have such hollow heads. A number of sinuses honeycomb the skull and act as echo chambers that magnify the sounds. One noise they exaggerate is teeth grinding. Some horses grind their teeth when they are annoyed and others just because they like the sound. It is sometimes a clue to pain in the GI tract, and may be an early sign of stomach ulcers.

Horses have a very long soft palate. It is so long that it hangs down and actually rests on the back of the tongue. Unlike us, you cannot open a horse's mouth and see the back of the throat because of that soft palate. This means that horses cannot mouth breathe. If a horse has a head cold which produces mucus, he will wheeze and rattle as the air goes through the mucus. You and I, with a good head cold are apt to breathe through the mouth. This anatomy also means that if the palate is torn, displaced upward, or swollen, it may make a fluttering noise when the air passes over it at the back of the throat. Sometimes the palate can be surgically trimmed when it becomes a problem.

An occasional horse may get into the habit of pulling his tongue far back into the mouth while being worked. This pushes the palate upwards into the airflow, producing a deep sound. Once a horse discovers this sound, he may keep making it as it is probably somewhat entertaining. This can cause a decrease in airflow, so this is mostly a racehorse problem. Toward the end of a race, horses need all the air they can get. There are a number of tongue devices on the track designed to keep the tongue in position. Every manufacturer of tongue ties claims that his product is the most comfortable and effective. If a trainer forgets to remove the tie after competition, the blood supply can be shut off with resultant tongue damage.

Long-necked horses are subject to a condition called "roaring," named after the noise that they make when being worked hard. It is a deep whistling tone that sounds something like air being blown across the top of a bottle. Listen for it when the horse breathes in. The sound is coming from the air sweeping around a portion of the larynx that is paralyzed and is protruding into the air steam. Muscles that are supposed to keep the larynx open aren't working because of nerve damage. As the air goes around the paralyzed portion, the roaring sound is produced. There is a surgery called "tie back" that involves pulling the paralyzed portion out of the way and tacking it down on the side, away from the airway. The surgery is usually effective.

The main part of a horse's diet is fiber, and when fiber is broken down, methane gas is produced. Some horses are very noisy in expelling the excess gas, and while it might be somewhat embarrassing to the owner, it is not a problem. If the situation is extreme, it can often be modified by changing the amount or type of grain or hay fed. Simethicone (Gas X) is also helpful. Depending on the strength, between 5 and 15 of the human pills are what most horse people seem to be using. There do not seem to be any side effects. It is also available as a paste.

Did you ever hear a sheath rumble? This is a noise peculiar to some geldings. It is a kind of hollow noise caused by air moving in the sheath when the horse is trotting. It is more common in geldings because the penis is smaller and often doesn't fill the sheath, so there is more room for the air to move around and make the rumble. It is totally normal and not a problem. Cleaning the sheath doesn't seem to make any difference.

Funny noises are just another thing that makes horses so different and *always* interesting.

103

Which Leg
(lameness evaluation)

○

The first part of any lameness exam is figuring out which leg is lame. This sounds obvious, but it is this first step that seems to throw so many people, even very experienced riders.

Let's say that your horse goes lame because he stepped on a nail. There will be no question which leg hurts. The horse will bear almost no weight on the leg while standing. When an animal has an early arthritis, it's not so easy. At first there might be some reluctance to work. Eventually it will become more and more apparent that he is a little off. He might stand solidly on all four and be sound at a walk, but trotting he will show lameness. It is at this point that people get confused as to which leg is the sore one.

If this has happened to you, you aren't alone. More often than not, when I am asked to look at a lame horse, the owner has pinpointed the wrong leg. At the beginning of our equine lameness course in vet school, we were shown films of ten lame horses and were asked to write down the off leg in each film. I got five wrong. Actually, as I didn't have a system, I think my correct answers were all guesses. If you don't have a system for evaluating lame horses, it is mostly guess work. All you know is that that you see a blur of four moving legs and that the horse isn't moving correctly.

To be sure that I could explain the system, I put a small stone in the heel of my right shoe so that when I walked it would hurt. Then I asked my wife, Bonnie, who has no real horse experience, to tell me which leg was being favored as I walked. She could only tell that I was limping, but didn't know which leg. Then I asked the key question: "When I walk, which foot is hitting the ground harder?" She could see that. In fact she could hear it. I shifted the stone to the other foot and asked the question again. Again, she was able to tell. I explained that if one leg is taking most of the weight, then the other one is taking less, and is the sore one. She got that, and then was able to tell which leg was sore. Try this with a friend. Again, the foot that doesn't hurt will hit the ground hardest. The good leg takes the shock. So, if the right one is coming down harder, then the left one is the sore one.

Believe it or not, that's all there is to it. If you get that concept, you are ready for lame horses. It's actually easier on horses because the head and neck of a horse weigh so much, and horses use this in favoring the lame leg. When a sound horse trots, the head stays on an even line. When he is sore, the head comes down when the *good* leg hits the ground and goes up when the *lame* leg hits the ground. In other words, the good leg is taking the weight of the head and neck. Watch for the head coming down. When it does, you know that the sound leg is hitting the ground, and the other leg is the sore one. This is called a head nod.

Don't let the fact that a horse has four legs confuse you. When you watch a horse go, first watch only the front end. If one of those feet is hitting the ground harder (the head nod), the horse is lame up front. Now watch the hind end. If one of those two feet is hitting the ground harder, you have a hind end lameness. For sure, there are refinements that come with time and experience, but if you start with these basics, and always ask which leg is taking the weight, most of the time you will know that the opposite leg is the sore one.

104

Winter Skinny
(winter feeding)

───────── ♘ ─────────

It's a deep, cold winter. I'm in your barn to check out one of your horses for one reason or another. I like to run my hands over every part of a horse that's reachable as part of my exam. In the process I slide my hands slide over his ribs. Whoops! I'm feeling way too many bony ribs. There is lots of hair, lots of bone, and very little covering in between. I ease into the topic. "How much feed is he getting?" I usually get a question back: "Why? Do you think he's too skinny?"

Winter skinny is pretty common. There are two reasons for it. The first is that that your horse burns a lot of calories just keeping warm. Those calories that would have put weight on in the summer are now being burned to maintain body temperature. The second is that horses grow this great hair coat as insulation. Even in a deep Maine winter most horses grow enough of a hair coat to keep warm. It's better than the best Baker blanket. The problem is that it makes your horse look like he's in great shape. All that hair could be hiding a thin horse.

The next time you are at the feed store, ask for a weight tape for every horse you own. They usually give them away. When you feel that your horse is in perfect condition, use the tape to get his approximate weight. Proper placement is just behind the elbows of the front legs and up over the withers. Pull it tight and mark the spot on the tape with the date. Bring the tape out again in a month and note the difference. For this purpose it really doesn't matter how many pounds you read on the tape. What *is* important is that you don't want your horse to be showing less pounds than you had earlier on. It's much harder and more expensive to *put* weight on than keep it on.

Contrary to what many think, it's the digestion of roughage

that keeps a horse warm. Winter feeding should be built around hay and not grain. Look on grain as a supplement and not the main source of nutrition. Most horses, if given the right amount of hay, (generally always available) need very little grain. Only if your horse has the naturally thin build of a Thoroughbred might he need extra grain, rice bran, beet pulp, or fat in the diet to maintain in the cold months.

If you've never used a weight tape, have a knowledgeable friend or your veterinarian show you how to properly place and read it. When the hair coat is the heaviest, you have to allow for that and subtract 20 or 30 pounds, depending on the thickness of the coat.

The weight tape is a tack trunk necessity, not used as often as a brush or foot pick, but certainly every month through the cold winter.

105

Wonder Drug
(Banamine)

———————— ♘ ————————

Banamine (generic name *Flunixin Meglumide*) became a veterinary drug about 30 years ago. Since then, just in our practice alone, many thousands of doses have been administered or dispensed. What's that all about? Banamine has become an important part of almost every equine vet's inventory, and while the term "wonder drug" may be a little strong, it is one of a handful of medications that I'd hate to be without. Banamine is in the NSAID (Non Steroidal Anti Inflammatory Drugs) class of drugs. That means that it isn't a corticosteroid like cortisone, prednisone or dexamethasone. Instead it is part of the family of medicines that include aspirin or Bute (pheynlbutazone). One research study showed it to be some four times stronger than Bute.

The word anti-inflammatory means that when given in proper dosage, aches and pains are remarkably lessened. Because movement of our horses is so important, we as owners and trainers are always interested in medicines or procedures that promise to relieve discomfort. However, you can only fool Mother Nature for so long. Give too much Banamine, and side effects such as stomach or large colon ulcers may result. Advice from your veterinarian as to when to use it, its dosage, and how long to administer it, is critical.

Although it is used routinely for acutely lame horses, its most frequent application for us is in the treatment of colic. The word colic means belly pain. The origin of the pain is usually from stomach or intestinal problems of some sort, and can range from simple gas to a twisted or trapped intestine.

In our practice our recommendations are as follows. First, we like all of our clients to have a supply of Banamine on hand. It comes in a paste syringe with three doses for a 1000-pound horse. If a client calls with a horse showing belly pain, we try to get some information over the phone. We are interested in the degree of pain, the heart rate, the color of the mucus membranes around the eye and in the mouth, and the intensity and location of gut sounds.

If the pain level is bearable, we usually advise giving several GasX and then waiting an hour. Often the pain is due to gas distending the intestine, and shortly the horse is fine. If GasX and waiting an hour brings no relief, we advise giving a dose of Banamine paste. More often than not, this quickly takes care of the pain. However, if a horse has a mechanical blockage from a twisted or entrapped intestine, the Banamine will relieve only some of the pain, and that relief is short lived. The horse soon starts to hurt again. These horses need veterinary attention with a full physical exam. This usually includes a rectal exam and passage of a stomach tube to determine what the problem is. The question to be answered is whether further medical treatment or surgery is called for.

Critics of Banamine insist that giving the drug just masks pain and does nothing to relieve the problem. It is true that when used in early colics, Banamine is for pain management. Think of the worst stomach ache you ever had. In an effort to escape the cramping a horse will throw himself down and then roll violently, perhaps smashing his head against the ground or stall floor with every new attack. So, I'm all for all for relieving pain. Again, in those serious problems that require surgery, Banamine will only lessen the pain temporarily. If the Banamine doesn't work for very long or well, I know that this horse needs additional support and perhaps surgery.

Banamine does come in an injectable form, but in my opinion this should only be used intravenously. If you use it in the muscle, the highly anti-inflammatory action of the drug will prohibit the body from fighting any bacteria that might be taken in with the needle. The result may be a very nasty abscess at the injection site. The paste works almost as fast as the injectable, and is safe. It is often astounding how well Banamine works. Wonder drug or not, I like to know that Banamine is in every stable's first aid kit.

106

Written Arrangements

♘

Marie owned a farm that was used as a turnout for race horses in the off season. She called me mid-morning one cold December day to come have a look at Popeye. She had just found him lying on a patch of ice in her lower pasture. Marie was nervously waiting for me in as I turned into her driveway around noon. I parked the truck and gathered what I might need. Fearing the worst I also put a bottle of euthanasia solution into my coat pocket.

It was a long walk from the barnyard to where Popeye was lying. As we made our way down to the pasture, Marie told me what had happened that morning. She turned the horses out early so that she could clean their stalls. A light drizzle was falling, and by mid-morning most of the horses were back up by the barn wanting to come back in. Popeye was missing. Marie walked the 10-acre pasture and finally found him lying on his side in a hollow which was not visible from the barn. Marie could see scratches on the ice where he had tried to get up, and after some prompting, she realized that he wasn't going to. She ran back up to the house to call me.

We found Popeye lying in the same spot that Marie had left him. I did a physical exam and checked his legs. Besides the weak heartbeat and subnormal temperature, there was a complete fracture of the femur right where it enters the hip socket. He had slipped on the ice and fallen on his hip. I told Marie he had to be euthanized. She knew I was right, but felt strongly that only the owner could give that permission. He was out of town and not reachable. We stood on that icy patch over Popeye who was shivering and going into shock. It took a few minutes to persuade Marie that we simply could not leave Popeye as he was. It wasn't until I assured her that I would be willing to take the heat and the possible law suit which might result that she agreed to my ending his life. As it turned out, the owner understood the situation, and that I did what had to be done.

This entire incident and a couple of similar ones over the years have made me realize how important it is to have specific arrangements in place whether you board horses or have yours boarded out. In this age of increased communication, it seems like we can be reached anytime, anywhere. The fact is, we can't. Cellphones are a great thing, but there are limitations. A couple of months ago, I was trying to trying to reach an owner who had just taken off on a six-hour plane trip overseas. In this case it wasn't a life or death situation, but a treatment that needed to be discussed. The conversation and treatment had to be delayed a week until she got back because there was no cell coverage in the country she was visiting. She had left without any instructions as to responsibilities for the animal. Even if your cellphone is attached at the hip and you don't happen to be on a plane, you probably don't take the device into the shower. As you know, there are also areas where there is no coverage.

Here is a recommendation. Draw up a contract between caretaker and owner. The word contract means a binding agreement between two or more people. Call it a written agreement if that makes it a little less scary. If you operate a boarding facility, you should take this responsibility. Sample agreements can be found on line. For more ideas, ask the owner of a well-run stable near you. If the barn where you are boarding doesn't have such an agreement, you should make one yourself to protect both parties.

The agreement should include exactly what is involved in daily care. This is not a complete list, but here are some questions that should be agreed upon: When is the board bill due? What services does it include? What will be fed, amounts and frequency? Who will arbitrate if there is a dispute about how much hay or grain a horse should get? If more is to be fed, how much extra will that cost? What are the blanket and turnout policies? Who makes arrangement for farrier and vet care? What happens if the owner can't be reached when medical and life decisions have to be made? Does each horse have a colic surgery plan? Who trucks the horse when it needs to go to a clinic?

These questions and others should be thoroughly discussed and agreed to before a horse walks into a boarding situation. It doesn't cost a lot to have an attorney review the language in the agreement. You draw up the points of the agreement; the lawyer's job is to look it over and make sure it is binding. Both parties should sign and date. Many a boarder has left a barn in the heat of an argument, which in most cases would have been avoidable had there been a standing agreement.

107

You Can't Miss It

(directions to your place)

───────────── ♘ ─────────────

Our veterinary practice shares emergency calls with four other practices. This means that when an urgent call comes in when I am on duty, I often don't know the person calling or how to get to her farm. All the displayed phone number tells me is the town. Our conversation at 11:00 PM might go something like this:

"OK Alice, you are right, this does sound like colic, and you seem to have done everything that you can. Perhaps I should come out and see him. What is your address?"

"We live in Durham. Do you know where the elementary school is?"

"Well, I know there's the old one and the new one. Tell you what, why don't you give me your actual address. I'll put it in the GPS on my phone and I should be able to find you."

"Well, I'm not sure that would work . . . they tell me that it isn't accurate to my place. So I'll give you some directions."

Alice apparently does not believe in road names, but instead gives me landmarks: the Hutchins place, the intersection with the tilted stop sign, and the old Smith place with all the window boxes. "Our place is about a mile from that big painted rock. We have lots of white fencing and a red barn. Really, you can't miss it."

Alice, I can assure you (I say to myself) *that I can miss it*. I have lots of experience trying to find horse farms at night and have not only driven miles out of the way, but have gotten totally lost in the process. Not as bad in the day time when you can stop and ask, but come night I pass all the dark houses telling me that everyone in the neighborhood has gone to bed.

A traveling salesman whose territory includes all of northern New England told me that all GPS systems are 99% accurate in the cities, but he estimates that it slips to 80% in rural areas. I agree. In fact, if you try to find my *own* farm using Google Maps you will end up 1 and 1/2 miles away, on a dead-end road. Calls and emails to Google have not resulted in change.

Here's something else I've found. If you have considerable road frontage some systems will put you at your property line, which may be hundreds of feet from your front door. Not a big problem in the daytime. It is a problem after dark when the GPS says I have arrived, but all I can see is woods.

Here are some things that I have learned about getting to your farm after the sun goes down.

1. It sounds sexist, but I find that men are almost always better at things like state road numbers and road names. If you are getting frustrated trying to explain how to get there, hand the phone off to an adult male who has lots of driving miles under his belt. For one thing, men almost always have a better concept of what a mile is.

2. Once it's dark, spare the color descriptions. Even that white fence doesn't show unless headlights are right on it. Actually all colors look the same in the dark. It's a black and white world when the sun goes down. The description of the yellow house or red barn doesn't help.

3. If you are aware that GPS doesn't pinpoint you, take a drive from your place to the post office. On the way home, write down the exact mileage and turns on how to get to your barn. I have found that post offices are always exactly located on GPS systems, and it's is a great place to start from. Enshrine that information in a plastic holder for everyone in the house and keep it by the phone. This will help every emergency responder, including fire trucks, ambulances, and the state police.

Over 40 years ago I was hired right out of vet school by a practice in the "north country" of the Connecticut River Valley. Back then this area was the definition of rural. Our clients were about equal in number between Vermont and New Hampshire. Over the course of a day, I regularly crossed the many rivers over three different covered bridges and two iron ones. When I first arrived, I didn't know the territory at all, and of course, GPS wasn't around then. At least today I always know what state I'm in! When my boss's wife would send me on calls, she would always tell the client to drape a towel over the mailbox, especially at night. For the first several months, I looked for and depended on those towels to bring me in. Now when I get confusing directions from someone I don't know late at night, I ask them to put out a towel. Many times it has saved me 15 minutes of frustrating road time, when I could have been at the barn.

My hope is that you never have a night emergency call and have to have a vet out that you've never met before. It happens, and if you are in the horse industry long enough, it may happen to you. Be prepared with exact directions for a vet you don't know. It's wise to have those directions down on paper by the phone before the incident happens, and you are in panic mode.

108

You Gotta Know How to Hold 'Em

(holding horses)

———————— ♘ ————————

Just yesterday I was vaccinating horses in a barn where there were four new owners, each with a recently purchased horse. These were mature horses that had no concept of barn manners, and worse, the owners had no idea how to handle them. The barn owner was on the property, but during most of my visit was in the house. I was in the middle of every veterinarian's nightmare. For the safety of all of us, I finally had to have two of the owners step aside and have my technician, Erin, handle the fractious animals. I was more than annoyed with the barn owner.

In contrast, I always feel safe in Sherrye Trafton's barn in Brunswick. Sherrye has made such a point of safety that she deserves recognition. She trains all her personnel and owners on how to hold horses. Whether the animals are getting vaccinated, massaged, or having their feet or teeth done, good horse handling is a real blessing for the equine professional who is attending them. When you as the horse handler do everything right, you create a far safer environment for everyone involved, including the horse.

The first rule is an obvious one. Each horse being worked on should have a handler. There are many horses that seem to be trustworthy on crossties, but I, for one, won't work on them that way. Horses are hardwired to escape in time of perceived danger. When 1000 pounds of scared horse backs up fast, crossties, snaps, and screw eyes are apt to break. A crosstie breaking under the tension can become a deadly whip capable of fracturing teeth or taking out an eye.

The second rule is to always use a lead instead of holding a horse by the halter, even when just bringing them in and out of their stall. If the horse goes up and you are hanging onto the halter, you are apt to suffer a shoulder injury. The lead gives a few feet of reaction space and far more control.

Finally, and this seems to be a forgotten piece, the handler should always stand on the same side of the horse that the vet or farrier is working on. For example: if your vet is giving a shot on the left side of the neck, or examining a leg on that side, you should be on the left side. If the vet moves to the right side, you should immediately move to that side. Correct distance to the horse is a foot or two to the side and somewhere between the head and the point of the shoulder, facing the vet. The hand holding the lead is about waist height. Now, should the animal attempt to strike, kick, or bite, quickly step sideways away from the horse and firmly pull the horse's head toward you. This throws the horse off balance, and his body will automatically shift to line up with his head. This pulls his hind end away from the vet. Done properly and quickly, this maneuver will abort the kick that was about to happen.

Everyone at Trafton's handles horses this way, and all the professionals working in that barn deeply appreciate the sense of safety this gives. When I am doing chiropractic work on horses, I continually move back and forth from one side of the horse to the other. When handlers actively participate by moving with me, I feel safe and better able to concentrate on my work. The handlers in this Brunswick barn are always aware and move quickly to keep everyone, humans and horses safe.

Want to stay on good terms with equine professionals? Consistently practice this stance and move until it becomes automatic. You will be appreciated and recognized as a savvy horse handler.

MAINE EQUINE
ASSOCIATES

About the Author

Dr David Jefferson is the owner of Maine Equine Associates, an ambulatory veterinary practice dedicated to keeping horses healthy and happy. He is originally from Pelham, New York, miles from the nearest horse. His interest in horses began at Cornell University where he earned his veterinary degree.

Before college he served as a U.S. Marine for three years. Dr J is a member of the Vineyard Christian Fellowship of Mechanic Falls and is part of a team that visits jail inmates weekly. He has been an Auburn, Maine, Literacy Volunteer, working with adults who have difficulty reading. He served as President of the Lewiston Auburn Rotary Club and is an active board member of the Maine State Society for the Protection of Animals.

Maine Equine Associates is run from the Jeffersons' home on their farm in New Gloucester, Maine, sharing the space with two donkeys, a cat or two, and a feisty male guinea fowl. David has been married to Bonnie for 52 years, and they have 2 adult children.

Made in the USA
Columbia, SC
25 July 2017